Delivering Research Data Management Services
Fundamentals of good practice

Also by Graham Pryor
Managing Research Data ISBN 978-1-85604-756-2

Delivering Research Data Management Services

Fundamentals of good practice

Edited by
Graham Pryor, **Sarah Jones** and **Angus Whyte**

f facet publishing

© This compilation: Graham Pryor, Sarah Jones and Angus Whyte 2014
The chapters: the contributors 2014

Published by Facet Publishing,
7 Ridgmount Street, London WC1E 7AE
www.facetpublishing.co.uk

Facet Publishing is wholly owned by CILIP: the Chartered Institute of Library and Information Professionals.

British Library Cataloguing in Publication Data
A catalogue record for this book is available from the British Library.

ISBN 978-1-85604-933-7
First published 2014

Text printed on FSC accredited material.

Typeset from editors' files by Flagholme Publishing Services in 10/14 pt Palatino Linotype and Myriad Pro
Printed and made in Great Britain by CPI Group (UK) Ltd, Croydon, CR0 4YY.

Contents

Preface

The generation of digital research output (let's generalize from the start and call it *data*) has been fairly commonplace in most if not all disciplines for some years now. More recently, the realization has emerged amongst those responsible for funding, hosting and supporting research that this data deluge could represent by far the most challenging aspect of 21st-century research administration that they are likely ever to encounter. As formative experiences go, it appears to be an eminently larger and more complex phenomenon, most acutely characterized by its exceptional rate of growth, than has previously been experienced in the engines of knowledge creation that are our universities.

Entering that rousing context, this book has a dual purpose: to build awareness amongst our readers of the principal drivers obliging them to focus on delivering a data management service infrastructure, whilst at the same time explaining the components and processes that will normally comprise the building blocks for such a service. These two strands are presented together with an explanation of the roles and responsibilities of those who will sustain, deliver and use the services. Hence, our topic embraces both the technical and human infrastructures necessary to effective service delivery, which are fundamentally inter-dependent. To complete the picture, a set of case studies supplements the 'how to' character of the main chapters by documenting real experiences and approaches to the creation of institutional and national services in leading organizations from the UK, Australia and the USA.

Anyone with an active stake in the generation, management and sharing of research data should find something of value in this book. You could be a researcher pursuing options for the secure and sustained storage of your data, seeking support to reliably managed access or the means to enable the greatest dissemination potential; or you might be viewing research undertakings from a management or policy perspective, with an eye for achieving maximum returns on investment, perhaps, through the introduction of improvements to the mechanism for knowledge exchange. It is as likely that you are a member of a support team handling the ingest, curation and archiving of research data, needing to understand not only the techniques involved but also the political or legal contexts and the relationships between those key stakeholders whose expectations will, ultimately, rest with you.

Whichever role best describes you, our message is that the design and introduction of sustainable research data management infrastructure and services must be addressed on an inclusive, whole-enterprise basis, since it will represent a significant change in both culture and practice for most if not all research stakeholders within a higher education institution. Correspondingly, the authors of this slim volume are optimistic that you will discover such a holistic approach to research data management services echoed within the succeeding pages of our book.

Graham Pryor

Contributors

Anthony Beitz is the General Manager of the Monash University e-Research Centre. He has extensive experience in the selection, development, deployment and support of e-research software infrastructure, especially in research data management. He directs the development and deployment of research data management infrastructure at Monash and has co-authored Monash's research data management strategy. Before joining the Monash e-Research Centre in 2008 he was a project manager for the DART and ARCHER projects, two key Australian e-research initiatives that explored and developed infrastructure for research data management. Prior to his appointment at Monash in 2006, he accumulated over a decade of experience in research and development with Telstra, Australia's major telecommunications provider.

Mark L. Brown has recently retired after 12 years as University Librarian at the University of Southampton. He led the development of the institutional repository strategy and a range of large-scale digitization projects, playing a significant role in shaping the institutional service model for research data management at the university. Chair of Research Libraries UK (RLUK) between 2007 and 2011, he was responsible for drafting the current RLUK Strategic Plan and is currently leading the strand on *Redefining the Modern Research Library*. He has acted as project director on several Jisc-funded repository and digitization projects and has had an active role in national initiatives on resource discovery. He has been a strong advocate for the green open access model and the active role of research libraries in the development of research support. A longstanding and active member of several Jisc committees and working groups, he has from 2013 become the Chair of the EDINA Management Board.

G. Sayeed Choudhury is Associate Dean for Research Data Management and Hodson Director of the Digital Research and Curation Center at the Sheridan Libraries of Johns Hopkins University. He is also the Director of Operations for the Institute of Data Intensive Engineering and Science (IDIES) based at Johns Hopkins. He is a member of the National Academies Board on Research Data and Information, the ICPSR Council, DuraSpace Board, and a Senior Presidential Fellow with the Council on Library and Information Resources. Previously, he was a member of the Digital Library Federation advisory committee, Library of Congress National Digital Stewardship Alliance Coordinating Committee and Federation of Earth Scientists Information Partnership (ESIP) Executive Committee. He has been a Lecturer in the Department of Computer Science at Johns Hopkins and a Research Fellow at the Graduate School of Library and Information Science at the University of Illinois at Urbana-Champaign. In 2013 he testified for the Research Subcommittee of the Congressional Committee on Science, Space and Technology.

Louise Corti is an Associate Director at the UK Data Archive, heading the Producer Relations and Collections Development sections for the UK Data Service. She is a research methodologist and her current expertise is in archiving and sharing social science data. She has held a number of research awards in the areas of research data management aimed at creating best practice and capacity building for researchers and research support staff. She has led the qualitative data archive since 1995 and is currently co-ordinating a working group and project on metadata and systems for systematically describing and presenting qualitative data.

David Groenewegen is the Director of Research Infrastructure at Monash University Library, where he is responsible for leading and developing the library's activities relating to research data management, research repositories, digitization and publishing. He was a foundation Director of the Australian National Data Service, where he was involved with the development and implementation of data management solutions across the Australian university sector. He has wide-ranging experience working in the areas of electronic information provision and related technology.

Cathrine Harboe-Ree is the Monash University Librarian. She is the past-President of the Council of Australian University Librarians (2009–13) and a member of the Australian National Data Service (ANDS) Steering Committee, representing Monash University, which is the lead agency. She has formerly been a member of the joint ministerial Australian eResearch Coordinating Committee and of the Australian eResearch Infrastructure Council (AeRIC) and was the Chair of the Commonwealth Government funded institutional repository project, ARROW, from its inception to its completion (2002–8). She has established and supervised the growth of Monash University Publishing, an innovative open access electronic press, and leads university-wide research data management policy, planning and co-ordination.

Simon Hodson is Executive Director of CODATA, an organization whose mission is to strengthen international science for the benefit of society by promoting improved scientific and technical data management and use. He also sits on the Board of Directors of the Dryad data repository, a not-for-profit initiative to make the data underlying scientific publications discoverable, freely reusable, and citable. From 2009 to 2013, as Programme Manager, he led two successive phases of Jisc's innovative Managing Research Data programme.

Sarah Jones is a Senior Information Support Officer with the Digital Curation Centre (DCC), a UK national service providing support to the higher education sector in all aspects of research data management. Since 2011 her principal focus has been on the DCC's institutional engagement programme, in which she has been leading the provision of support to a range of universities, helping them to scope researchers' requirements, delivering training, advising on the customization of the DMPonline tool and assisting the implementation of research data management services. She also develops guidance materials for the DCC, specifically on research data policy and data management planning, and has been involved in a number of projects from the Jisc Managing Research Data programme.

Wilna Macmillan is the Director of Client Services – Science Health and Engineering at Monash University Library. Her portfolio includes oversight of the library's engagement with the university's research agenda, including research data management and capability building, working with a number of faculty areas and with broad oversight of several branch libraries. She has been at Monash University since 2006. Prior to this she held various library and communication positions at CSIRO and worked in the university, research, community college and health sectors, including seven years in the USA and UK.

Laura Molloy is a researcher at the Humanities Advanced Technology and Information Institute (HATII) at the University of Glasgow, working in the areas of digital curation and research data management. A member of Digital Curation Centre staff, she has experience in the design and delivery of training and skills development for researchers and support professionals, including work on the Jisc-funded Incremental project and the Data Management Skills Support Initiative (DaMSSI). She also gathers and analyses evidence of benefits from the Jisc Managing Research Data programme. EU-funded work includes the delivery of outreach and training events for the Planets project, online outreach materials for Digital Preservation Europe (DPE) and development of a curriculum framework for digital curation in the cultural heritage sector for the DigCurV project.

Graham Pryor is Information Management Consultant with the Amor Group, following six years as Associate Director with the Digital Curation Centre (DCC), where he designed and managed the e-Science liaison and institutional engagement programmes. Until his departure from the DCC in mid-2013 he also developed the highly inclusive Research Data Management Forum, a medium for the bi-annual exchange of knowledge and experience in the more urgent topics surfacing from the broader data community. Prior to the DCC he spent nine years as Director of Information Systems and Services at the University of Aberdeen, which followed a number of senior information management posts within the UK's defence and energy sectors.

Sam Searle has been the eResearch Senior Specialist (Information Management) at Griffith University since October 2012. From August 2008 to May 2012 she was the Research Data Coordinator at Monash University. In that role, she co-ordinated a range of institutional activities relating to research data management and contributed to the community of data librarians emerging out of projects sponsored by the Australian National

Data Service (ANDS). She has also worked on audits of government agency compliance with privacy and right to information legislation at the Office of the Information Commissioner (Queensland), in e-research business development at Victoria University of Wellington, on digitization projects at the National Library of New Zealand, and in other research, library, archives and publishing roles in universities in Australia, New Zealand and Scotland.

Wendy White is Head of Scholarly Communication at the University of Southampton, where she leads the co-ordination of cross-service research data management support. She has been involved with a range of Jisc projects relating to initiatives in open access, repositories, research data and digitization. Most recently, from 2011 to 2013, she was Principal Investigator for the DataPool project. Her work embraces strategic, policy and service developments across all elements of the research lifecycle and she has contributed to a range of national committees. For many years she was a member of the SCONUL Working Group on Information Literacy and she represents Research Libraries UK on the Research Information and Digital Literacies Coalition, where she is currently leading a strand of activity on open data. She was an advocate for green open access on the Repositories Sub-Group of the Finch Working Group and has recently contributed to HEFCE's REF Data Collection Steering Group.

Angus Whyte is a Senior Institutional Support Officer in the Digital Curation Centre (DCC). He works alongside partners in UK universities to improve services that support researchers and other stakeholders in data management, and has authored guidelines and articles on a range of data issues. He has a PhD in Social Informatics from the University of Strathclyde and before joining the DCC was for ten years a postdoctorate researcher, working on requirements discovery and the evaluation of information systems to support engagement in policy-making.

Matthew Woollard is Director of both the UK Data Service and the UK Data Archive at the University of Essex. He has practical and theoretical experience in all aspects of data service infrastructure, providing leadership in data curation, archiving and preservation activities. From 2002 to 2006 he was the Head of the History Data Service and from 2006 to 2010 an Associate Director and Head of Digital Preservation and Systems at the UK Data Archive. He currently provides leadership and strategic direction of both the

UK Data Archive and UK Data Service, developing and enhancing the organizations' national and international reputation and ensuring their effective management, operation and development.

CHAPTER 1

A patchwork of change

Graham Pryor

1. Evolution in an age of technological revolution

After a number of years in which the stock response to the accelerating data deluge was simply to throw larger and larger volumes of storage capacity to the university research community, the provision of planned and structured research data management (RDM) services has at last begun to gain a foothold across the higher education sector. So what has been going on in those most recent decades of the information age, since around 1990, and why has it taken so long for the sector to accept that it needs to introduce a new kind of support infrastructure, both technological and human?

A full nine years after Tim Berners-Lee launched the world wide web, an act that introduced the first truly public data search and retrieval service to the internet, the UK government's spending review of 2000 delivered its original and unprecedented e-science initiative. This was designed to encourage the development of an IT infrastructure sufficient to support the increasingly global research collaborations emerging from science and engineering disciplines. Such collaborations, in fact e-science itself, were characterized by the shared use of some combination of very large computing resources, enormous data collections and fast and ubiquitous access to remote facilities or sensor data. Three years later, in its *Circular 6/03 (Revised) Digital Curation Centre,*[1] the UK's Joint Information Systems Committee (Jisc) called for proposals 'to pilot the development of generic support services for maintaining digital data and research results over their entire life-cycle for current and future users'. The analysis that Jisc used to promote this initiative was that the 'current generation of "e-Science" experiments and computations will create more scientific data in the next five years than has been collected in the whole of human history. Properly curated, this data will form a major resource for future generations of scientists.'

From these beginnings, one may assume that the active curation of primary data had been recognized as a core requirement of the e-science community. The corollary was that some new kind of service provision would be devised to manage the challenges inherent in not only the long-term preservation of electronic documents, databases and publications, but also to ensure that data users now and in the future could discover the data they need and make effective use of their preferred data manipulation tools and methodologies. As *Circular 6/03* most perceptively determined, data curation 'includes all the processes needed for good data creation and management, and the capacity to add value to generate new sources of information and knowledge'; the consequence of which, inescapably, must involve a sustained 'interaction between creators and providers of data, the archivers of data, and most importantly the consumers of data'.

So far, so good. A further nine years on from that formative observation by Jisc, the Royal Society report *Science as an Open Enterprise: open data for open science*[2] referred to the 'rapid and pervasive technological change that has created new ways of acquiring, storing, manipulating and transmitting vast data volumes', a revolution that has stimulated 'new habits of communication and collaboration amongst scientists' and challenged 'many existing norms of scientific behaviour'. Yet in the view of the report's distinguished authors, six further changes in research practice are still necessary before there can be a truly successful exploitation of these new technologies and collaborations:

1 A shift away from a research culture where data is viewed as a private preserve.
2 An expansion of the criteria used to evaluate research in order that credit can be given for useful data communication and novel ways of collaborating.
3 The development of common standards for communicating data.
4 The mandating of intelligent openness for that data which is relevant to published scientific papers.

5 The creation of a strong cohort of data scientists to manage and support the use of digital data.
6 The development and use of new software tools to automate and simplify the creation and exploitation of datasets.

According to the Royal Society's report, the 'means to make these changes are available' but they have not yet been achieved due to the lack of 'an effective commitment to their use from scientists, their institutions and those who fund and support science'.

Whilst acknowledging that the Royal Society's particular focus in this report is to promote the principle of openness and to generate new momentum in open science, this assertion could be taken by those who have made real advances with standards, tools and the foundation of openness as the cause for some alarm. If one infers that between the late 1990s and the present day there has been little progress by the higher education community in its response to the transformational changes being experienced in research data generation, sharing and curation, then a number of significant initiatives have most certainly been overlooked. The Society's key message, however, is expressed by the phrase 'effective commitment', which we shall interpret as the coherent and pervasive adoption of those measures necessary to the implementation of RDM processes, protocols, standards and services; further, this potentially universal adoption has to demonstrate that institutions have accepted these measures as fully funded, established and sustainable components of their institutional structures and business. In that case, yes, the Royal Society is spot-on, as the distance between the few who occupy the vanguard and the majority that has yet to address what is meant by a serious commitment to data management and sharing appears to have widened in the past few years. This is not an unexpected state of affairs; nor is it in any way a static one. In the large, diverse and complex organism that is a research-led university, the pursuit of such a course of action will be associated with considerable cultural change. This will be the transformational process that the Royal Society recognizes has still to be secured, but which even in the most agile and risk-disposed of institutions cannot be achieved in haste.

The development of institutional RDM services has already been likened to 'an iterative cycle similar to business process redesign' (Jones, Pryor and White, 2012) where, borrowing terms from the business sector, one would expect the introduction of any new mission-critical philosophy, principles and structures to be grounded in a fundamental rethinking of existing processes, in order to deliver greater productivity and value to the customer. Typically, in business, this will involve the radical and rapid simplification of organizational layers and the elimination of unproductive or redundant activities. Not so in higher education. In all but the most 'managed' of universities, the prevalent culture will generate significant resistance to the unchallenged achievement of these goals. Here, the 'iterative cycle' that defines the process of redesign will prove to be exactly that, with an inevitable need for extensive repetition, in numerous forums, of the argument for RDM; the consequent intromission of recurrent adjustments to the parameters for change; and the persistent necessity to advocate change when you may have felt that your manifesto had already received the community's assent. We do not mention this merely to paint a negative view of higher education or lay blame, but to point out how important it is to be aware of these challenges from the outset and not to be discouraged by the prospect, since the underlying movement for change that will eventually strengthen your cause is slowly but surely under way.

2. Six necessary changes?

Take, for example, the first of the Royal Society's six necessary changes: a shift away from a research culture where data is viewed as a private preserve. This is already well established as a necessary practice in some of the 'big sciences', like physics, where the analysis of huge volumes of research data depends on its being shared internationally; and in the field of genomics, the rapid access to sequence and other kinds of genomic data has been a guiding principle of the Human Genome Project. In the UK, in 2009, the Panton Principles[3] were written by a group of scientists convinced that 'for science to effectively function, and for society to reap the full benefits from scientific endeavours, it is crucial that science data be made open'. The Principles were subsequently refined and taken to a broader public platform with the help of the members of the Open Knowledge Foundation Working Group on Open Data in Science,[4] a diverse group of scientists, publishers, students and others with an interest in promoting open science. So, whilst this is all still indicative of a culture of self-regulating scholarship and not the large-scale public enterprise being promoted in the Royal Society's report, it is nonetheless a real representation of the shift in attitude and practice that will in time demand platforms and structures for support on an institutional, national and global scale.

It is as feasible to provide evidence of progress in each of the other five areas of necessary change. In the area of research evaluation, for example, Main Panel C of the UK's Research Excellence Framework (REF), the new national mechanism for assessing research undertaken in higher education institutions, plans to accept a wide range of research output, including digital artefacts such as datasets and multi-use datasets. This is a small beginning in the move away from the traditional submission of research publications, and it applies to only one of the four main assessment panels, but it is a very significant change. In a consultative document issued on 25 February 2013, the Higher Education Funding Council for England (HEFCE) prepared to take further steps after the 2014 REF by seeking views on the submission of scholarly publications delivered as open access. Speaking on behalf of the four UK funding bodies for higher education, and with an objective to increase considerably the proportion of research outputs published in open-access form, HEFCE declared their intention to require that outputs meeting the REF open access requirement shall be accessible through an institutional repository. They are of course talking here about publications, rather than data, but they make clear that in practice each submitting institution will 'maintain a web facility through which all relevant outputs might be identified and accessed (including items available through a link to another website)'.[5] Even more significantly, having made explicit the requirement for all submitting institutions to provide enabling infrastructure, there follows particular reference to the role of data in making the research process more effective, with respondents to the consultation being invited to comment on whether sufficient progress has been made to implement a requirement for supporting open data as well as open publications.

The growth in specialized national services is also an indication of gathering momentum. We have already remarked the creation of the Digital Curation Centre (DCC) and, if you are pondering the need for standards or other authoritative guides to data management frameworks, a simple search on the Centre's web pages[6] will quickly reveal the extent to which benchmarks for metadata and data communication protocols have advanced internationally. If help in deciding what software platform best meets your needs is what you are seeking, OSS Watch,[7] funded in the UK as a free, national service, provides unbiased advice and guidance in the use, development and licensing of open-source software. If cloud services are going to feature in your infrastructure portfolio, the JANET Brokerage Service[8] provides independent guidance, collaborative purchasing power and due diligence to help institutions move towards cloud storage and external data centre services.

The success of the Jisc's Managing Research Data Programme[9] is further evidence of the determination of national bodies to persuade and assist institutions in meeting the data challenge. In particular, its 2011–13 programme has enabled 17 large institutional projects to focus on developing and extending RDM infrastructures. An additional eight projects are helping research groups, projects or departments fulfil disciplinary best practice and the requirements of research funders by implementing data management plans and supporting systems.

These are indeed all significant footholds and, as more initiatives are sustained, there is already evidence of increasing cross-fertilization of ideas, experience and the exchange of good practice right across the sector. Yet projects are notorious for their inability to gain the critical mass and momentum that will ensure their sustainability before project funding is exhausted. Although the Jisc Managing Research Data Programme expects that the data management projects it has funded will each be part of a recognized institutional mission to provide high-quality support for research, in an environment where there is heavy competition for limited resources that shift is not everywhere guaranteed. But the kind of change envisaged in *Science as an Open Enterprise*, which has been further invested with the weight of government resolve in the *Open Data White Paper: unleashing the potential* (Cabinet Office, 2012), including Tim Berners-Lee's proposed Five Star Scheme for data standards, presupposes that universities will themselves have committed to sophisticated mechanisms of support and unrestrained measures for delivery of their research output. After several years of best efforts on the part of national agencies, in order to move more nimbly to that happy state now requires something of revolution rather than the long, slow particulate motion of evolution. History is witness to the fact that such a transition is normally enabled by the intervention of some fresh external stimulus.

3. Policy frameworks, mandates and expectations

Major stimuli were in no short supply during the year prior to publication of the Royal Society's report. Research Councils UK (RCUK) set the tone for 2011 with its *Common Principles on Data Policy*,[10] which although lacking teeth was unique in giving common cause to the seven councils' commitment to transparency and for the first time described a coherent approach across the research base. Publicly funded research data was declared a public good, 'produced in the public interest, which should be made openly available with as few restrictions as possible in a timely and responsible manner that does not harm intellectual property'. Actions for institutions were implied by the assumption that they would have data policies and plans in place and that measures would be taken not only to preserve data of acknowledged value but that it would also be assigned sufficient metadata for other researchers to understand and reuse it. It was even recognized that the use of public funds to support the management and sharing of publicly funded research data would be legitimate, although no new funds were being offered for that purpose – but, after all, these were principles, not plans.

More instructional policy frameworks were soon to follow, however. Having released a revised *Research Data Policy*[11] in September 2010, the Economic and Social Research Council (ESRC) brought a new requirement into force in spring 2011, whereby research grant applicants would be required to submit a statement on data sharing and provide a data management and sharing plan. What softened this new obligation for institutions was the knowledge that the ESRC already offered extensive support to its funded researchers in the shape of the UK Data Archive (UKDA) at the University of Essex. As explained in the revised policy document, data centre staff will happily assist researchers to plan their data management and sharing, and providing ongoing support throughout their project, including final deposit and reuse. As we shall explore later in this book, the availability of national data services should always feature in deliberations concerning the deployment of institutional resources for RDM service provision.

But if one is looking for the moment when university managers woke up to a more revolutionary flavour in research council data policy that, too, occurred in 2011, when on 1 May the Engineering and Physical Sciences Research Council (EPSRC) published its *Policy Framework on Research Data*. The Framework described seven core principles, which were directly aligned with the core RCUK principles, two of which were deemed to be of particular importance: first, 'that publicly funded research data should generally be made as widely and freely available as possible in a timely and responsible manner'; and second, 'that the research process should not be damaged by the inappropriate release of such data'.[12] Both imply actions to be taken by institutions and their researchers, both assume that mechanisms do or will exist to enable those actions. Neither sounds extraordinarily radical except that, unlike the ESRC, the EPSRC provides no support infrastructure, meaning that universities in receipt of EPSRC research grants would themselves have to supply the appropriate services and support.

By itself, that realization was not likely to persuade institutions that they must commit to the development of RDM services; after all, higher education is awash with principles of one kind or another. The moment of epiphany came, though, with the accompanying nine 'clear expectations' that the funder lay at the door of the 100-plus organizations in receipt of its funding. Most rousing of them all was expectation number nine, which plainly stated that those organizations 'will ensure adequate resources are provided to support the curation of publicly funded research data; these resources will be allocated from within their existing public funding streams, whether received from Research Councils as direct or indirect support for specific projects or from higher education Funding Councils as block grants'.

To ensure that, having gained everyone's attention, the attention did not immediately slip away again, the EPSRC had written the previous month to forewarn all university vice-chancellors and principals of the EPSRC policy timetable. As reiterated in a second letter, sent in February 2012, the timetable was dependent upon two deadlines: by 1 May 2012 each institution was to have a clear roadmap in place to align policies and processes with EPSRC expectations, which by 1 May 2015 should have led to full compliance with those expectations. If by that later date any institution is found not to be fully compliant and it can be shown either to be deliberately obstructing the proper sharing of research data or otherwise seriously failing to comply with EPSRC's expectations, this will initiate a process that could ultimately lead to it being declared ineligible for EPSRC support. Since the EPSRC supports about 8000 academic researchers from a £4 billion portfolio, this could not be ignored.

What, then, do the other eight EPSRC expectations mean for universities required to ensure there are 'adequate resources . . . to support the curation of publicly-funded research data'? The self-analysis involved in the creation of a roadmap will enable an institution to discover its current condition and the steps it needs to take to achieve compliance. In other words, it will need to ask what actions are necessary to support research data curation, who will take them, when should they be taken and how much is this activity expected to cost. Effectively, as demonstrated by Table 1.1, the creation of an EPSRC roadmap could be the kernel of a larger RDM service plan.

Table 1.1 EPSRC expectations and university responses

EPSRC expectation	Potential university response
1. Research organizations will promote internal awareness of these principles and expectations and ensure that their researchers and research students have a general awareness of the regulatory environment and of the available exemptions which may be used, should the need arise, to justify the withholding of research data.	• Provide publicity and guidance, possibly through workshops and training including induction for new researchers and postgraduates. • Provide a mechanism via the institutional repository (where one exists) to add a statement / link to data. • Reflect funder and regulatory obligations in policies for research and research data.
2. Published research papers should include a short statement describing how and on what terms any supporting research data may be accessed.	• Publicize this requirement, include it in induction for new researchers and reflect it in policies for research and research data.
3. Each research organization will have specific policies and associated processes to maintain effective internal awareness of their publicly-funded research data holdings and of requests by third parties to access such data; all of their researchers or research students funded by EPSRC will be required to comply with research organization policies in this area or, in exceptional circumstances, to provide justification of why this is not possible.	• Implement measures to record and make discoverable all publicly-funded research data that cannot be treated as an exception. This could have far-reaching consequences – e.g. the creation and maintenance of a data catalogue that also records the details of third-party access requests.
4. Publicly-funded research data that is not generated in digital format will be stored in a manner to facilitate it being shared in the event of a valid request for access to the data being received (this expectation could be satisfied by implementing a policy to convert and store such data in digital format in a timely manner).	• Undertake an audit to identify such physical material. • Consider the cost, benefits and risks involved in conversion to digital format, compare with alternative 'physical' measures and select preferred option.
5. Research organizations will ensure that appropriately structured metadata describing the research data they hold is published (normally within 12 months of the data being generated) and made freely accessible on the internet; in each case the metadata must be sufficient to allow others to understand what research data exists, why, when and how it was generated, and how to access it. Where the research data referred to in the metadata is a digital object it is expected that the metadata will include use of a robust digital object identifier (for example as available through the DataCite organization – http://datacite.org).	• Identify appropriate and acceptable metadata standards and protocols. • Implement processes and responsibilities for adequate metadata assignment. • Establish and sustain a mechanism to enable data discovery on the internet. • Advise researchers of requirements and the support to be provided. • Provide guidance and training to data custodians and/or researchers in the assignment of metadata. • Include requirement in research data policy.
6. Where access to the data is restricted the published metadata should also give the reason and summarize the conditions which must be satisfied for access to be granted. For example 'commercially confidential' data, in which a business organization has a legitimate interest, might be made available to others subject to a suitable legally enforceable non-disclosure agreement.	• Provide guidance, particularly in induction for new researchers. • Include requirement in research data policy.

Continued on next page

Table 1.1 *(continued)*	
EPSRC expectation	**Potential university response**
7. Research organizations will ensure that EPSRC-funded research data is securely preserved for a minimum of 10-years from the date that any researcher 'privileged access' period expires or, if others have accessed the data, from last date on which access to the data was requested by a third party; all reasonable steps will be taken to ensure that publicly-funded data is not held in any jurisdiction where the available legal safeguards provide lower levels of protection than are available in the UK.	• Long-term measures will have to be decided in order to archive, curate and enable discovery and access. • Need to assess the extent to which available options will be deployed (i.e. an institutional repository, national data centres, cloud services) and investment made. • Identify roles and responsibilities for the preservation of data, its periodic review and methods for secure and appropriate disposal.
8. Research organizations will ensure that effective data curation is provided throughout the full data lifecycle, with 'data curation' and 'data lifecycle' being as defined by the Digital Curation Centre. The full range of responsibilities associated with data curation over the data lifecycle will be clearly allocated within the research organization, and where research data is subject to restricted access the research organization will implement and manage appropriate security controls; research organizations will particularly ensure that the quality assurance of their data curation processes is a specifically assigned responsibility.	• Effectively, expectation number 8 is requiring institutions to create a comprehensive research data management service! • As implied by the second half of this expectation, the service is likely to involve a broad range of actors and activities with new roles and responsibilities to enable the gamut of data management planning, the assignment of metadata for discoverability and access, long-term preservation, et al. • Extensive planning and investment will be required, with the potential for new recruitment where essential skills are lacking, together with the introduction of new routines for governance and communication.

Such an analysis makes plain that meeting these not-extraordinary expectations for data management will involve not only the research process but a diverse range of associated activities, roles and organizational constituents. At least three key perspectives would have to be represented and agreements forged between them for a fit for purpose service to emerge: (1) the internal community engaged in research practice, (2) institutional management and (3) the providers of information systems, services and support. Each of these perspectives will in turn be multifaceted, potentially adding to the complexity of the undertaking. Most heterogeneous will be the research support perspective, which could embrace staff from the library, information technology services, research administration and the records management functions, not forgetting the various kinds of specialist support staff located within individual research teams. As a rule, these groups will not have worked together previously as coherent teams and they may know little about each other's activities; it is equally unlikely that they are already pursuing shared routines and objectives. Thrown together by the *force majeure* of funder mandates they will have to face a wholly new set of interpersonal subtexts and organizational dynamics that will need to be addressed, in addition to the main challenge of familiarization with the tenets of research data management.

4. Supporting modernization and institutional focus

Meeting that challenge is not a prospect that has to be faced in isolation. Also in spring 2011, with funding from the Higher Education Funding Council for England (HEFCE), the DCC rolled out the first of its institutional engagement programmes. This initiative was but one feature of yet another funding body's attempts to tackle current issues in higher education. Although HEFCE's initial focus here was not on research data, its Universities Modernisation Fund, set up to support 10,000 extra student places in 2010–11 and encourage universities and colleges to adopt efficiencies and savings through shared services and other innovative practices, provided the DCC with sufficient resource to embark on a series of unique collaborations with 21 UK universities. These collaborations, called institutional engagements, were designed with the sole purpose of improving institutional capabilities (their ability to articulate and achieve RDM objectives) and capacity (the creation of sustained and effective infrastructures) in the conduct of effective research data management. These free, 60-day engagements have provided the selected 21 universities with assistance in making the case for RDM services and infrastructure, in re-engineering the roles of support staff and equipping them with new skills, and in the transfer of knowledge about available tools and techniques. Moreover, whilst this chosen clutch of institutions represents around only a fifth of the research-led universities in the UK, a condition of each engagement was that the experience and outcomes would be openly promulgated and actively shared with the wider community.

Whilst the first phase of that programme has drawn to a close, the DCC has maintained its links with the candidate institutions. It has also commenced a second tranche of engagements that reflects the needs of a more mature data management environment, whilst at the same time recognizing the growth of a rearguard 'long tail'. This refined engagement process now offers a series of thematic modules covering specific technical solutions to policy and infrastructure questions, which are likely to appeal to institutions that have already begun to shape their RDM service. But in addition there is a package of complementary products designed to assist latecomers in conducting advocacy, building strategies and re-engineering the skills base. With this broadening base the Centre remains a key source of advice and guidance, acting increasingly as a medium for exchange between multiple layers in the emerging community of data practitioners.

5. Global perspectives

Membership of that community is increasingly international, although the pace outside the UK has been set mainly by Australia and the USA. Both have witnessed pressure brought to bear on researchers and institutions from funders, from government and from within the research community: pressure to share and make data open as well as to select, appraise and preserve data for specific periods as a condition of the compact between funders and grant holders. The tension between these aspirations and mandates and the ability to resource appropriate responses has been addressed rather differently in the case of these two nations.

The national research data strategies of Australia and the USA have already been contrasted (Treloar, Choudhury and Michener, 2012) as responses to two very different government and research sector environments. The approach taken in Australia has been to develop a national data service, ANDS, which exploits a collaborative framework of data stores, federations and services across these sectors. Through the provision of guidance and instruction on internal institutional data management, ANDS's institutional partners are expected to move forward together in the implementation of data management planning frameworks, tools for data reuse and the development of teams with data management skills.

Taking this common approach, with considerable central funding and a three-year high-level project plan, raised the profile of RDM through 'a combination of national services and coherent institutional research data infrastructure, combined with the ability to exploit that infrastructure with tools, policy and capability' (Treloar, Choudhury and Michener, 2012). In Chapter 8 we provide a closer look at one of those institutional infrastructures with a case study from Monash University.

Although ANDS was created to drive improvements in the Australian research environment, the data registry solution that has been developed under its auspices, Research Data Australia,[13] which provides a discovery service for Australian research data collections, has emerged as but one element of the ANDS service that is influencing service development elsewhere in the global data community. As UK universities become more involved in the management of research data and their capacity to contribute develops, the case for a UK Research Data Discovery Service is also growing, adding a further potential building block to the transformation of research practice. Recognizing that the ANDS approach has demonstrated success and that the software is relatively mature, Jisc and DCC will in 2013 complete a pilot registry service that aggregates records of research data held by UK universities and by key national and discipline-orientated data centres.

Notwithstanding the National Science Foundation's requirement from 2011 for grant submissions to include data management plans, the movement for change in the USA has come about less as a consequence of mandates or dictates than from initiatives arising within the research support community itself. There, far-sighted librarians in particular have noted the implications for their services from the rise of data-intensive research and have responded quickly by re-engineering their technical and human infrastructures. Whereas in the UK the gap between researchers and the library has been widened by the availability of the internet, which has nurtured a research culture of increasing self-reliance in terms of information retrieval and use, in the USA libraries have seized the initiative by retraining staff as data scientists and by taking the lead in such multi-disciplinary, multi-partner programmes as Data Conservancy,[14] a $20,000,000 project involving ten partner institutions. Notably, Data Conservancy, with its objective of scientific data curation, perceives a library-led organizational framework delivering cross-disciplinary discovery. In February 2013, President Obama's administration required research funding agencies to ensure that the public can access publications and data produced as an output from Federally funded research. This unusual high-level intervention will give further strength to the Data Conservancy mission to preserve data and make it available for scientific use. Any such pronouncements are there to be exploited by enterprising librarians keen to reinvent themselves as more active partners in the research agenda.

This and other data enterprises are by no means inward-looking and will provide a further source for the designers of RDM services of exemplars in infrastructure and service provision. The DataONE project,[15] for example, with a team sourced predominantly from the digital library world, is charged with delivering a federated data network to preserve and improve access to data in the biological and environmental sciences. The DataONE plan talks in terms of implementing global infrastructure by allowing a number of nodes to be added to the network on continents outside North America.

In simple terms, DataONE will provide a place for researchers to store data and its associated metadata but, to equip them with the means to use this service effectively, the project is addressing a raft of interrelated activities. Data management planning, the techniques, protocols and methods for data acquisition and back-up, data analysis and workflow are but a small example of the areas under development and any institutions engaged in the design of RDM services would sensibly add this and similar international projects to their knowledge base.

6. Unfamiliar territory

Planning for the creation of RDM services not only brings together groups and functions that previously were separate and distinct, it very probably brings them into contact with a whole register of management and financial terms and procedures that previously were remote. Sometimes these can become confused and certainly they can seem confusing. We have therefore included in this introduction a brief explanation of some of the terms you are more likely to encounter. Their inclusion here does not necessarily imply that each of them will feature in your own start-up processes; for example, you may choose to develop a business case to secure the resources necessary and elect only to use a simple roadmap in place of full business and operating plans. Your approach will depend on the organizational structures and procedures already in place. What follows is meant to clarify terminology not dictate the manner of its use.

Strategy

Logically the starting point, an RDM strategy should be an aspirational statement setting out your long-term goals and objectives and the courses of action necessary to achieving them. It may include reference to the human and financial resources needed for meeting objectives but, essentially, it is more to do with setting the scene than setting detailed budgets. Endorsement of a strategy can in most circumstances be taken as approval to proceed within an institution's overarching business mission. It also legitimizes the development of policy and serves as an invitation to submit a business case.

Business case

The business case will formally present the argument for resourcing the RDM project or programme. Typically, it will be a detailed but accessible document submitted for consideration by senior management, although it may also be delivered as a presentation. It will describe the background and context to implementing RDM infrastructure and services, the anticipated benefits, options considered (including the reasons for their adoption or rejection), predicted costs, a gap analysis and expected risks (including the costs and risks of doing nothing). By formally endorsing a business case, senior managers are consenting to the deployment of resources and the preparation of forward budgets. From this point it is also appropriate to commence work on a policy to underpin the strategy.

Business plan

As a summation of the overarching direction for RDM development and the activities to be resourced and undertaken, within a specified timeframe and well defined context, the business plan serves as the main reference document for the programme. Whilst business plans may be externally or internally focused, in terms of developing institutional RDM services it is probable that the principal focus will be internal, although external interests could exist on global scale in the form of consortial partners, research funders, commercial investors, publishers and discipline collaborators.

The business plan will reflect the terms of engagement approved by management, by drawing together all the components of the RDM programme into a coherently structured process and timetable. It will include the RDM vision, a summary of strategy, critical success factors and a description of perceived benefits, together with detailed plans for financial and human resources, the roadmap and operational plan, an explanation of measures to comply with legal, statutory and funder obligations, and a sustainability and exit plan. Although the RDM business plan is likely to cover a period of five to ten years, it should be reviewed annually to ensure that the identified critical success factors remain appropriate (and are being achieved). Resubmission within the institutional planning cycle is recommended to ensure that confirmed budgets are carried forward.

Roadmap

The term 'roadmap', recently associated with EPSRC's data management expectations, has been used to describe the series of actions necessary to achieving a particular level of RDM effectiveness. Ideally it will explain key expectations, current arrangements and gaps in provision; the milestones to be achieved over a specific timeframe to meet expectations and mend those gaps; the roles and responsibilities of individual actors and groups; and the costs. Whilst it has been used specifically to identify the measures that will deliver compliance with EPSRC policy, the roadmap is likely to feature as the baseline for a broader development of RDM service strategy and, as such, it could be treated as an element (and potential surrogate) of the business case and of the business plan.

Operating plan

An operating plan works as a subset of the business plan and will describe the goals and activities of the contributing parts of the RDM programme or organization (e.g. the working group or project team, the library or IT department) over a given operational period, typically a budgetary year. It is usually constructed (or revised) annually and is the basis for the annual revenue budget request. However, whilst the focus will be upon the next year's budget submission, operating plans should include the predicted activities and budgets for between one and three years, in order to allow the institution to develop rolling forecasts and balances. The operating plan is also the mechanism for highlighting (and seeking ratification) of modifications to the business plan that may have arisen from changes in policy, movement in the fiscal environment, or adjustments to the strategy.

Since the implementation and growth of RDM will involve a diversity of stakeholder groups within an institution, the operating plan is the means by which they can each prepare for resource allocation at a team or departmental level (where the development of RDM is likely to depend on separate departmental budgets), at the same time acting as the medium for enabling a coherent and inclusive request for funding. The need for significant cross-departmental dialogue in the development of operating plans is therefore crucial. In practice, where RDM services are being grafted on to existing units and functions, each party may present its own contribution to the RDM strategy as a component of a discrete departmental plan.

Policy

An RDM policy describes the principles that an institution has agreed will guide the decisions and the actions necessary to achieve desired outcomes. It is not to be confused with either a strategy or a plan, since it does not explain what will be done to achieve those outcomes. Nonetheless, an RDM policy is valuable as a public statement of intent and an expression of the commitment of management and senior stakeholders. Furthermore, it identifies such decision-makers as accountable for not only the policy but also the implementation of measures to deliver the resources and infrastructure required to enable the policy.

Capital budget/expenditure

Capital budgets are prepared to enable long-term investment in major items such as new or replacement equipment (e.g. servers and networks) or physical facilities (e.g. a data centre or repository). Other non-recurrent costs may be eligible for capital funding; it is advisable to seek advice on this matter from the finance department. Some funders allow research grants to contribute to capital budgets for the development of data centres and RDM services. It is recommended that clarification of funder policy is sought before funds are committed in this way.

When considering proposals for capital expenditure, an institution is likely to rank submissions to determine which will be the most financially rewarding. It is therefore important to have laid the groundwork in the endorsed business case for demonstrating the cost-benefits of the RDM development programme.

What constitutes a capital item can differ between institutions and it is always worth checking whether designation as a revenue item is both achievable and more beneficial. It is also important to remember that capital items will depreciate in value and will require maintenance. Both aspects of purchase should be described here but the actual budget for maintenance will appear in the revenue budget.

Revenue budget/expenditure

The revenue (or operating) budget covers the cost of those annual activities necessary to the development and delivery of RDM services, including estimates of the cost of human and other resources but excluding any capital items. As acknowledged above, the potentially diverse nature of an RDM team can call for significant cross-department collaboration in the creation of revenue budgets.

7. Summation

In this chapter we have introduced the provision of RDM services as an unfolding patchwork of challenges. For the higher education sector in the 21st century the development of digital technology has irrevocably altered research practice; it has also changed the context, having been instrumental in enabling new research methods that have accelerated the globalization of research. The impact of the digital age on traditional research support services, which were primarily understood in terms of the university library, is a leading motivation for change; some might say almost a case of do or die for the library profession. Certainly, for the time being, there is a gap between service provision and customer needs, although this is not only to be seen as a gulf between the library and the research agenda but is also evident in the marked impotence of some IT services when faced by enormous data scale and diversity. But as we have pointed out, the challenge is not only for these more obvious contenders, since it embraces a wider and uniquely heterogeneous ensemble of service and support.

This challenge demands a whole new way of thinking. In his summary of the report *Data-driven Infrastructure*,[16] in which a number of approaches are suggested for managing both corporate and research data, the author Max Hammond explains that, while universities have begun to address the growing demands for data management by creating a variety of architectures, 'one concept that is emerging is that of data-centric architecture which focuses primarily on organizational data rather than systems, and is designed to facilitate the sharing of data between the processes handling institutional data'. It is not just a technology challenge that we are facing, although it is a socio-technical one, but principally it is a data challenge. That is what is new.

In a context of increasing regulation by government and greater levels of intervention by research funders, institutions can no longer procrastinate and must act to find a sustainable approach to RDM services that is fit for their own purposes. This book provides a step by step guide to the components of an RDM service, concluding with case studies that describe several innovative approaches to the development of data-driven infrastructures. There are a number of approaches to consider and many decisions to be taken. We wish you well as you embark upon them.

8. References

8.1 Websites

1 www.jisc.ac.uk/fundingopportunities/funding_calls/2003/09/funding_ digcentre.aspx.

2 Royal Society, *Science as an Open Enterprise: open data for open science*, Royal Society Science Policy Centre report 02/12, http://royalsociety.org/policy/projects/science-public-enterprise/report.

3 http://pantonprinciples.org/about.

4 http://science.okfn.org.

5 www.hefce.ac.uk/media/hefce/content/news/news/2013/open_access_letter.pdf.

6 www.dcc.ac.uk.

7 www.oss-watch.ac.uk.

8 https://www.ja.net/products-services/janet-cloud-services.

9 www.jisc.ac.uk/whatwedo/programmes/mrd.aspx.

10 *RCUK Common Principles on Data Policy*, www.rcuk.ac.uk/research/Pages/DataPolicy.aspx.

11 www.esrc.ac.uk/about-esrc/information/data-policy.aspx.

12 www.epsrc.ac.uk/about/standards/researchdata/Pages/default.aspx.

13 http://researchdata.ands.org.au.

14 http://dataconservancy.org.

15 www.dataone.org.

16 http://blog.observatory.jisc.ac.uk/techwatch-reports/data-driven-infrastructure.

8.2 Citations

Cabinet Office (2012) *Open Data White Paper: unleashing the potential*, HM Government.

Jones, S., Pryor, G. and Whyte, A. (2012) Developing Research Data Management Capability: the view from a national support service. In iPRES 2012, *Proceedings of the Ninth International Conference on Preservation of Digital Objects*, https://ipres.ischool.utoronto.ca.

Treloar, A., Choudhury, G. S. and Michener, W. (2012) Contrasting National Research Data Strategies: Australia and the USA. In Pryor, G. (ed.), *Managing Research Data*, Facet Publishing.

CHAPTER 2

Options and approaches to RDM service provision

Graham Pryor

1. Carrots, sticks and the prospect of marginalization

Chapter 1 concluded with the assertion that, as a consequence of pressure from government and the major funders, institutions need quickly to identify measures that will deliver a sustainable approach to research data management (RDM) service provision. That said, it would be wrong for the selection of any such measures to proceed simply on the basis of an arbitrary tick-box response to the various carrots and sticks being proffered or waved by the agents of authority. There are other sound and persuasive reasons why research-intensive universities need to give serious thought to the development of RDM support, not least the benefits we shall outline in this chapter, during which process precedence over all other considerations must be given to the understanding that any measures adopted will be deemed fit for the specific needs and purposes of the individual institution. To ignore that caveat would be to guarantee wasted resource and an unpopular service.

Yet, faced with the potential loss of funding that is implicit in the EPSRC gambit, many institutions have felt compelled to develop roadmaps that will secure their compliance with this particular funder's expectations for data management. In some quarters of the sector this action has been taken in spite of an evident reluctance to accept that traditionally self-regulating organizations are being obligated in such an abnormally direct manner.

Attitudes towards this obligation, and by association towards the perceived merits of research data management, were revealed in a survey of EPSRC grant holders conducted by the Digital Curation Centre (DCC) during August and September 2012. Whilst all responding institutions claimed either to have completed or to be in the throes of developing a roadmap, only 34% indicated that their roadmap would feature as a core component of a broader research data management strategy. Whilst a number of individual and generally positive comments suggested that the EPSRC's action had galvanized institutions into addressing a topic that until now had been widely neglected – even, it was said, offering a firm foundation for the development of good practice – there was also considerable resentment towards the imposition of yet another apparent administrative hurdle that research institutions would have to negotiate. Perhaps most significantly, 43% found that meeting this funder's expectations *per se* would be difficult to reconcile with prevailing financial conditions, where budgets were being cut and staffing levels reduced. The perceptible low priority being given to the subject of data management, coupled with a certain irritation at being forced down a particular path by a third party, could explain why most of the responding institutions had included in their roadmap a timetable and list of tasks but only 22% have described the resources required to deliver them. One is left with the sense that some at least had indeed approached the creation of a roadmap as a tick-box exercise designed only to keep them in the EPSRC fold, or at best to create a holding position whilst they decide what actual steps can be taken.

They are perhaps right to exercise caution. In practice, following those plans, or roadmaps, will in most cases necessitate a considerable investment in some level of new or reorganized service provision, which typically will be investment that was previously unplanned or unforeseen prior to the EPSRC intervention. Whilst to some extent the level of that investment may be dictated by the selection of only those basic measures deemed necessary for meeting the nine EPSRC expectations, if they are to work more positively not only as a framework for compliance but also to provide real value for money in the institutional context, any plans for the investment of capital or human resources will have to be achievable, meaningful and effective as a reflection of local needs and aspirations. This will prove most patently to be the case when they are judged against other competing demands for expenditure on research, teaching and the estate in general.

In his letter to vice-chancellors dated 10 February 2012, EPSRC's Director of Communications, Information & Strategy made clear that it was not the intention of the funder to be prescriptive, that measures deemed appropriate for one institution may not be so for another and that the EPSRC had no desire to evaluate the appropriateness of institution-specific plans. This ought to suggest a fair margin of wriggle room, even when, as in the case of some medium-sized UK institutions, as much as one-third or more of their research income is provided by the EPSRC. So if there is an argument for the introduction of RDM services that is greater than mere compliance with the expectations of a single, if very significant, funder, however compelling those expectations may or may not be judged of themselves, what are the more fundamental reasons for pursuing such a strategy and how far should an institution go in meeting them?

2. From innovation to transformation

Organizations such as Jisc in the UK, or the USA's National Science Foundation (NSF), proselytize the effective management of research data with the promise of real rewards through and beyond the lifetime of individual research programmes or projects. For Jisc and NSF, and indeed for most national organizations engaged in the process of improving their research environments, the argument for effectively managing research data is well rehearsed. They acknowledge and respect a requirement for the investment of public funds to deliver some form of public good; they are well versed in the challenges inherent in the scale and complexity of the data being generated, which beg the presence of custodianship, order and the imperative of standard methodologies; and they have plenty of evidence from the globalization and increasingly cross-disciplinary nature of research to argue for better platforms for collaboration, sharing and the exchange of data. But not all the drivers for improving the management and sharing of research data are 'top-down', says Jisc. Researchers 'who have experienced the innovative and transforming potential of data intensive research through data reuse, recombination or meta-analysis, are also calling for data to be as open as possible'.[1] Key benefits culled from Jisc's Research Data Management Infrastructure (RDMI) projects, part of the broader Managing Research Data (MRD) programme, which funded eight projects to provide examples of good practice, have been identified[2] as both direct and indirect (i.e. costs avoided). The programme has logged a catalogue of institutional benefits, pointing to an improved environment for developing fresh research opportunities, combined with a greater potential for securing research funding; an ability better to organize for economies of scale; larger and higher quality output of publications; and mitigation of the organizational risk inherent in a poorly managed data asset.

There are also benefits for individual researchers and research teams, including the availability of built-in support for research tasks, dependable mechanisms for achieving rapid access to results data and derived data, savings in time and efficiency and an expansion to the volume of reliable citations to their data. This brings us in the direction of a more personal argument concerning the transformational nature of data as an instrument of research and new knowledge, which carried to its natural conclusion will promise that researchers who are ready to share well managed data are also by implication practising higher-quality research, since they will have no qualms about making it open. In return, they can confidently aspire to an increased personal visibility and as a result look forward to enjoying a boost to their reputation and status.

For the research support services, lessons from the Jisc RDMI programme suggest that a coherent approach to managing research data will enable infrastructure to be reused across multiple projects, whilst an improved awareness of researcher needs will lead to an enhancement of the guidance provided for the use of and development of data management tools.

For each of these constituent groups, lower long-term costs for the preservation of datasets are perhaps the largest shared benefit. But whilst it is important to ensure that data is invested with the qualities of discoverability, accessibility and intelligibility in order to enable its long-term future usability, perhaps even after the originating programme of research has ceased and the research team has disbanded, such measures are equally crucial to the proficient organization and use of data during the research active phase. The argument, then, is not simply about the archiving of data but is very much to do with improving and enriching the whole research process, which is surely axiomatic for any research-led organization.

By now, if you were not already convinced, we should have persuaded you that the practice of coherent and effective research data management techniques should be an option of choice. That does not, of course, necessarily imply that universities each need to build and install a full, comprehensive and monolithic research data management *service*. Before embarking on that journey all assumptions should be tested, in line with true scholarly method, focusing initially on the basics of what it is an RDM service might be expected to provide and, where particular features of such services are deemed necessary, how they should most appropriately be delivered – through corporate mediation and stewardship, for example, or as measures devolved throughout the organization, or perhaps contracted to a third party? Decisions here will need to take account of the availability of national or international services, which may be regarded as alternatives or as complementary to institutional infrastructures. But how an institution responds to these questions will increasingly be determined not merely by its particular culture and mode of governance, but by the accuracy of its perceptions concerning a research data landscape in which complexity and the pace of change now represent colossal and unprecedented challenges. Facing up to those challenges whilst maintaining a balance between predicted costs and cost benefits can, we would argue, only be achieved by breaking them down into individual themes and modules, as we shall explain and illustrate throughout the remaining chapters of this book.

Perhaps closer consideration of the extent and nature of *value* that may be gained from managing and sharing research data would be another way of judging how far an institution wishes to invest in services and infrastructure. The Royal Society report to which we referred in the previous chapter, *Science as an Open Enterprise: open data for open science*,[3] described four ascending tiers of infrastructure, with the value of data broadening into a greater number of contexts the further one pitched it up the data pyramid. In Figure 2.1 we present the concept of broadening value and permanence as ripples spreading out across a pool. Most institutions will have broken the

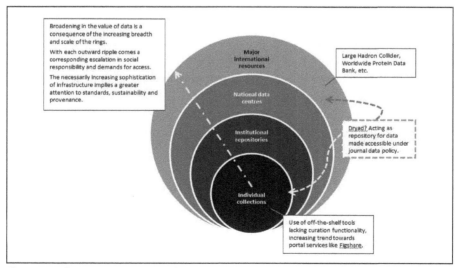

Figure 2.1 The Data Pool, a journey through increasing value and permanence (Developed from a concept used in *Science as an Open Enterprise*, Royal Society, 2012 and previously explored by Fran Berman in *Communications of the ACM*, December 2008, 53)

surface of this pool at the level of individual collections; not all will aspire to spread further to the reaches of a major international resource. But awareness of this potential for extensibility and the exposure and responsibilities that travelling outward will bring, should assist the definition of appropriate institutional goals for research data management. As well as helping to match research data aspirations against institutional objectives for presence and significance in the broader community, exploring these widening pools of activity should also produce evidence of the kinds of services and resources that sustain them[4] and, as will be explained in subsequent chapters, a number of options exist for enabling data storage and sharing that do not limit one to investment in institutional infrastructure. The further one goes in aspiring to greater breadth of value, the greater the complexity (and cost) of infrastructure; but if strategic data management decisions take matters of value into account, selecting from these options will be influenced as much by institutional readiness, ambition and strategy as by the demands of the research community itself.

3. The boundaries of aspiration

Speaking in October 2012 about her experiences when defining RDM needs at the University of St Andrews, Research Computing Team Leader Birgit Plietzsch asked 'Is the journey the destination?'[5] As she went on to explain, St Andrews is a university with 600 years' accrual of institutional culture in which the individual schools have acquired a high level of autonomy; its recently reorganized IT Services was still trying to find its feet, data management skills gaps had been identified throughout the organization, and to address some or all of these issues required focus and involvement from otherwise busy academics. In terms of a procedural framework with which the project might claim legitimacy or relevance, there existed an institutional strategy and an IT strategy but no formal guidance covering research data. This situation is easily recognizable as common to many institutions – except for the 600 years' history, of course.

In the end, faced with promoting a major development initiative in an unfamiliar area of activity, St Andrews decided to develop an RDM roadmap based on the university's established aims for achieving excellence and impact: world-class infrastructure, skills and knowledge, a commitment to integrity and professionalism and a devotion to leadership and collaboration. Consequently, the exercise provided a context that needed no translation from technical jargon; but quite dramatically this value approach to developing a roadmap served to illustrate the significant impact upon the university that could be expected from the introduction of an RDM policy and plan. It has subsequently led to data asset audits being undertaken in order to substantiate the requirements for RDM policy and service provision. As Birgit concluded when considering the lessons learned, one should take care not to underestimate the extent to which institutional culture influences RDM implementation; not all support can be developed from an existing strategy or policy; and RDM service implementation requires robust support structures within the institution.[6]

At another point on the spectrum of preparedness, the approach to RDM being taken at Queen Mary, University of London (QMUL) has had the advantage of being attached to an established programme for the transformation of IT service provision. Designed originally to resolve particular challenges when managing the research lifecycle, such as the provision of post-research support to websites and databases, or meeting demands for a catalogue and price list for centrally supported IT solutions,[7] newly emerging demands for solutions to data management routines could logically be absorbed into the work plan. The transformation programme already enjoyed a platform of governance, approved funding and senior sponsorship, as well as a sense of shared ownership and inclusion. It has therefore been highly beneficial to attach QMUL's RDM roadmap (see Figure 2.2) to the larger project, particularly in the enabling phase, where the RDM building blocks quite distinctly reflect established aims for governance, resourcing and support.

Despite the advantage of being able to treat RDM as the extension to an existing initiative, the core issues of policy alignment, planning, skills development, the introduction of RDM tools and infrastructure and organizing the entire prospect so that it resolves issues of cost and sustainability are as unavoidable at QMUL as they were at St Andrews. The inference to be drawn here is that a model set of activities could be assembled for application in multiple contexts, irrespective of the cultural and organizational differences when viewed institution by institution. Wherever the institution, planning for RDM services at its most specific level will always include consideration of questions such as whether sensitive data will be produced and how it will be looked after, what storage requirements there will be and how these will be provided, where finalized data will be deposited and how it will be curated until eventual disposal.

RDM Theme		Phase 1: Enabling RDM	Phase 2: RDM skills and tools	Phase 3: Best practice
RDM Governance	Policy review	Policy alignment Definition of data, data types, roles and responsibilities	Set up policy review	
	Business planning	Inclusion of research data in publication process Allocations of resource to RDM training	Demand forecasting	Integrate to REF reporting
	Registration of research	Tools for registration of research	Integration with grant applications, publications and resource management systems	Encourage registration of unfunded research
RDM Resourcing	Consultancy support	RDM services and consultancy Catalogue of IT services for researchers Tools to support data management planning	Tools for curation, preservation, metadata and obsolescence	
	IT planning	Align skills to RDM requirements Plan for appropriate technologies	Forward planning and managing technology change	
	Costs and sustainment	Build simple transparent cost model grant application Build considered, scalable, mechanisms for re-charge		
RDM Support	Data repository	Build research data repository	Build links to external data repositories standards and tools	Develop statistics and analytical for REF
	RDM infrastructure	Develop central infrastructure, networks, storage and processing capacity, back-up and continuity facilities, security and integrity	Build sharing capabilities, collaborative tools and specialized services	
	RDM tools	Develop guidance for RDM utilizing independent external tools	Tools for curation, preservation, metadata and obsolescence	Continual development of tools and best practice

Figure 2.2
QMUL's RDM Roadmap Delivery Plan (reproduced by permission of Paul O'Shaughnessy, Programme and Project Manager, QMUL)

4. A modular framework

Addressing the eighth International Digital Curation Conference with a report on progress from Jisc's 2011–13 MRD programme,[8] Simon Hodson described a set of five discrete components that could represent the essential building blocks for a research data management service. From a starting point of data management planning, through to data storage and the mechanisms for recording and identifying data, these activities are contained within an enabling context consisting of policy, sustainable business planning, training and guidance. If you are about to embark on planning new RDM services, this collection of activities (developed further in Chapter 5) may well provide an effective basis upon which to begin defining fundamental requirements.

In what were noted in his presentation as areas of both significant progress and challenge, the development and approval of institutional policies and strategies came top of the list, since in the generally hierarchical yet diverse environment of a British university these will be as essential to the credentials of RDM standard-bearers as they will be slow in their achievement of consensus and approval. Other aspects of progress and challenge experienced by the MRD programme – an enterprise that latterly included 17 large institutional projects, all designed to develop and extend some very real RDM infrastructures – can be expected to recur in almost any institution engaged in building RDM services: the presentation of business cases for sustaining an ongoing service, the development, adaptation, piloting and (in most cases) embedding of training and support services within institutional structures and the join-up of institutional systems (for example, the exchange of information between research administration systems, the CRIS, the data repository, etc.)

In case study 5 (Chapter 10 of this book) Simon describes how projects from the MRD programme have been active in the piloting of RDM systems and solutions represented in Figure 2.3, particularly in the areas of managing active data, data deposit and the development of data repositories, and reference to these real-life trials should be salutary. In Chapter 5 we provide a more detailed explanation of the core components of a typical RDM service structure, how they relate to one another and how they may be put in place.

The relationship between policy and the components of infrastructure is indivisible, with the roadmap performing the function of a helpful go-between. As described by the project Data Management Rollout at Oxford (DaMaRO)[9] (see Figure 2.4), the creation of a research data management

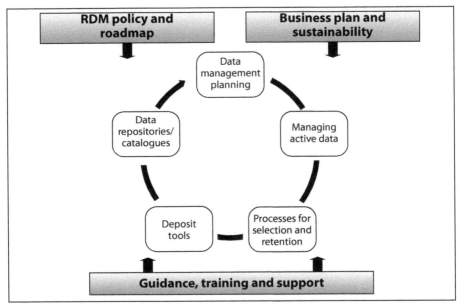

Figure 2.3 Components of research data management support services (*redrawn with permission from a diagram by Simon Hodson, Jisc MRD Programme Manager*)

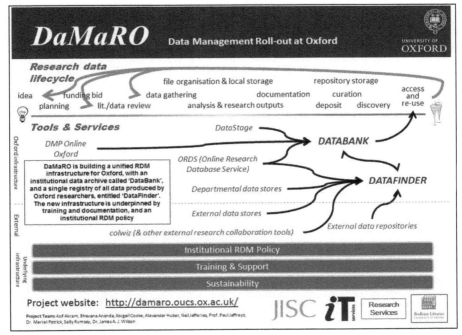

Figure 2.4 The DaMaRO unification initiative (*reproduced by permission of James Wilson, IT Services, University of Oxford*)

policy for the University of Oxford and the infrastructure to enable researchers to comply with it go hand in hand; and when thinking of policy, the DaMaRO team is looking beyond the boundaries of research data, with a high-level Research Data Management Working Group convened to ensure that the project's activities are co-ordinated with the broader strategic interests of the institution.

Here, at Oxford, one again finds the strength of the argument for building on what has gone before, with the modular components of an RDM service being assembled using the outputs from a series of individual research data management projects that the University has been engaged in over the last few years. Following a workshop in July 2012, when these original elements of existing digital infrastructure were appraised alongside further speculative options for future infrastructure, the DaMaRO project has proceeded to combine tools and discovery mechanisms into a unified institutional research data management framework. The benefit from having such a head start is perhaps exceptional but it is not unique, and where existing undertakings can be further developed they will have the advantage of momentum, proof of concept and, not least, a certain amount of credible acceptance.

In case study 3 (Chapter 8 of this book), the issues of relevance and acceptance are explored in some detail. In this case, at Monash University, the development of research data management capability has been attributed to a pincer movement coming on one side from the research community and, on the other, from institutional management, resulting in a highly strategic approach to investment. For the researchers, contextualized by the rapid globalization of research and heightened competition, there had been a growing acceptance of the need to achieve new research outcomes and higher research impact, which in turn meant taking more deliberate steps to safeguard and validate their data whilst at the same time finding ways of facilitating collaboration and enabling reuse. University management shared some of that motivation, wishing to enable leading-edge research in order to achieve the university's aspirations by increasing research outcomes and impact. They were also concerned to reduce risks, particularly legal ones, and to attract the best researchers and the best possible level of research income. The consequent ambition for the institution to be a leader in the application of good data management, as a direct means of leveraging research practice, has resulted in the emergence of collective responsibility for improving research data management in a co-ordinated and integrated way. Embedding this new commitment within institutional culture has been fostered further by its inclusion in Monash Futures,[10] a programme of staff-led reform that aims for transformational improvement across the full range of Monash University's education, research and administration activities. Comparisons with the IT transformation programme at QMUL may be drawn, but with the difference that at Monash research data management has been built from the ground up, for its own distinct purposes, rather than having enjoyed development as an extension of an existing technical services programme.

The inherently businesslike doctrine that is inspiring developments at Monash is perhaps more akin to that of a private sector organization than is usually encountered amongst the UK's public universities, yet the two principal drivers for institutional management are the same in both countries: the desire for maximum income and optimum research profile. Ultimately, therefore, the issues that institutional management will weigh when considering how far to go in the development of RDM services will come down to where best to invest in order to secure long-term advantage. Anyone wishing to make the case for RDM must acknowledge and build upon that basic fact of life.

5. Investment as a dynamic of excellence and scale

Income (and by corollary the ability to spend) and the dimensions of one's research profile are generally regarded as inseparable in the minds of university managers. But in an article posted in *Guardian Professional*, Zoë Molyneux suggests that we are at risk of becoming obsessive about the scale of research funding. This obsession focuses on two specific questions: 'how do we as a sector prevent a future claw-back from the research budget by the Treasury in a climate where higher education is perceived to have "done well" in recent funding announcements and, secondly, should the research budget avoid painful cuts, what is the most effective way to allocate funding which will support high-quality research activities?'[11] She points out that government policy 'relies on an equation between excellence, as measured by various quality indicators, and scale. Institutions which strike the right balance between the two are rewarded'. In terms of individual research projects, she explains, this balance is most conspicuously represented when it is possible to demonstrate not simply that they are of high quality but also that they possess the critical mass to define them as excellent in a global context. The argument for diverting funds to research that has the potential for global impact is, she recognizes, a compelling one, but it is a mistake to assume that global impact can only be achieved by concentrating one's resources on developing scale. As she warns, there is a risk that 'excellence and scale are . . . in danger of being made synonymous in the minds of higher education funders'. It is a threat that institutional management will already be aware of, particularly in the smaller research-intensive universities. But it also presents a dichotomy to the proponents of effective research data management, who may find that whilst resources for investment are initially constrained, the argument for developing RDM services as a means of securing research excellence and subsequently winning critical mass of a different kind can be greatly strengthened. At the institutional level, therefore, planning for RDM services will manifest itself as a case of achieving balance between laying the foundations for long-term aspiration and securing the nearer term exhibition of novel successes.

The probable solution is to work incrementally and, where possible, collaboratively. Patricia Cruse, Director of the University of California Curation Center (UC3), describes her own experience in terms of needing to start small, providing simple solutions 'that build up to solve more complex problems', deploying 'simple and flexible infrastructure and services that can be used in diverse ways' and prioritizing 'the use of scarce resources to support emerging initiatives'.[12] She also stresses that now, as one reaches into broader and more complex territory, is the time seriously to develop partnerships. Building the community by working with researchers from the outset, determining and meeting a whole mesh of expectations, understanding what is achievable and demonstrating relevance, are all keys to achieving sustainability.

The approach taken at UC3 has been to invest time and resources in the development of five services that will have appeal across a highly diverse community and, it is anticipated, attract a broad and solid swath of buy-in. Their first RDM service, DMP Tool, has been devised to provide the resources necessary for creating a data management plan, directly assisting researchers by giving them the means to meet new funder requirements, whilst at the same time reassuring those funders (such as the NSF or the National Institutes of Health) that their data management mandates are being taken seriously. The value of such a service was immediately apparent and between October 2011 and August 2012 the number of institutions using it had rocketed to almost 600. That success has led to further investment, with US$590,000 being awarded by the Alfred P. Sloan Foundation for the development of DMP Tool as a means of providing support across the full data management lifecycle, to nurture the emergence of an engaged open source community of users and developers, and to connect individual stakeholders to each other and each other's institutional resources, including services, expertise and guidance.

Similarly, Merritt, a curation repository open to the University of California community and beyond, has by starting its life as both discipline- and content-agnostic, with a technical architecture that allows for diversity, allowed for future growth from small beginnings. The long-term success of these services will of course be dependent upon their technical, administrative and, most importantly, financial sustainability. With respect to Merritt, it is already planned that there will be a partial recovery of UC3 service costs achieved by either one-time payments or using a pay-as-you-go model. Patricia Cruse's parting shot is that one must always 'be entrepreneurial'.

6. Whose money is it anyway?

Being entrepreneurial is not the whole story, of course, particularly in the UK environment, where high volumes of research are funded by the seven research councils and a handful of other key players, such as the Wellcome Trust, and where certain expectations are predetermined as a condition of grant (in Chapter 1 we have already considered the policy frameworks, mandates and expectations of this powerful group). The research councils alone invest around £3billion annually in research conducted at UK universities, which gives them considerable clout when declaring that 'publicly funded research data are a public good, produced in the public interest, which should be made openly available with as few restrictions as possible in a timely and responsible manner that does not harm intellectual property'.[13] Until recently, however, they have not been at all explicit in their advice as to how measures to preserve data – or how to make data discoverable and reusable over the long term, or how to protect against the inappropriate release of data, all of which they expect – should be funded. Admittedly, it is stated in the seventh of the Research Councils UK (RCUK) *Common Principles on Data Policy* that 'it is appropriate to use public funds to support the management and sharing of publicly-funded research data', yet this does not explain which particular public funds can be used in this way or clarify whether there are any constraints over the manner of their disbursement. Consequently this declaration has tended to be interpreted in a muddled way, as reference to the availability of a certain but undefined proportion of a research grant or, more circumspectly, being taken as an implied and usually unwelcome call on the hard-pressed budgets of research institutions. On a case-by-case basis it has often been difficult to say which. What is clear is that it could not refer exclusively to the provision of infrastructure by the research councils themselves, since the availability of national data centres is irregular, with only a few funding bodies offering a full service to their researchers. The principal exceptions are the ESRC and the Natural Environment Research Council (NERC), both of which provide comprehensive preservation and support services through the Economic and Social Data Service (ESDS) and the NERC data centres. But even where provision is made it needs to be borne in mind that these national services are selective: they may not necessarily accept data from a research project even if they fall within their scope of discipline, and institutions can still find themselves looking after data in those subject areas simply because they do not meet data centre selection criteria.

In these circumstances, what we are left with is an awareness that the responsibility for decisions concerning the appropriate provision of RDM services rests with the research institutions themselves, whether they choose to provide their own infrastructure entirely or in a mixed mode that incorporates other external services.

The decision process is, thankfully, becoming less opaque. At a national meeting convened by the DCC in April 2013,[14] a panel of representatives from the major UK research funders sought to explain what is allowable in terms of the use of research grants to fund data management. Whilst making it plain that they were not in the business of paying twice – i.e., where national or discipline repositories are supported by them, the use of money from research grants to enable institutional infrastructure would not be seen as legitimate – they conceded that, in accordance with RCUK Common Principle number seven, the costs of data management are indeed payable from a grant so long as they are within the lifetime of the funded project. Beyond that period, where national or discipline repositories do not exist, the responsibility for data preservation, curation and sharing lies with the employing institution. There are of course, exceptions and the Medical Research Council for one is happy to negotiate over longer-term requirements where these can be justified by the nature of the research.

If indeed there are RDM costs to be met within the lifetime of a project, these must be declared in the funding bid. Here, the onus is very much upon the individual researcher, who needs to be very clear what it is the funders are being asked to pay for through the grant. They, the funders, have confirmed that there is no rule of thumb to be used to measure the proportion of a grant that may acceptably be spent on research data management; it all depends on the kind of work to be undertaken and, to ensure that needs are recognized and met, each element of anticipated data management activity should be listed in a research proposal. There are no penalties for doing this!

So, a mixed approach to funding is both feasible and endorsed by the funders. They see little difference between meeting institutional obligations for good research governance *per se* and providing effective measures for managing research data, since the latter is but one component of the larger brief and not an optional addition. Indeed, where research is undertaken using public funds, institutions have long been required to apply high standards of research governance, putting quality processes in place to safeguard and optimize such investment. In the context of the digital era, those processes will now include RDM and any institution in receipt of public funding for research needs to set aside resources for enabling effective RDM as part of its overall service to its researchers.

In an environment where university funding can be severely constrained by the rigours of fiscal policy and where the focus of institutional investment tends to follow a route determined by short-term stratagems, setting aside sustainable resources for the long-term undertaking that is typified by data management and curation is easier said than done. The advice from those institutions that have taken up the RDM baton is not to wait around for new monies to materialize but to do what one can with the resources at hand. This will, in general, mean repurposing staff and restructuring service organizations, diverting funds from less strategic initiatives and using the challenge of assembling a budget as the opportunity to rethink the goals of the broader service, whether that is library- or IT-based. At Bristol, despite the university having granted funds for a two-year pilot research data service, the team has been kept at a minimum (one service director, three research data librarians and one technical support) and is made up from staff already employed in the library and IT services. Non-staff costs are marginal, comprising one web server, a Datacite licence and other peripherals. It is hoped that the anticipated success of the pilot will generate incremental growth. A similar situation can be found at the University of Edinburgh, where a forward RDM service budget of £2 million is split 50:50 between expenditure on staff and expenditure on 'stuff', much of the former being reskilled library, IT and research office personnel for whom a budget already existed.

Notwithstanding the positions being taken by the UK funders, the 4C initiative (Collaboration to Clarify the Costs of Curation), a consortium sponsored by the EU under its 7th Framework programme, has brought together 13 agencies in seven different European countries to help organizations approach their investment in data curation and preservation with an assurance of greater certainty. The main objective of the 4C project is 'to ensure that where existing work is relevant . . . stakeholders realize and understand how to employ those resources. An additional aim of the project is to examine more closely how existing functions might be made more fit-for-purpose, relevant and useable by a wide range of organizations operating at different scales in both the public and the private sector.'[15] Key outputs from 4C will include an analysis of the state of the art in cost modelling and an analysis of needs; an online curation costs exchange tool; a roadmap of analysis and recommendations for future action; and investment strategies for the promotion of affordable digital curation solutions and services. Due for completion on 31 January 2015, 4C should equip institutions with the tools necessary to developing a convincing case for investment in digital curation, by showing how to predict costs more accurately and how to define the benefits of curation, currently a major headache when the potential impact of investment in curation activity is dependent upon long-term uncertainties and the 'known unknown' of actual cost. You may not have to wait that long before looking for help from 4C, since its Curation Costs Exchange prototype is due for release in January 2014.

7. Alliances and partnerships

One way of spreading the cost and the risk is of course to invest in RDM services on a collaborative basis. Patricia Cruse's Merritt repository includes a design to integrate with distributed data grids, specifically the DataONE project, with a view to participation in ONEShare, a data repository open to the community at large. In the UK, the White Rose Consortium, a partnership among the universities of Leeds, Sheffield and York, which was established in 1997, is actively exploring options for the development of shared research data management infrastructure and services. Within the Consortium, the libraries have already developed White Rose Research Online, a shared, open-access repository that contains a growing collection of research outputs from across the three institutions. The next step they are considering is whether the level of trust, focus and reliability they have built can form the basis for a White Rose data service. At the level of resourcing, for both the technical and human infrastructure, such collaboration makes a strong economic argument. Yet, assuming that the integration of existing systems proves feasible and cost-effective, the spectre of individual institutional cultures and ambition may still militate against the emergence of a data management co-operative. Even so, should that prove to be the eventual outcome, the ability to work together on the design, testing and validation of a research data management framework must surely pay dividends from the exercise of shared strengths.

Partnerships between universities will always be complicated by the diverse range of stakeholders involved, their expectations, preferences and limitations. That is a given. But more crucially, if in this instance the decision is made to proceed with a White Rose shared infrastructure and service, it will be all the more critical to establish the working parameters for sustained funding that can satisfy all of the players, within the three participating universities and amongst their principal funders.

In a field inhabited by pilots, trials and emergent technologies, the opportunity for working collaboratively exerts a strong attraction. It is an approach that comes highly recommended for anyone embarking on the design and implementation of services in a rapidly evolving field. This need not imply arrangements as closely melded as a consortium or shared services, but is a sensible approach to evaluating options. For example, in 2012 a number of the Jisc MRD projects had, on an individual basis, been examining the Open Knowledge Foundation's CKAN,[16] an open source platform that provides tools to streamline publishing, sharing, finding and using data. CKAN is widely used internationally for governmental data portals, and for the MRD projects it had the potential to support research data management in universities. In February 2013, the Orbital[17] and data.bris[18] projects, with the Jisc MRD project cohort, facilitated a workshop for the community to learn more together about CKAN as a platform for managing active data, as a data portal or as a catalogue. It was planned that the presentations and discussions should feed into a requirements gathering exercise that in turn would enable an evaluation of CKAN for academic use, but with one additional outcome being that the future development of CKAN itself could be influenced in a way that would benefit the higher education sector. The lesson here is that such convergences will always offer new introductions and avenues of opportunity that are denied to developers working remotely.

8. Websites and explanatory notes

1   www.jisc.ac.uk/whatwedo/programmes/di_researchmanagement/
    managingresearchdata.aspx.

2   Beagrie, N. (2011) *Benefits from the Infrastructure Projects in the Jisc Managing
    Research Data Programme: final report*, Jisc,
    www.jisc.ac.uk/media/documents/programmes/mrd/RDM_Benefits_
    FinalReport-Sept.pdf.

3   Royal Society, *Science as an Open Enterprise: open data for open science*, Royal Society
    Science Policy Centre report 02/12, http://royalsociety.org/policy/projects/science-
    public-enterprise/report. Data pyramid diagram based on an original concept by
    Francine Berman in *Communications of the ACM*, December 2008, **51** (12).

4   The examples shown are Dryad, an international repository of data underlying
    peer-reviewed articles in the basic and applied biosciences; Figshare, a service
    allowing researchers to publish all of their research outputs in an easily citable,
    sharable and discoverable manner; the Large Hadron Collider, the renowned
    international collaboration in high-energy physics; and the Worldwide Protein
    Data Bank, a group of organizations that act as deposition, data processing and
    distribution centres for protein data.

5   Title of a presentation given at the Components of Institutional Research Data
    Services workshop organized by Jisc and the DCC, Nottingham 24–25 October
    2013, www.jisc.ac.uk/whatwedo/programmes/di_researchmanagement/
    managingresearchdata/events/ComponentsofInstitutionalResearchData
    Services.aspx.

6   In the blog *RDM within the University of St Andrews IT support*, dated 28 January
    2013, Birgit Plietzsch provides a concise explanation of her RDM experience
    (www.dcc.ac.uk/blog/rdm-within-university-st-andrews-it-support).

7   A typical range of services to be covered by the catalogue included access to
    backed-up and maintained storage space, the provision of appropriate levels of
    processing power, security solutions, databases and GIS tools.

8   Hodson, S. (2013) *Institutional Research Data Management Services: progress and
    challenges in the Jisc managing research data programme*, January, www.dcc.ac.uk/
    sites/default/files/documents/IDCC13presentations/HodsonIDCC13.pdf.

9   http://damaro.oucs.ox.ac.uk.

10 www.monash.edu.au/news/monashmemo/assets/includes/content/
    20100922/stories-uni-news2.html.

11 www.guardian.co.uk/higher-education-network/blog/2013/jan/02.

12 Cruse, P. (2013) *Building Services, Building Communities, Supporting Data
    Intensive Research*, January, www.dcc.ac.uk/sites/default/files/documents/
    IDCC13presentations/1145CruseIDCC2013.pdf.

13 RCUK *Common Principles on Data Policy*,
www.rcuk.ac.uk/research/Pages/DataPolicy.aspx.

14 RDMF special event: Funding Research Data Management,
www.dcc.ac.uk/events/research-data-management-forum-rdmf/
rdmf-special-event-funding-research-data-management.

15 http://4cprojectdotnet.files.wordpress.com/2013/03/
4c_briefing_march2013_final.pdf.

16 http://ckan.org.

17 http://orbital.blogs.lincoln.ac.uk.

18 http://data.blogs.ilrt.org.

CHAPTER 3

Who's doing data? A spectrum of roles, responsibilities and competences

Graham Pryor

1. A broad community of interest

Any institution reaching for the goal of well managed research data will, from the outset, have to consider how best to achieve a coherent association of the diverse group of actors, organizational processes and embedded systems that, once they are effectively melded together, will deliver the necessary technological and human infrastructures. In this chapter we focus on probably the greater part of this challenge, the creation and direction of a research data management (RDM) team. In practice, as with the more technical measures described in Chapters 4 and 5, it is not possible to prescribe a single and unyielding model for such an association, since it will always reflect the needs of individual organizations, cultures and traditions, yet it is feasible to describe a suite of structural components that can be used in building towards a fully functional arrangement, from which any institution may select and assemble its own approach.

The DCC Curation Lifecycle Model (Figure 3.1) provides a graphical overview of the stages involved in the successful curation and preservation of data from the point at which a research project is conceived. It is meant to assist in planning required activities so that all necessary stages in the lifecycle are managed in the correct sequence. It also provides a means of identifying the roles and responsibilities that will come into play at each of the separate stages, which as illustrated here can involve several types of actor or referral at any one time.

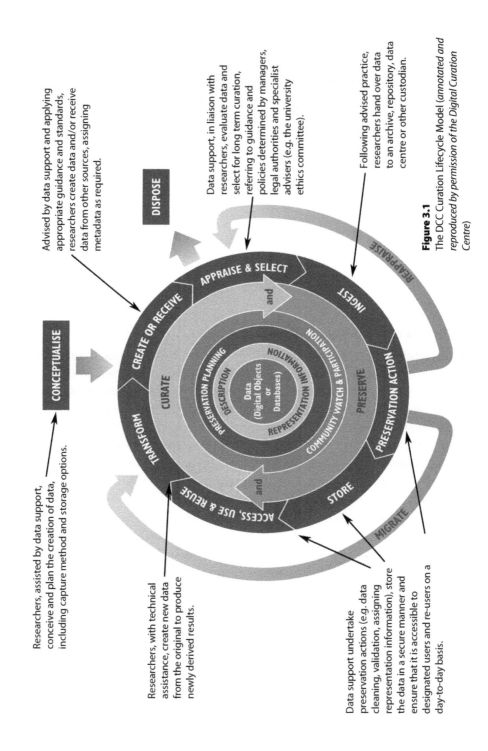

Advised by data support and applying appropriate guidance and standards, researchers create data and/or receive data from other sources, assigning metadata as required.

Researchers, assisted by data support, conceive and plan the creation of data, including capture method and storage options.

Researchers, with technical assistance, create new data from the original to produce newly derived results.

Data support undertake preservation actions (e.g. data cleaning, validation, assigning representation information), store the data in a secure manner and ensure that it is accessible to designated users and re-users on a day-to-day basis.

Data support, in liaison with researchers, evaluate data and select for long term curation, referring to guidance and policies determined by managers, legal authorities and specialist advisers (e.g. the university ethics committee).

Following advised practice, researchers hand over data to an archive, repository, data centre or other custodian.

Figure 3.1
The DCC Curation Lifecycle Model (*annotated and reproduced by permission of the Digital Curation Centre*)

CONCEPTUALISE

DISPOSE

CREATE OR RECEIVE

APPRAISE & SELECT

and

INGEST

REAPPRAISE

TRANSFORM

CURATE

PRESERVATION PLANNING

DESCRIPTION

REPRESENTATION INFORMATION

Data (Digital Objects or Databases)

COMMUNITY WATCH & PARTICIPATION

PRESERVE

PRESERVATION ACTION

ACCESS, USE & REUSE

and

STORE

MIGRATE

The term 'data support' is used in this diagram to describe a sometimes broad grouping of information and systems professionals, specialist administrative staff and records managers, to name only the more conspicuous elements from that cohort. Their roles will be described more explicitly in subsequent pages.

Typically, then, the responsibility for managing a Higher Education Institution's (HEI's) research data will be distributed amongst a heterogeneous range of actors situated both within and outside the institution. The exercise of that responsibility will, for some, extend across an exponentially protracted timescale, with the data generated from research representing a long-term series of technical and organizational challenges that cannot be left to any one individual or group. When, for example, the Engineering and Physical Sciences Research Council requires data to be kept for ten years after it is generated, which may then be repeated for a further ten-year interval following last use, the actions necessary to sustain that data in an accessible form may demand the intervention of data custodians, systems support and even the data originator. Only a sustained service organization could be expected to plan for such events in a way that will ensure continued compliance. Yet in many institutions the responsibilities for research data will remain distributed across several independent functions, including the research teams that are the originators of the data. So when data is to be made available to other researchers for reuse, the competent service team that will ensure it remains discoverable and intelligible in the long term, and with the rights of the original researcher protected, may in fact comprise a fluid body of staff whose roles are not primarily to do with data management.

Even in those situations where the data management 'team' has a diverse and distributed membership, someone has to take responsibility for the delivery of the whole service against an agreed level of execution. In most cases this will not be an issue that should or can burden researchers and divert them from their principal business of undertaking research. The University of Edinburgh's research data management policy[1] answers this conundrum by providing ample examples of where the provision of a centrally managed service has to be preferred over the delegation of responsibilities to individual stakeholders. By reference to contexts and timescales, the range of indispensable human and technology infrastructures, the parameters for data management planning and the need for appropriate safeguards, each aim of the policy connects until there is a clear sense of need for organized support. The key phrases that create this framework of responsibilities have been italicized here to demonstrate the orchestration achieved by the policy:

1 Research data should be managed to the highest standards *throughout the research data lifecycle* as part of the University's commitment to research excellence.
2 The *University should provide training, support and advice, as well as mechanisms and services for storage, back-up, registration, deposit and retention of research data assets* in support of current and future access, *during and after completion* of research projects.
3 All *new research proposals must include research data management plans* or protocols that explicitly address data capture, management, integrity, confidentiality, retention, sharing and publication.
4 Research data management plans *must ensure that research data are available for access and reuse*, where appropriate and *under appropriate safeguards*.
5 The *legitimate interests* of the subjects of research data *must be protected*.
6 Research data of future historical interest, and all research data that represents records of the University, including data that substantiates research findings, *should be offered and assessed for deposit and retention in an appropriate national or international data service or domain repository, or a University repository*. Such research data deposited elsewhere should be registered with the University.

Implicit amongst these six policy requirements is the understanding that whilst researchers will have a specific role in the planning and execution of data management, and that the university will support them by providing training and guidance, there will inevitably be a need to pass responsibility for data curation to services that are equipped to meet requirements beyond the active data stage. A simple analysis of the six statements demonstrates the range of skills and services that will be needed to deliver against such a set of policy requirements, which could not easily or economically be replicated across the many individual schools or departments of an institution:

- At pre-award:
  - help in the preparation of data management plans, including the expert use of online tools and guidance over legal and ethical constraints.

- Throughout the project:
  - guidance on measures for storing, managing and manipulating data, for achieving regulatory compliance and in applying essential data curation
  - advice and/or provision of data storage facilities that meet the needs of a wide range of data types and formats throughout the phases of the research lifecycle.
- During and after the project:
  - an expert advisory service to assist with the creation and assignment of appropriate metadata
  - help in making research data visible and/or available to defined audiences.
- Post-project:
  - data archiving, including help to researchers in deciding how to archive data at the end of a project (or at any other appropriate point), local ingest to a repository or hand-off to a third party
  - provision of a data catalogue to record the location and availability of the institution's data assets.

It is worth remembering, too, that specialized discipline services have existed for a number of years at a national level in the UK and may offer an appropriate voice to anyone seeking support for a managed institutional data service. The longest-established of these national facilities, the UK Data Archive, explains in its Managing and Sharing Data[2] that 'looking after research data for the longer-term and protecting them from unwanted loss requires having good strategies in place for securely storing, backing-up, transmitting and disposing of data. Collaborative research brings challenges for the shared storage of and access to, data'. Indeed! – and the execution of such an undertaking begs the provision of a properly structured and expert resource, whether at a national or an institutional level.

2. A three-way division of responsibility

Having established that meeting the range of needs arising throughout the data lifecycle cannot be delegated to a single unit or function, it is still possible to identify three groups that will normally share the roles and responsibilities for defining, enabling and delivering RDM services:

1 University management.

2 Support and administrative services.
3 Researchers/data producers.

2.1 Management

They may not be expected to undertake data curation duties but university management have a key role to play in the introduction of RDM services, and without their commitment and support any initiative to introduce new ways of working will be weakened. Making that commitment has to be on the basis of their good understanding and critical evaluation of the prevailing issues, in order that the proposed services can be judged and found desirable, achievable and made sustainable. Consequently, it is crucial that the proponents of an RDM service conduct a thorough programme of advocacy and information provision so that senior university staff can be equipped to respond by giving clear, informed and unequivocal support.

It is highly likely, particularly in times of budgetary constraint, that the stumbling point for university managers will be the requirement to allocate funding for long-term investment in RDM infrastructures, which is when the issues of compliance, benefits and strategic advantage discussed in the previous chapter will need to be carefully rehearsed by those who are making a service proposal. As already remarked in Chapter 2, to invest in digital curation is to risk capital against outcomes that are unlikely to be realized in the short or medium term, since curation and preservation are firmly anchored to the long-term view. This is a problem when assembling a business case that will compete with institutional submissions having a far shorter interval before payback and with more reliably assured and costed outcomes.

At the time of writing, successful RDM business cases – i.e. those that lead to the recruitment of staff and long-term investment in infrastructure – sadly, are rare. A survey of 63 HEIs conducted by the Digital Curation Centre (DCC) in March 2013 revealed that a number of RDM working groups were seeking funds in the current budget round, usually quite modest sums of up to £45,000 for training or to employ a dedicated member of RDM staff, but in many instances they had received feedback early in the process indicating that they were unlikely to be successful. That is not to say that all such funding bids are doomed: a detailed business analysis and proposal at the London School of Economics has resulted in the allocation of £100,000 for a 12-month pilot project, whilst at the University of Bristol senior management have approved the business case for a 2½-year project that will build on the Jisc data.bris pilot to establish a permanent university-wide research data service.[3]

Here, a key success factor was the argument that a relatively small investment in this fast-changing area would pay for itself; first of all, by helping to retain current levels of research funding through the application of measures to deal with growing funder requirements and, secondly, by increasing the university's competitive advantage as a consequence of quickly moving ahead of the game, especially in terms of preparedness for 'big data' projects.

When making your case to university managers it will be important to understand what is going to give the greatest resonance to your pitch. For this you need to know what RDM actually means to senior management and what there is about it that they value (or otherwise). Only by appreciating their perspective can you take positive steps to appeal to it. Vice-chancellors and pro-vice-chancellors may be familiar with issues such as open access and open data, and they should be conversant with the growing pressure from the research funders and academic publishers, but you will need to explain what these can all mean for the institution when taken together. The provision of clearly presented risk assessments, for both action and inaction, will speak far more persuasively than detailed explanations of the need for specific roles and services.

In terms of their specific role in RDM service development, the principal responsibilities to be met by senior management are to:

- provide a champion at pro-vice-chancellor (PVC) research level or equivalent, who will be a persuasive and influential advocate of the RDM cause and who will chair RDM steering/working group business
- establish a representative, balanced and appropriately equipped steering/ working group that will reflect the interests of essential stakeholders
- appraise and approve proposals, plans and strategies, lending support to budget submissions and any necessary organizational restructuring
- advise on the higher level strategic issues that must be addressed during service design, including obligations to government, funding and other agencies
- support and enable the ratification of an RDM policy that articulates the institution's core RDM principles and provides a realistic framework for guidelines and service design.

2.2 Support and administration services

We have already commented on the heterogeneous nature of the support teams that will deliver RDM services, although in a majority of cases they may be categorized as comprising the library, information technology, repository, records management and research administration functions. This list is not exclusive! For each of them, managing research data is likely to be a relatively new challenge for which the responsibilities and practices have yet to be firmly established. Those traditionally engaged in information and computing service provision will, however, be customarily recognized as the groups best fitted to lead in the identification of requirements, standards and solutions. For library staff, research data management is already being seized upon as an opportunity to refresh and re-orientate service portfolios that have dwindled in recent years as a consequence of the internet, which has encouraged self-reliance amongst even the most conventional of library users. At the University of Bristol, the data.bris research data service, whilst piloted by IT Services, is going forward under the management of the library, 'since opening up data is seen as an extension of the wider open publication practices already being developed by the Library'.[4] The core activities of Bristol's library-driven service will include assisting with data management planning, delivering training in RDM, advocating the opening up of research data across the university and managing the data.bris repository.

To these established information-orientated groups we must add research administration, the function that involves the management of grants and contracts, commercialization and the support of innovation, which comes in a variety of forms across the sector. In most cases the 'research office' will have a key role to play as the link between researchers, university management and the research funders.

Although we may be able quickly to identify these potential members of the RDM service community within our own institutions, it is important to recognize that in most cases they will not have previously worked together as a cohesive unit or partnership or even share the same aims; yet to deliver RDM services effectively they will be expected to work collaboratively in providing the effort to:

- establish and function as an RDM team to undertake the actions defined by the steering group
- undertake analyses of policy requirements at a national, funder and institutional level
- identify the current status of the institution's data assets and data management practices, including an appraisal of the gaps between existing and planned arrangements

- develop and implement proposals, plans and budgets for the technological and human infrastructures necessary to deliver RDM services
- retrain, reorganize and otherwise acquire the skills for providing effective RDM services
- plan and undertake a programme of advocacy to promote the key aspects of effective research data management, explaining in universally accessible terms its obligations, benefits and the services anticipated
- facilitate training opportunities for managers, support staff and researchers
- reorganize and re-orientate from an assembly of traditionally independent units into a working partnership that can deliver a seamless RDM service.

For the library and IT service members of this group, supporting RDM will include the not unfamiliar challenge of providing varied layers of guidance, with resources and training designed to meet a range of audiences. These will be delivered through established web pages carrying basic guidance, with more sophisticated measures provided via audience-focused workshops, group meetings and small-group consultations, the latter being preferred as a means of dealing with specific discipline or team approaches to creating, managing and sharing data. The role of the help desk is also one that can be extended, possibly using a new generic e-mail address to filter RDM enquiries. Given that RDM is generally a topic that will be new to a large proportion of the research community, where there may be a reluctance to admit ignorance, it will also help to identify named contacts in addition to the generic help desks, in order that questions may be posed and help sought without more public scrutiny. By making contact details more visible and introducing support staff at training events, the RDM service will be seen as having a human face, making it far more approachable than the anonymous presence at the end of an Ethernet cable or telephone wire.

2.3 Researchers/data producers

As our third group of participants in the data management enterprise, the creators and users of research data, researchers may not at first seem be the most obvious candidates when one is thinking about who will be responsible for the actual delivery of services, yet their active engagement in the development of RDM services is in fact crucial. Any service provision has to be built upon a close understanding of the researchers' work, its patterns and timetables, motivations and priorities. Of course, development of this understanding has to be a reciprocal undertaking, since it cannot be achieved without commitment by the research community to contribute fully and willingly to the definition of service requirements, and without their active involvement and support the relevance and success of any RDM service is bound to be limited. Whilst management will define its expectations and quantify what level of service is sustainable, and whilst the support services will design and deliver a range of measures to meet the institution's needs and obligations, it is the responsibility of the research community to:

- ensure their views are represented by contributing to steering/working groups
- collaborate in the gathering of requirements and the testing of solutions and methods
- clearly articulate the particular requirements, opportunities and obstacles encountered within their disciplines when creating, using and sharing data
- champion the adoption of approved data management methods and services within their communities
- support and sustain initiatives to train new researchers in good data management practice.

In practice, much of the responsibility for RDM within the active research community will be devolved to the principal investigator (PI) for a project. PIs are normally perceived as being responsible for the quality of the research being undertaken by their teams and will similarly be deemed accountable to the university through their research group, department or school for the management of research data created throughout the life of those projects or programmes. That accountability does not necessarily mean they must be hands-on with the data at all times but it does provide a good reason for them to work to good advantage with both the senior policy makers and the support teams. Co-opting enthusiastic PIs to an RDM working group would therefore make a lot of sense.

3. New skills for old: some competences in data management

Training will not be reserved to the postgraduate or early career researcher.

Support staff from the library or computing services may be regarded as having the closest natural affinity to the new realm of data management; but the required skills and techniques of these newly emerging roles are sufficiently distinct to make the transition from more traditional practices highly dependent upon fresh or refresher training, and not only in the principles and methods of data curation. Professional training in digital curation is itself in its infancy and it will be some time before institutions can recruit wholly competent staff directly from the marketplace, which means that training will have to be arranged for existing staff to be reskilled into their changed roles. That said, in the medium-to-long term such programmes as the new Aberystwyth University MSc/PG Dip in digital curation,[5] launched in 2013 and promising to equip students 'with the strategic, practical and technical skills for a career in digital curation', will eventually be feeding a new breed of data manager into the research community. Similar programmes are emerging in the USA, for example the Certificate in Digital Curation offered by the University of North Carolina at Chapel Hill,[6] the Certificate of Advanced Study in Data Science offered at Syracuse University[7] and the Digital Stewardship Certificate, a fully online programme offered by Simmons College in Boston.[8]

Sources for training materials and training programmes can be found online. The Jisc Call for Projects 04/10 led to five initiatives under the RDMTrain programme[9] that aimed to create a body of discipline-focused postgraduate training units. It was envisaged that these could be reused by other institutions in order to stimulate curriculum change and create a greater awareness of the need for research data management skills training. Research Data MANTRA, for example, which focused on the geosciences, social and political sciences, and clinical psychology, has made available a series of online chapters for self-paced RDM training, plus software-specific training modules.[10] For UK institutions as a whole, the DCC provides free half-day workshops that give an introduction to research data management and curation, the range of activities and roles that should be considered when planning and implementing new projects, and an overview of the tools that can assist with curation activities.[11] Training and guidance is also on offer from the funder-supported national data centres. The list of training resources in Table 3.1 is reproduced with permission from the DCC's working level guide to the development of RDM services.[12]

These are mainly UK resources, although they can be used anywhere. In the USA, training in research data management techniques is frequently provided for researchers as an internal institutional service, such as the

Table 3.1 RDM training resources

Name	Description	Target audience	Link (URL)
UKDA training materials	Slides and exercises for a course covering all aspects of the data lifecycle	Researchers	www.data-archive.ac.uk/ create-manage/training-resources
Research Data MANTRA	An online RDM training course with quizzes, videos and software tutorials	Researchers	http://datalib.edina.ac.uk/ mantra
CAiRO	An online RDM module for creative arts researchers	Researchers	www.projectcairo.org/ module/unit1-0.html
DataTrain	Slides and training materials for archaeology and social anthropology researchers	Researchers	www.lib.cam.ac.uk/dataman/ datatrain/datatrainintro.html
DATUM for Health	Slides with speaker notes and audio recordings for health science researchers	Researchers	http://findjorum.ac.uk/ resources/20963
Introducing research data	A 27-page handbook with case studies and associated presentation	Researchers	http://eprints.soton.ac.uk/ 338816
Leeds RoaDMaP	Presentations, handbook and feedback from courses aimed at engineering researchers, social scientists and research support staff	Researchers and support staff	http://library.leeds.ac.uk/ roadmap-project-outputs
TraD – Training for Data Management at UEL	Online modules, slides and exercises for a variety of audiences	Researchers and Librarians	www.uel.ac.uk/trad
DCC roadshows	Case studies, presentations and exercises aimed at support staff establishing RDM services	Research support staff	www.dcc.ac.uk/events/ data-management-roadshows
RDMRose	Eight sessions with presentations, case studies and activity sheets	Librarians	http://rdmrose.group.shef.ac. uk/?page_id=10
Data Intelligence 4 Librarians	Online content used to run face-to-face courses with homework activities between sessions to reinforce learning	Librarians	http://dataintelligence.3tu.nl/ en/home
DIY Research Data Management Training Kit for Librarians	Audio-synced presentations and exercises demonstrating how the MANTRA module can be reused for academic liaison librarians	Librarians	Overview slides at www.slideshare.net/ edinadocumentationofficer/ jisc-managing-research-data-liaison-librarian-training

workshops provided at the University of Minnesota,[13] whereas the Australian National Data Service (ANDS) hosts an articulated suite of guidance, training and tutorials.[14]

If you are only now engaged in sketching out the extent to which existing staff will need to be 're-engineered' into new RDM roles, or if you are fortunate enough to be able to recruit additional expertise, it would be helpful to define what skills and knowledge will be needed at start-up and for the operation of a full service. In a briefing paper published in August 2011, the Repositories Support Project attempted to provide such a definition for institutional repository staff,[15] which it was acknowledged had begun to accept responsibility for managing data as well as publications. As can be seen, individually the majority of these requirements reflect some fairly well known capabilities, but when assembled together to represent the skills portfolio of a fully functional role they will challenge the routine skill set of a more traditional librarian or member of computing support:

- **Management** – an ability to manage the set-up, development and ongoing maintenance of the repository including strategic and financial planning and engagement with relevant groups, individuals and stakeholders
- **Supervision** – an ability to oversee the work and day-to-day activity of any colleagues directly working on the repository
- **Software** – familiarity with relevant web-based systems and repository software; the ability to implement and modify systems and software to meet the needs of the repository and institution, often in collaboration with a technical developer
- **Metadata** – familiarity with relevant and emerging standards and an ability to monitor and ensure metadata quality is maintained
- **Curation preservation** – familiarity with current best practice and an ability to liaise with other departments to ensure storage and digital preservation and curation procedures meet best practice
- **Rights** – familiarity with current intellectual property rights (IPR) and related copyright issues, interpretations and best practice; possesses an ability to develop content policies and engage with key stakeholders to maximize quality and quantity of content
- **Advocacy** – an ability to liaise and advocate with various groups, departments and individuals both within the institution and externally to promote the deposit and use of items in the repository
- **Training and support** – an ability to meet the needs of the repository

and its users in terms of training and awareness of OA, the repository, deposit routes and continuing scholarly communications evolution; additionally the institutional repository must be able to provide support for users requiring assistance or information in using the repository's resources and other open-access sites

- **Current awareness and CPD** – familiarity with current trends, standards and emerging best practices in the repository and research community; it is essential to maintain an awareness of developments in repository software and associated technologies.

This document was further refined in October 2011 to explain in greater detail what software, metadata standards and IPR issues would be involved, to name but three of the nine aspects covered, and what duties repository staff might be expected to perform. When one considers the topic of metadata alone, which begs familiarity with relevant metadata standards including (but not limited to) Dublin Core, MARC, METS, MODS; general interoperability protocols such as OAI-PMH, OAI-ORE, and standards for the interoperability of research information, particularly CERIF, it is easy to concede that for some this could prove to be a formidable list.[16] It also recognized that some 'institutions spread the work over several posts or over several departments; typically including library cataloguers, subject librarians, other library, teaching and administrative staff as well as IT services', a complex situation in which the maintenance and exchange of a balanced level of skills will be particularly challenging.

But to return to the design of RDM training for researchers, this is best undertaken in collaboration with academic staff or, where they exist, data experts working in the disciplines, to ensure that both content and approach are relevant and meaningful. To embed good RDM practice in the research environment as a matter of routine it is also important to incorporate these new aspects of the research process workflow within existing induction and training programmes, so that they are communicated as fundamental components rather than optional additions. As an appropriate theatre for the development of an RDM culture, doctoral training centres and graduate schools that are active in the development of researcher skills can be recruited as principal agents for achieving change in researcher practice, since they will be dealing with an annually replenished and cross-disciplinary cohort of postgraduate students.

4. Establishing a niche: RDM as a value prospect

Providing a service that is meaningful to researchers on a personal level is bound to create more of a welcome than the imposition of an impersonal corporate regime. Recognizing this, the Penn State University libraries have, for example, undertaken a study of the disciplinary practices and needs for managing the personal data lifecycle, asking such questions as how do faculty create, manage, share and archive personal information collections. This may appear to be a fairly obvious thing to do but the initiative has proven invaluable in uncovering researchers' significant levels of frustration with the fragmentation and redundancy of data, the lack of linked data and linked practices, and the absence of reliable mechanisms for data preservation. As a direct consequence of having taken the trouble to ask their research community, it is now planned to introduce measures that will unify the scholars' online workflow and address 'faculty members' cognitive and affective needs with regard to information curation, management and personal archiving'.[17] In this way, by 'getting up close and personal' with the research community, library staff have demonstrated that they have a valuable role to play in making the research process an easier place to be. But in terms of formally developing a suite of service components, perhaps an even stronger example can be given in the area of data management planning.

For researchers, the recent and expanding requirement for data management plans (DMPs) to be submitted as part of a grant proposal have proved to be an occasionally bewildering and generally burdensome addition to the bid writing experience. For the aspirational data support service, on the other hand, they represent an opportunity to lend expert assistance and the means to demonstrate the value of an organized and researcher-focused service. In the UK, support teams (most typically from the library) have been promoting the use of DMPonline,[18] a flexible web-based tool for the creation of personalized plans according to the specific characteristics of the proposed research or the expectations of the research funder. DMPonline is locally customizable and can be re-badged and enriched with locally derived guidance materials, thereby providing a framework upon which the service providers can design a product that meets the needs of individual groups. Similarly, in the USA, several universities and organizations have been developing DMP Tool to help researchers meet these new funder requirements.[19] Its fast-paced success has already been described in Chapter 2.

In a white paper published in January 2013, the ACTI Data Management Working Group within Educause claimed that an 'institutionally supported service will not only result in more accurate and comprehensive DMPs but will also generate a broader knowledge-base and community-minded environment in support of this service within the institution'.[20] Whilst, they said, the organization of DMP services will vary by institution and will be shaped by a number of factors, including institutional culture, organizational make-up and geographic dispersion, the paper identifies two emerging models: (1) a small group of designated staff who are 'embedded in an existing department whose activities are closely aligned and/or impacted by these efforts (i.e. library, research, IT, or in some cases an independent office supported by all three of these and possibly others)'; (2) an advisory committee 'charged with the responsibility of providing guidance and assistance to individual faculty and departments for a collection of tasks related to data management (e.g. developing DMPs for grant proposals, including discipline-specific guidance, providing DMP review services in the pre-proposal phase, identifying IT costs related to proposed research projects, etc.)'. In the UK we are seeing the emergence of a model that draws upon both of these, with central services making overtures to schools and departments without necessarily becoming embedded within them.

At the University of Edinburgh, during the consultative process that led to publication of its research data management policy, emphasis was placed upon having something real and meaningful that could be taken to the research community as a means of enhancing the research experience, rather than deliver a series of 'rules' that the researcher would be expected to observe. One might even describe it as a service-based policy; certainly implementation of that policy is now following such a course by addressing the four stages of a research project in terms of the kinds of assistance required, as described earlier in this chapter.

5. Inclusivity and the bounds of human infrastructure

We have in this chapter covered the gamut of roles and responsibilities that might be expected of an RDM service and what they could mean for the individuals who will deliver them. As the extent of individual involvement can be potentially far-reaching it is crucial that roles and responsibilities, once recognized, are formally assigned and not just defined. This is especially important in the context of collaborative research, where the roles and responsibilities for managing the data generated and gathered will need to be agreed between partners, whether they are within the same institution or dispersed across separate institutions.

As almost the final word on this subject, the UK Data Archive reminds us[21] that the range of people involved in research data management may include each or all of the following:

- principal investigators designing research
- research staff or students collecting, creating, processing and analysing data
- external contractors with a role in data collection, collation or processing, e.g. transcribers
- support staff managing and administering research
- institutional IT services providing data storage, security and back-up services
- external data centres or archives that facilitate data sharing.

A similar observation is given in Liz Lyon's seminal report, *Dealing with Data*:

> Whilst particular named individuals in key roles will have responsibility for data management within their own organisation, the importance of co-ordination with peer groups and peer organisations is of critical importance. Institutions, funders, data centres and disciplinary communities all have a responsibility to work together to derive shared and agreed policies and good practice, to ensure the continuing effective provision of data curation and preservation services, and a more open approach to data sharing.[22]

The success of an RDM service will, quite evidently, rest upon the inclusivity and connectivity of its human infrastructure. It will call for some considerable management talent.

6. Websites and web resources

1 www.ed.ac.uk/schools-departments/information-services/about/policies-and-regulations/research-data-policy.
2 www.data-archive.ac.uk/media/2894/managingsharing.pdf.
3 https://data.blogs.ilrt.org.
4 www.dcc.ac.uk/blog/making-business-case.
5 www.aber.ac.uk/en/dis/courses/digitalcuration/#d.en.126862.
6 http://sils.unc.edu/programs/certificates/digital_curation.
7 http://coursecatalog.syr.edu/2013/programs/data_science.

8   www.simmons.edu/gslis/programs/postmasters/digital-stewardship/index.php.

9   www.jisc.ac.uk/whatwedo/programmes/mrd/rdmtrain.aspx.

10 http://datalib.edina.ac.uk/mantra.

11 www.dcc.ac.uk/training/dc-101.

12 Jones, S., Pryor, G. and Whyte, A. (2013) *How to Develop Research Data Management Services – a Guide for HEIs*, www.dcc.ac.uk/resources/how-guides/how-develop-rdm-services.

13 www.lib.umn.edu/datamanagement/workshops.

14 www.ands.org.au/support/index.html.

15 www.rsp.ac.uk/documents/briefing-papers/2011/RepositoryStaffandSkills_RSP_0811.pdf.

16 www.rsp.ac.uk/documents/Repository_Staff_and_Skills_Set_2011.pdf.

17 www.dcc.ac.uk/sites/default/files/documents/idcc13posters/poster184v2.pdf.

18 https://dmponline.dcc.ac.uk.

19 https://dmp.cdlib.org/about/dmp_about.

20 Fary, M. and Owen, K. (2013) *Developing an Institutional Research Data Management Plan Service*, http://net.educause.edu/ir/library/pdf/ACTI1301.pdf.

21 http://data-archive.ac.uk/create-manage/planning-for-sharing/roles-responsibilities.

22 Lyon, E. (2007) *Dealing with Data: roles, rights, responsibilities and relationships*, www.ukoln.ac.uk/ukoln/staff/e.j.lyon/reports/dealing_with_data_report-final.pdf.

CHAPTER 4

A pathway to sustainable research data services: from scoping to sustainability

Angus Whyte

1. Introduction

This chapter describes the phases involved in developing and establishing research data management (RDM) services. It draws on the Digital Curation Centre's programme of engagement with universities in the UK, and from working alongside related projects developing RDM services.[1] The chapter envisages a development cycle that involves a range of the stakeholders and actors discussed in Chapter 3.

The RDM development cycle is viewed here as a recurring sequence of six phases, familiar from other forms of service design. The first involves envisioning the need for change, then initiating a process to bring that change about. Next is a discovery phase, characterizing the data management lifecycle and its stakeholders to scope their requirements for change. This enables the design of policies and services to address gaps between what is currently done and what is needed. Alpha and beta stages of the design phase test the ground for the implementation phase. Lastly, evaluation of the process and its outputs should ensure that what has been learned feeds into the continuous improvement of services provided to researchers and other customers, such as funding bodies, research users and the broader public.

In section 2 we describe the six phases identified in Figure 4.1: envision,

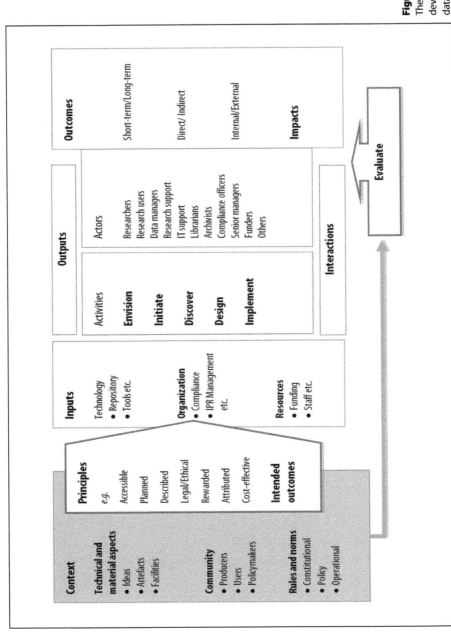

Figure 4.1
The process of developing research data services

initiate, discover, design, implement and evaluate. These are informed by service design principles[2] and established practice in business process re-engineering (BPR) (Kettinger et al., 1997).

Developing a research data management service in a university is like business process re-engineering in some respects. For example, senior management need to support it, customer requirements need to be met, and internal stakeholders' buy-in is essential. RDM is also like BPR in that its outputs typically include tools for transforming digital data and the workflows around data production. Also like BPR, cultural change may be at least as significant to success as the enhanced capabilities that are on offer from changed systems.

There are also important differences between the RDM context and business process change. Section 3 considers the research data management context, including the norms of practice with which service development must contend. Research contexts are unlike business processes in that they are typically more complex – i.e., the activities involved are difficult, uncertain, and with highly variable levels of interdependence and standardization.

On top of that, research domains are fuzzily defined and tribally organized (Fry, 2006; Becher, 1989). Research is typically organized through informal networks crossing national and institutional boundaries, operating to norms that allow academic independence to pursue high-risk ideas and resist institutional control – e.g. of intellectual property rights (Bos et al., 2007). The research expertise needed to understand data may be shared among members of such networks but difficult to communicate as broadly as policy makers expect. In section 2 we review factors likely to indicate opportunities and barriers to the productive engagement with research communities.

The fourth section of this chapter describes tools for initiating change and discovering requirements to support data practices. These steps are highly interdependent and likely to be less familiar to university managers and service providers than the design and implementation stages, which arguably draw on more generic capabilities. The main tools described are CARDIO[3] and the Data Asset Framework (DAF) (Jones, 2009), and the section identifies ways to use these in combination.

The fifth section deals with planning for sustainability: making a case for an RDM service, and business planning to ensure the service continues to engage with the research community and to renew itself. Finally, in section 6 conclusions are drawn about how the development process needs to take account of the likely shape of RDM services to come.

2. Development phases

2.1 Envision

This stage is mainly about establishing a shared vision at senior level in the organization. Senior management will need to establish a steering group or advisory board to assist them, unless one already exists with a closely related remit (such as records management). Ideally, a member of the senior management group responsible for research should chair the group (in a UK institution this might typically be the deputy/pro-vice-chancellor for research). There may be an existing champion or group already taking initiatives towards improved RDM, and it may be they can be co-opted to a steering group. In any case, senior management backing for the steering group is essential to successful development.

A steering group's overall goals may include establishing policy principles for RDM, to help communicate where it fits within the organization's overall mission, and to define roles and responsibilities for researchers and the institution. (Chapter 5 looks in more detail at how to establish a policy.) The steering group will also devise a strategy or roadmap for high-level approval, considering the institution's research strategy, external policy drivers, service priorities and technology opportunities.

Depending on preferences and the size of the organization's research base, the RDM strategy may be a separate document or a short statement prefacing an operational plan. In either case the steering group's overall goal will be to identify a business case to be presented to the research committee, or whichever organizational body can commit funding towards establishing the necessary services. Once this case has been made, the steering group may be reconstituted to plan and guide a project through to an established service.

Key elements:

- establish management commitment and vision
- discover research policy and strategic opportunities
- identify technology drivers for change
- scope initial investigation.

2.2 Initiate

Having secured the necessary commitment for an initial investigation, the steering group's work will focus on raising stakeholder awareness and obtaining 'buy-in' for further development. It is often the case that RDM steering groups bring together service providers that communicate about their support for teaching and learning, but rarely about research support or anything directly relevant to data.

Some initial work to gain mutual understanding and identify the salient issues is likely to be needed. As well as reflecting on the organizational opportunities and technology drivers, the steering group may find case studies and examples from other institutions useful. The policy requirements of funding bodies and regulators will frame the capabilities required in broad terms and various models of the capabilities that are needed for RDM support are available. CARDIO is a tool to help benchmark how the capabilities compare against such models; it is discussed in more detail below in section 4.2.

Benchmarking to identify capability gaps may help the case for change as well as identify the range of outputs needed to achieve desired outcomes; it can also be used to determine what factors will be used to evaluate success. The outcomes are likely to include some or all of the services or infrastructure components described in the next chapter (e.g. guidance, training, support to data management planning and active storage management). How these are framed, prioritized and related to existing practices will of course depend on the local strategy and context.

Analysis of the benefits and risks – to researchers, the institution and to external customers and stakeholders – will help to identify the desired outcomes and criteria for success. Models of RDM benefits and risks e.g. KRDS,[4] are useful at this stage as well as in evaluation, as we discuss below in section 2.6. It will be vital to engage with researchers at all levels, and senior researchers should be included in the steering group. Also valuable is input from research users or knowledge exchange experts to understand the implications for them in making research data workflows more formalized, or from opening them up.

Diverse priorities are likely to emerge. While service providers will be familiar with managing change in the context of the institution's administrative processes or teaching practices, research practices are more diverse and fluid; it will therefore be essential to understand the real needs of the data producers and users by conducting focus groups or workshops, surveys and structured interviews. This is likely to demand a broader resource than can be provided from the steering group. Operational teams will also be needed to supply effort, with input principally from the library, IT and research support services. Tools to support this stage include the Data Asset Framework (DAF) and generic project scheduling and budgeting techniques.

Key elements:

- identify, consult and inform stakeholders
- identify researcher and customer priorities
- identify desired outcomes and success criteria
- organize operational team(s)
- conduct project planning.

2.3 Discover

The next phase involves more in-depth investigation within the identified priorities. The objective is to diagnose the need for change in current practice and discover requirements. It is important to appreciate some of the disciplinary landscape and the prevailing norms around data production, sharing and use. The study will also consider the support service landscape, who that involves and what issues researchers and other stakeholders encounter. The discovery phase should set out what the RDM service will need to do, in the form of use cases or user stories.

Research naturally involves highly specialized knowledge and non-standard techniques for data collection. Different research groups, even within similar disciplines, will have their own methods. Given the number and diversity of research groups in an institution, the RDM Steering Group or project manager will need to be selective in who they can try to involve in a study to scope researchers' requirements. Ideally the groups engaged with should span different funding sources, data types and scale of research team (i.e., from lone researchers to large consortia), so that the study can account for variation across the factors highlighted in section 3. It is also good to involve researchers from different career stages, as PhD students' needs and concerns will differ from those of senior professors. In practice the sample will likely be opportunistic, as participation will depend on researchers' levels of interest or concern. The selection of methods for requirements discovery should therefore include a spectrum of approaches, from those that are quick and easy for researchers to engage with to those that take more time but yield more in-depth information.

The aim here is to appreciate enough about current RDM practices, how they are shaped by disciplinary factors, and the use of available sources of support, in order to identify the appetite for change, how needs are framed and the likely barriers to aligning them with RDM strategy and regulatory requirements. The discovery phase may therefore include an assessment of the awareness of relevant policies, and chart the lifecycle of typical data assets and associated research objects (software, protocols, logs, etc.)

Typically, a project manager or group with operational responsibility will undertake this work in a series of short studies involving selected research groups and the current providers of any relevant services such as back-up, storage or library support. As described in section 4 below, methods to help document the landscape include *Data Curation Profiles* (Witt et al., 2009), *Stakeholder Profiles* (Michener et al., 2012), and the Data Asset Framework (DAF) approach (Jones, 2009).

Interviews and workshops can yield a great deal of qualitative description that will need to be distilled to identify the activities most in need of support. Models of data curation activities such as the *DCC Curation Lifecycle Model* (Higgins, 2008) can support this analysis. Models can help map the service to be designed, by providing an initial framework for summarizing the large amounts of qualitative information that emerge from requirements gathering. Nevertheless, the map needs to fit the actual terrain – what the potential service users actually say and do, rather than by superimposing models onto current practice. The CARDIO tool can usefully complement this analysis by relating stakeholders' assessment of current support provision to a model of the capabilities an RDM service should have.

This analysis should then feed into more standard design approaches that are used to document user needs, such as use cases (Cockburn, 2001) and user stories (Cohn, 2004). The acceptance criteria that will be used to judge how well use cases are fulfilled are an equally important output from this stage. Benefits frameworks for RDM are likely to be helpful here; a Benefits Analysis Tool from the Keeping Research Data Safe project[4] identifies how RDM services can provide a return to researchers, service providers and external stakeholders, a topic we return to under 'Evaluate' below.

Key elements:

- document existing data practices and support
- analyse existing data practices and support
- identify required organizational, technical and resource capabilities
- identify user needs and acceptance criteria.

2.4 Design

Design of an RDM service is often an iterative process, starting from early prototypes established in the discovery phase and taking these further through alpha and beta stages. As in any other service design project the basic concepts of the new service will be identified through the discovery phase. The design should begin with a clear idea of what purpose each service fulfils for its users/customers, what functions will be needed to do that, what value is provided as a result, and how that value will be known. These elements (purpose, functions, quality and performance) can be used to describe the services to be provided (Taylor, 2011).

RDM is a novel area for most institutions and is evolving in a rapidly changing environment. Defining services in a fine-grained and modular way, as in the 'curation micro-services' approach, should build in the flexibility to minimize the impact of changes in costs and availability. For the same reason agile design methods are likely to pay dividends.

Whether or not the 'system' involves software development, establishing what roles and responsibilities are needed to provide the required functions at the right level is a key design step. The 'human infrastructure' aspects of service design are just as important, and changing existing support roles or developing policy guidance will address some RDM requirements. Where new processes are being put in place it will be critical to identify their ownership – e.g. with library, IT, or research support functions, which might be provided centrally or distributed to faculty or other organizational levels. Data management planning (DMP) is a good example of a cross-functional service area. DMP support could, for example, include linking online DMP tools to processes for pre-award support, or harvesting information from the resulting plans to help estimate the take-up of post-award support services.

The alpha phase will require a detailed operational plan for taking any online RDM system through to beta and live phases. Whichever design approach is taken the alpha phase should implement a basic working prototype from the use cases and any wireframe or paper prototype, aiming to solicit user feedback. If this indicates that a workable approach can be established with the resources available, the beta phase will take forward what has been learned and produce a fully working prototype of the online service (see, for example, the *Government Service Design Manual*).[2]

The design phase will also address requirements for integration with other services. These are likely to include, *inter alia*, the institution's grant costing system, its current research information system (CRIS), and the research output repository. The design process will also need to take account of existing or planned lower-level infrastructure such as network-attached storage or external cloud-based storage-as-a-service.

As is explained in Chapter 5, many researchers will use common off-the-shelf cloud services for storage and collaboration, such as Dropbox. Research groups in disciplines with mature infrastructure for RDM (such as astronomy, or genomics) may have well established platforms and workflows for using and depositing data in externally based archives and virtual research environments (VREs). There may be home-grown specialist repositories, presenting opportunities to integrate these with any central data repository the RDM service is to provide. All such established practices should be examined and considered within the design prospect.

The institutional RDM project will also need to take account of any current workflows for metadata management, and work towards integrating them with workflows for publishing metadata in an institutional catalogue. Tools available for workflow modelling include Research Activity Information Development (RAID) diagrams (Darlington et al., 2011), Web Curator Tool and MyExperiment (see entries in DCC Tools and Services Catalogue[5]).

Key elements:

- define and analyse new service concepts
- prototype and detailed design of new service
- design human resource structures
- analyse and design data management tools and infrastructure.

2.5 Implement

There will be both human and technical aspects to delivering and joining up the services that are developed. For example, the design beta phase should establish which support functions (e.g. IT, library or research office) are the 'owners' of which services, and any needs for restructuring of individuals' roles within these services. It should also identify the need for new relationships and workflows to be established between these roles.

Implementing these changes will call for a programme of advocacy, training and professional development. As new workflows are put in place, any published guidance may need to be updated to communicate these changes. Implementation of these changes is unlikely to be without complication, as it is liable to disrupt the existing norms of service providers as well as impose on practices that have long been the sole responsibility of principal investigators (PIs).

For data management tools and software-based services the critical issues are likely to be around integration with other systems and compliance with standards. For many universities the institutional systems to which RDM support will interface, such as research information systems and output reporting, are both new and the subject of shifting policy demands from funders (e.g. in the case of delivering open access). This will in particular affect the requirements for metadata exchange between these systems. Tools should also be flexible enough to allow support for standards-based profiles, particularly those based on CERIF for research information (see EuroCRIS[6]), as these become more widely used for information about research datasets.

There may be a need for the institutional RDM service to comply with the ISO 2700 series of information security management systems standards (ISO 27000 Directory[7]). For example, to help ensure the security of medical data University College London (UCL) in 2012 became the first UK institution to be audited on the ISO 27001 standard, with support from the Jisc-funded project Data Management Planning for Secure Services.[8]

Of course, the need to comply with standards for web accessibility and the conditions of local information governance should be identified in the discovery phase. However, standards in the RDM domain are still emerging, and as take-up of the service improves and standards become more widely adopted there will be further demands for compliance. So while at the time of writing few institutions have sought accreditation for their RDM services to the 'trusted repository' standards, such as the Data Seal of Approval and ISO 16363 (see APARSEN, 2012), this may well change.

Implementation of data management tools and infrastructure should be to a defined level of service, reflecting, for example, expectations for availability and reliability. Acceptance measures and testing plans for these and other performance criteria will have been defined in the beta phase. These need to be included in the business model and operating procedures for the service in its live phase.

Key elements:

- reorganize support services
- implement data management tools and services
- ensure compliance with relevant standards.

2.6 Evaluate

A decision to 'go live' with an RDM service will depend on the case being made to senior management for offering a fully operational service. Decisions on resourcing may hang on the availability of evidence showing measurable benefits to users and other stakeholders. If these are identified early, in the discovery phase, they can be refined through later phases in light of the practicalities of gathering meaningful data. This should provide the groundwork for setting in place feedback mechanisms and analytics that will allow continuous improvements to be made to the service.

The project team will have a roadmap or operational plan to monitor progression against milestones. Beyond this, benchmarking can help the project team and others to maintain an overall picture of how well capabilities are improving, and guide decisions on readiness to move from alpha to beta stages and make the business case for more funding. The CARDIO tool guides users on capabilities that are considered good practice, but other generic models are also available (e.g. Crowston and Qin, 2010). These are not heavily prescriptive, so the assessment can be mapped to the specific project's needs. Priorities may, for example, be identified from user and stakeholder expectations that have been identified in the discovery and alpha stages. Then, when expected benefits have been scoped for the beta service in terms of performance indicators, user feedback and analytics can feed into further benchmarking assessments. For example, the CARDIO tool has options to assess capabilities against the data policy expectations of UK funding bodies, such as support for data management planning. An assessment of this capability could use a range of more specific metrics – e.g., satisfaction with online guidance, or how frequently users need direct support with their DMP.

A benefits analysis toolkit (KRDS/I2S2[4]) was developed to support institutions in RDM advocacy and business case development. The toolkit comprises the KRDS Benefits Framework and the Value-chain and Benefits Impact tool. Each tool lists a wide range of potential benefits to different stakeholders. The Framework uses the three main dimensions shown in Figure 4.2 for focused discussion of the RDM service's value proposition.

The first of these dimensions, 'What is the outcome?', considers benefits that are direct and indirect. *Direct benefits* can be demonstrated to provide a value as a result of the

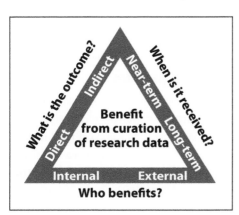

Figure 4.2
The KRDS Benefits Framework (*reproduced with permission, from KRDS/I2S2*)[4]

outputs of RDM development (for instance, researchers becoming more aware of their DMP obligations to funders) or as a result of online advice being provided. *Indirect benefits* typically arise as a 'knock-on' effect, through later costs and/or risks being avoided. Funding a DMP advice service, for example, may indirectly benefit the institution's flow of research income, by limiting the number of research grants delayed when peer reviewers reject inadequate DMPs.

The dimensions can be further subdivided when relevant. For example, the 'Who benefits?' dimension is split between internal and external stakeholders. This can be expanded, as in an example produced by the University of Bath's Research360 project. This listed potential benefits first to the *university community*, the academic staff and researchers, students, professional services and the institution; and secondly to *external partners*, including industry and commerce, public and voluntary sectors, government and society (Beagrie and Pink, 2012).

Wide consultation on anticipated and expected benefits, and the indicators used to provide evidence of whether or not they are being achieved, will help to ensure that evaluation serves the practical needs of the service and its users. For example, in the Jisc Managing Research Data programme a team of 'evidence gatherers' consulted individual projects on the evidence of benefits they could realistically produce from narratives and short case studies as well as quantitative metrics such as downloads (Whyte et al., 2014).

Key elements:

- evaluate benefits and costs of service improvements
- link to continuous improvement programme.

3. Appreciating the context – norms of data practice

Developing new research data management services and infrastructure requires an appreciation of the existing landscape. As mentioned earlier, this comprises researchers' use of existing services as well as their own practices for dealing with data. However, cross-disciplinary RDM infrastructure development is relatively new and there is little guidance for the information professional wanting to know how data practices may shape the development of support. An approach that can usefully relate contextual factors to RDM is the 'Institutional Analysis and Development' (IAD) framework (Hess and Ostrom, 2005).

The IAD framework has a broad scope; to help analyse how organizations and communities can make decisions and rules effectively to sustain a resource or achieve a desired outcome, such as the 'knowledge commons' envisaged by research data-sharing policies. The framework highlights factors that may help one appreciate current norms and the 'patterns of interaction' that relate everyday research practice to RDM principles, capabilities, service components and their outcomes. Norms may be embedded in everyday practice in a take-it-for-granted way. It makes sense to identify these in early design phases, to avoid costly changes to the research process or the support service that may result if norms only become apparent when a new process breaches them. Norms are 'external variables' to development; included in the factors discussed below.

3.1 Ideas, artefacts and facilities

Research data begin as traces or impressions that result from the expression of ideas, and lead to further ideas being expressed; '. . . data is the primary building block of information, comprising the lowest level of abstraction in any field of knowledge, where it is identifiable as collections of numbers, characters, images or other symbols that when contextualized in a certain way represent facts, figures or ideas as communicable information' (Pryor, 2012).

It is easy to take for granted the 'factual' nature of data, but it is important to remember that it becomes research data through its relationships to other things, its 'representation information' in the terminology of the Open Archival Information System (CCSDS, 2002). In particular, it becomes research data through an assertion that it is evidence for research findings, as when related to a model, for example (Edwards, 2010). Some of the information needed to frame a stream of bits as research evidence may be available in the research application, or the instruments used to capture those bits or package them in files and metadata. To work as a 'public good', researchers need to package data with enough contextual information for it to be understood by peers in their research field, using standard formats, which will allow it to be deposited in a formally governed archive or repository.

Information practices in research fields vary in terms of the mutual dependency of researchers and the degree of uncertainty in their tasks (Fry, 2006). Less technical uncertainty means standards are more likely to be viable, and data or code more replicable. Greater mutual dependence is accompanied by economies of scale and centralization of resources around large-scale facilities (Fry, 2006). It is probably no coincidence, therefore, that data management and sharing are better established in fields with these characteristics, such as astronomy, earth sciences and genomics.

Research facilities, instruments and analysis platforms shape data production and management. Their location, capacity and capabilities will set boundaries on what more can be achieved by developing new RDM infrastructure to support the institution as a whole, as well as offering examples of good practice. These need to be considered in identifying requirements and evaluating results. Considering institutional back-up solutions, for example, users' requirements for data retrieval may vary across different instruments that produce different file quantities, sizes, complexity and overall volumes. Consequently, it is important to recognize limits on the feasibility of 'one-size-fits all' approaches.

The *artefacts* that embody data and relate it to its producers' expressed ideas will define the possibilities for harvesting and pooling data. RDM tools or services can facilitate more use of 'digital research objects' that link digital workflows to data. These could include, for example, electronic laboratory notebooks. A range of dimensions can be considered when assessing the options and benefits of digital research objects, including the extent to which they need to be 'reusable, repurposeable, repeatable, reproducible, replayable, referenceable, revealable and respectful' (De Roure et al., 2011). When introducing tools or services that replace physical artefacts such as notebooks with digital ones, careful attention also needs to be taken to ensure the digital artefacts do not introduce unexpected limitations as to how users can interact with them (Hartswood et al., 2012).

Repositories can help to manage research objects in a more formal and collaborative manner, just as they can be used to manage software code used for data analysis. However, the research environment limits the scope to introduce standardized 'enterprise' solutions, as these may not meet the needs of research to explore novel ways of working with data. Information professionals need to *co-design* with research communities, to build on the platforms they already use, and minimize the effort to share data by extracting metadata automatically (Beitz, 2013).

3.2 Communities – producers, users and policymakers

Data producers may be anyone involved in producing outputs, including those working on the supporting infrastructure, as well as researchers and 'citizen scientists'. In most research fields there will be a range of stakeholders involved in data production, including companies, policy-makers, non-governmental organizations and individual citizens. Their participation in RDM development may be considered desirable, whether on a steering group or as representative users to be consulted during design, or simply to be informed about the service when it is implemented.

To scope and evaluate an RDM service the information professional will need to establish which stakeholders in data production and management the service needs to accommodate. For example, the developers of the DataONE infrastructure for biological and environmental research identified primary stakeholders as 'scientists', with a further range of secondary stakeholders represented by those who regularly interact with scientists during the research process. As Figure 4.3 shows, librarians were identified as key secondary stakeholders, as they are present in each of the institutional environments in which scientists work (Michener et al., 2012).

We also need to ask how an RDM service will interoperate with other service providers. The landscape that repositories operate in is becoming more complex, with a diverse range of organizations involved in providing infrastructure. Infrastructures for RDM can be thought of in terms of layers. At the bottom we have networked computing and storage providers, including commercial providers of cloud services as well as public NRENS

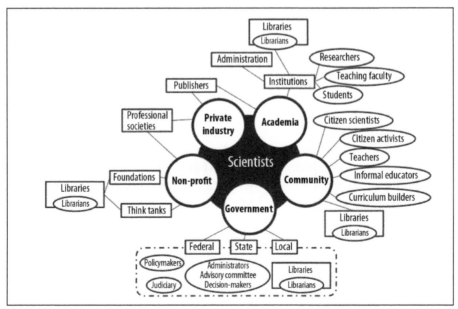

Figure 4.3 RDM Stakeholders: an example from DataONE. Individual roles are shown as ovals and organizations as boxes (*reproduced with permission, from Michener et al., 2012*)

(National Research and Education Networks); on top of this we see 'cyber-infrastructure' such as DataONE emerging in the USA, and 'research infrastructures' like OpenAire in Europe, providing increasingly standardized services that are federated across national borders (Whyte, 2012).

Policy-making bodies are well established in some research communities, which have developed sophisticated data practices and curation resources that are largely self-governed. Committees comprised of scientists and research users plan large-particle physics experiments and astronomical studies, for example. This is likely to become more common across all disciplines with the trend towards larger and more inter-disciplinary research teams (Wuchty et al., 2007).

3.3 Rules and norms – constitutional, policy and operational

In recent years 'top-down' data governance applied through public funders and regulatory bodies has become more pronounced, reflecting the need to address technology changes in science, coupled with broader public interest in research transparency and integrity (Royal Society, 2012). Common principles are being adopted across national boundaries and between funding bodies. In the UK, for example, the seven research councils jointly issued common data principles that set out the shared roles and responsibilities of the institutions and researchers that they fund.[9]

Principles such as these help identify the capabilities an institution needs in order to contribute to a research data commons. The IAD framework makes an analytic distinction between such 'constitutional rules' and 'collective choice' policies. The latter are formulated at an operational level to define, for example, who may submit research data to a repository and who may access it.

Norms of data sharing are a contentious subject and will strongly affect the take-up of data repository services. There is a wide gulf between top-down policies that require researchers to adopt a default position of sharing data publicly, and researchers' widely held beliefs and established practice. Many see it as the PI's right of moral ownership to offer data access only on conditions that directly benefit their research, such as collaboration or joint authorship (see Tenopir et al., 2011). This makes it especially important to link mechanisms for public sharing to evidence of the benefits to researchers – e.g., from achieving greater visibility of the research and, in the longer term, data citations that earn professional kudos and quantifiable career rewards.

Sustaining common-pool resources like repositories depends on community take-up. It also demands 'nested levels of governance'. This is most effective when higher-level authorities set parameters that allow self-determination by relatively smaller communities of providers and decision-makers, each 'unified as to the purpose and goals of the information resource or knowledge commons at hand' (Hess and Ostrom, 2005). In practice this means that institutional policies may work best when they allow details to be worked out at a lower level such as the faculty or department.

Examples of this 'nested' governance include repository certification and data appraisal. Criteria in use for both of these are similar across disciplinary data repositories (see the criteria listed in Whyte and Wilson, 2010). Yet they are different enough in their detail to accommodate differences, for example in the kinds of contextual information needed for reuse, or the methods used for quality assurance. Compare, for example, the criteria used by the UK's environmental and social science data centres (NERC, 2012; Van den Eynden, 2013).

The organizational level that is best placed to support data management will also depend on other norms, such as how existing library, IT or research support and training services are delivered. The organizational and funding body norms for cost accounting will also have a bearing here, and we return to that at the end of the chapter.

4. Tools for initiating change and discovering data practices

4.1 In-depth case studies

Case studies of research groups' and other stakeholders' data practices represent a high-value and high-cost approach. The case studies may be 'immersive', involving information or data science specialists following researchers and the story of the data they produce from observation of their work. This will typically require several weeks of intensive study or months of regular involvement. Case studies can also involve interviews with researchers on data policy issues and support requirements. Lighter-weight approaches, such as that enabled by DAF/CARDIO (see section 4.2), also do this. Clearly, balance of effort and return is needed. Lightweight approaches will often be preferable, but at the risk of missing key challenges to RDM by shoehorning responses to fit a limited set of questions, or not sufficiently addressing inconvenient truths. For example, some recent studies point to substantial challenges in the reuse of data, especially for new purposes or across disciplines (Hartswood et al., 2012; Faniel and Zimmerman, 2011). Other studies demonstrate that, even within disciplines, data practices and support requirements vary widely between research groups (Lyon et al., 2010).

In-depth study can be easiest to justify where it will help in understanding areas of practice where significant and substantial changes are planned. That may apply to a specific workflow as a subset of a larger programme. For example, automating the procedures around depositing data into a repository might justify an in-depth analysis of workflows to ensure that requirements are properly understood. In-depth studies across a broader scale are also possible. For example, the RDM programme might involve large-scale development and integration of new software across a variety of institutions and data centres; particular examples would be the US cyberinfrastructure programmes such as DataOne, or European research data infrastructures that provide for specific disciplinary needs (see Whyte, 2012).

The skills needed to carry out in-depth studies are usually supplied from two directions: the information specialist with social research skills in observation and interviewing, and software specialists with skills in working closely with users to co-design systems. Studies like this may be undertaken as collaborations with academic staff from computing science or library/information science or with e-research centres.

In situations where in-depth studies cannot be resourced, the RDM development programme might benefit from a literature review of relevant published studies. For example, data archives have been around for decades in some disciplines, notably in areas such as astronomy, geosciences, genomics and particle physics, where there are strong drivers towards sharing access to large, expensive instruments and facilities. These domains have been the focus of insightful studies on e-infrastructure (or cyberinfrastructure) developments to support collaborative research (e.g., Cragin and Shankar, 2006). Smaller science and scholarship communities are also using data-intensive methods, as in the analysis of digital images or large public datasets (Wilson et al., 2011).

4.2 Surveying data practices and benchmarking service capabilities

Many institutional RDM projects benefit from online surveys of researchers and other stakeholders in data management. These typically draw on similar questions to larger scale surveys of common practices and attitudes towards data sharing and reuse. For example, the DataONE project surveyed thousands of scientists in 2009–10 to produce a 'baseline assessment', following this up with more detailed work on stakeholder profiles (see section 4.4 below).

DAF (Data Asset Framework) offers a quick and lightweight approach to discovering data management practice though online and face-to-face surveys, whereas CARDIO is a benchmarking approach that can be used to assess the gaps between current and required support capabilities. The two approaches were developed independently and may be used that way, as more fully described elsewhere (Jones, 2009). They can also be used to complement each other, as suggested below.

Both DAF and CARDIO employ surveys, structured interviews and workshop techniques. DAF can fulfil an 'intelligence-gathering' role, collecting evidence of researchers' current practices and views on service provision. The benchmarking and gap analysis requires evidence, whether assessments are made online or in a workshop. The evidence that DAF studies can provide is typically in the form of a landscape report based on online surveys and interviews, as follows:

- **Online surveys:** typically these contain 10–20 questions covering research-active staff awareness of policy requirements, responsibilities for data management planning, expectations of benefits, needs for training and guidance, current practices for back-up and storage, providing access to working data and sharing data of longer-term value, plus their priorities for support service provision.
- **Semi-structured interviews:** typically these consist of individual or small group interviews involving a number of pilot groups. These should span a number of disciplines, funding sources and scale of research teams. Studies normally involve 3–6 researchers, depending on group size, from PhD students to group leaders at professorial level. The interviews cover similar topics to survey questions, but aim for a more conversational approach to understand the researchers' current field of research and context. This covers aspects as outlined in section 3, e.g. instruments and artefacts used in data collection, the tools, standards and infrastructure used to work with data, views on data reuse and policy drivers towards that.

CARDIO workshop participants may then draw upon this evidence. These workshops typically involve RDM steering group representatives, plus representatives from all functions involved in service provision and academic colleagues from the research groups selected for DAF studies.

CARDIO employs a 1–5 rating scale to assess the level of service provision against 30 criteria representing organizational, technical and resource capabilities. These may be capabilities expressed in terms of the whole institution or at the level of faculties or smaller units, depending on whether service provision is devolved or centralized. Broadly the levels represent service maturity. In the context of a programme of RDM service development they can be interpreted as a progression through the initiation, discovery, alpha and beta stages of design and then a live service that can demonstrate engagement with its users:

1 There is initial recognition at institutional level of the need for a service.
2 Requirements are being assessed through discovery or evaluation studies.
3 New solutions are being tested through small-scale trials.
4 Solutions are being piloted across the institution.
5 Services are established and process is in place for continuous improvement.

The steps in the benchmarking exercise initially involve a co-ordinator or project manager making an initial assessment, then recruiting the participants and inviting their individual assessments. The collaborative aspect involves comparing and discussing assessments with a view to agreeing where responsibilities are clear or otherwise. Individual assessments can be surveyed online using the CARDIO tool. Face-to-face workshop settings may offer better opportunities to benefit from drawing together individuals with different perspectives and from diverse research and service backgrounds, especially if they do not ordinarily interact.

Using CARDIO in workshop settings can involve different profiles or sets of criteria. For example, a CARDIO profile of nine groups of capabilities was matched to the data policy expectations set out by the Engineering and Physical Sciences Research Council;[10] this was co-designed with participants in the DCC's 2012–13 programme of institutional engagements.

The studies are carried out by one or (preferably) two information professionals from library, IT or research support roles. Local support counterparts may also be involved, both as interviewers and as interviewees. A DAF study will follow similar protocols to those of a qualitative research case study. For example, although the purpose is development rather than research, ethical review may be required of interview questions, informed consent forms and any steps taken to anonymize the results.

Resourcing these studies demands careful planning. Notes or any transcripts of recordings will need to be analysed, and while this will not be to the same level of rigour as research (which typically takes around 6 hours' analysis per hour of interview), it will still involve at least as much time as carrying out the interviews. Involving more researchers per interview, reducing the length to 15–30 minutes, or using fewer open-ended than closed questions can of course reduce the effort needed, although each of these approaches will also reduce the richness of the results.

A report is then produced, summarizing the analysis and offering recommendations to the RDM steering group on which service development priorities to address. In some institutions DAF studies have supported consultation on draft RDM policy, feeding into the university's formal decision-making processes through committees dealing with information governance and research.

4.3 Documenting data lifecycles with data curation profiles

A data curation profile (DCP) is described as an outline of the 'story' of a dataset or collection, describing its origin and lifecycle within a research project.[11] The approach was developed to address the challenge of determining '. . . which disciplinary and sub-disciplinary distinctions need to be attended to in shaping curation requirements and services' (Cragin et al., 2010). The approach has a primary focus on analysing differences in data-sharing practices across specific research communities, and how these are affected by, for example, the data types used and the stage of the data lifecycle.

The DCP approach is close to DAF in some respects, including the scope of the questions asked. As with DAF, the profiles are intended for librarians and others to use to inform decisions. However, where DAF aims for a general awareness of datasets and practices across a department or institution, DCP takes a more rigorous look at the data associated with a sub-discipline.

The process of using a DCP in a librarian–researcher 'data interview' can be useful in training and development, to build the participants' confidence to engage in discussions about data management – e.g. see MANTRA.[12] Curation profiles can inform decisions applied to particular collections, for example in the selection of datasets for retention, and in the provision of metadata (Witt et al., 2009).

Data curation profile interviews are designed to take place across two one-hour sessions. Like DAF, the approach uses a semi-structured interview format, with questions about the interviewees' research process, types of data collected, accessibility and ownership issues, how data is transformed through the research process, and any practices relating to sharing the outputs of the various stages. A toolkit is available, comprising a profile template, a worksheet that researcher and interviewer will complete during the interview, a manual for interviewers and a user guide.[11] Completed profiles may be submitted for publication in a reference resource, the *Data Curation Profiles Directory*.[13]

4.4 Stakeholder profiles, personas and scenarios

It is standard practice for user-focused service designers to characterize the stakeholders in a proposed service, build 'personas' representing key characteristics thought to affect their use of the service, and develop scenarios representing typical use cases (see Design Council, 2011). In terms of the design phases referred to in this chapter, *stakeholder profiles* help to scope user needs in the discovery phase. In the design phase *personas* help align the archetypal user characteristics with the emerging design concepts. *Scenarios* then support design and implementation by fleshing out how the service will work for its users.

These approaches are exemplified by the DataONE project's design process (Michener et al., 2012). DataONE is a large-scale US-based federated data network designed to provide a foundation for innovative environmental research. The network supports scientists and other stakeholders to engage with the relevant science, data and policy communities. It also facilitates easy, secure and persistent storage of data, and disseminates tools for data discovery, analysis, visualization and decision making.

DataONE followed up their stakeholder analysis (see section 3.2) with 'baseline assessments' of the stakeholders' current practices, perceptions and 'needs relevant to all stages of the data lifecycle' (Michener et al., 2012). These were online surveys, similar in scope to DAF surveys and data curation profile questions. The DataONE survey is very detailed when it comes to individual roles and demographic characteristics, and highly revealing on data-sharing practices and the conditions that researchers would prefer to attach to reuse (Tenopir et al., 2011).

Based on the survey findings, personas were written to describe 'typical' stakeholders in both primary and secondary categories. According to Michener et al., they included 'research scientists in early, mid and late career; a scientist at a field station; a modeler; a data librarian; a citizen scientist; and a university administrator' (Michener et al., 2012, 11).

The personas were then related to a set of use cases representing the intended functions of DataONE tools and services, which were then fleshed out into scenarios describing how particular capabilities would be used at a specific point in the data lifecycle, such as enabling searching across multiple data sources.

5. Planning for sustainability

Making the business case to sustain a service can be challenging when institutions are under constant pressure to do more in a highly competitive funding environment. Inevitably institutions will have developed their own practice for approving business cases, but the approach to justifying an RDM service is not essentially different from any similar information-based service (see e.g. Currall and McKinney, 2007).

As a result of pilot implementation and beta testing of the online components of the service, it should be possible to identify basic elements of the business case, including the proposed scope, an appraisal of the options for providing it, and identification of who it is proposed will provide it. A description of the scope should be consistent with how the RDM service would appear in a service portfolio or catalogue, describing for each component:

- **Purpose:** what the service aims to deliver, its goals or use cases; outcome statements from the discovery phase that will drive it (e.g., 'a service to support data management planning')
- **Functions:** what the service must do for its customers/beneficiaries in order to achieve its purpose (e.g., 'provides institution-wide guidelines on handling sensitive data')
- **Quality:** what value the service provides to its users (e.g., 'clarity on data management roles and responsibilities')
- **Performance:** how the service will be monitored using criteria that express its value (e.g., availability, capacity, responsiveness, reliability) and impact (e.g., take-up, satisfaction, research visibility).

The business case will, in effect, provide a story to illustrate Figure 4.1. This will summarize what the pilot implementation will establish, or has already learned, to justify investing the resources needed to make organizational and technological changes. It will set out the opportunity presented to the organization, in terms of strategic objectives and attendant benefits and risks. It will justify a commitment to invest in the preferred option, and identify how costs may be recovered and how the service performance can be evaluated against how it fulfils its objectives.

Since the RDM service will likely include a range of service components or tools, the implications of different service level options will need to be outlined for each. For example ADMIRe, a University of Nottingham institutional pilot project supported by the Jisc Managing Research Data Programme, identified three service levels for six 'core service activities', as shown in Table 4.1.

The potential benefits from RDM were discussed earlier under evaluation (section 2.6). Risks will also be addressed: these will include risks to the availability of data that an operational RDM service would help to mitigate. Risks to the organization from the service not meeting its objectives will also help make the case. For example, there may be risks to institutional reputation if research is discredited and oversight has been poor, or there may be reduced funding opportunities from inadequate data management planning.

Table 4.1 An example of service options for an RDM business case (reproduced with permission from Williamson, 2013, ADMIRe RDM service models. Retrieved from http://admire.jiscinvolve.org/wp/2013/03/29/jisc-managing-research-data-programme-workshop)

Core service activities	Level 1 Minimal	Level 2 Mediated	Level 3 Consultancy
Data Management Plans	PI with website guidance	Training, advocacy and some one-to-one	Tailored approach, subject-specific advice and training
Active data management and storage	IT Support, Schools and PI (ad hoc)	Training, advocacy and some one-to-one	Tailored approach and subject-specific advice
Data archive and preservation	IT Services with IT Support	Training, advocacy and some one-to-one	Tailored approach and subject-specific/funder requirements
Data sharing and publishing	IT Services with IT Support	Training, advocacy, CPD at University of Nottingham	Tailored approach and on-going training
Copyright and IPR	PI with website guidance	Training, CPD at University of Nottingham	Tailored approach and on-going training
Compliance and reporting	PI responsible	Institutional overview and mechanisms	Systemized reporting
	Website advice and self-supporting	*Focused support and capacity building*	*Consultancy, subject-specific and embedding*

A key issue to address will be how the service fits with existing service groupings, and whether these are centralized or faculty-based. Some combination of the two is likely and the balance may vary across service components, since these vary in how far they require disciplinary expertise.

Financial factors will come into play, as some components or activities (e.g. training) may fit well with established cost centres and charging mechanisms. The desirability of establishing new cost centres will take into account factors such as the feasibility of usage charges, which has to take into consideration the willingness of PIs to pay, the challenges of estimating take-up, the level of transparency needed by the institution and by funders, and the need to minimize any impact on overhead rates charged by central services.

Beyond the 'pump-priming' of set-up costs, it is likely that services will be resourced through a combination of the following:

- providing online open source resources with no charge and minimal support (e.g., online guidance, software tools)
- charging to grants either as indirect costs (e.g., for data management planning) or calculated according to usage of a research support facility (e.g., database hosting)
- embedding services in existing funding channels (e.g., training)
- absorbing costs by making savings elsewhere (e.g., through reskilling and repurposing library staff)
- deploying grant funding to develop or sustain a community resource (e.g., a curated reference dataset or data management tool).

The strategic objectives outlined in the business case can make the key difference to winning over senior management. For example RDM may support institutional research strategies to offer a competitive research environment and infrastructure for collaborative research. Inter-disciplinary capabilities to address 'grand challenges' are also commonly on the strategy agenda, and here RDM can emphasize capabilities such as cross-disciplinary metadata searching and data visualization tools.

6. Summary

In this chapter we have shown how developing RDM services can be approached in a similar way to any other service design project. At the same time, RDM services are unlike other kinds of service that institutions provide, because research can involve wider networks of stakeholders than are normally supported. Development is made more complex by the need to take into account varying requirements for policy compliance and data governance. It is also necessary to recognize but not be overwhelmed by the uncertainties and complexities of research itself, which by its nature breaks rules.

The essential point of difference in RDM service development is the need to plan for continuous improvement. Indeed, RDM services may grow from small beginnings, such as the provision of online guidance to services that already exist under other names, and lists of helpful external resources or pointers. It is important, too, to recognize that the need for institutional data repositories will be shaped by the norms of research practice and the realities of institutional funding, and it is likely that economies of scale will drive specialization, both within and across institutions. Requirements will change as a consequence of further development in the technologies underpinning RDM and digital research. With researchers' growing awareness of the services available to them will come new expectations and demands, most likely for better support to collaborative research and data publication, and for easier methods of tracking of the impacts from effective RDM, including that from improved data citation.

The chapter has also surveyed tools to assist in requirements discovery and the early phases of design. The road to a sustainable RDM service will be easier if the path followed from discovery to design is broad enough to encompass the real needs of users and stakeholders. If so, it will have generated a clear idea of the functions that should be implemented and the value they should provide, and crucially these will have been tested with users against criteria that they accept. Ensuring clarity when describing predicted value and benefits will certainly help make the business case. At the time of writing, the models used to cost and resource RDM activities are far from mature, and resourcing an RDM service remains a challenge. Ultimately the bottom line may prove to be that doing nothing is a strategy that will deliver unsustainable costs to any institution that wants to maintain a credible research capability.

7. References

7.1 Websites

1   Jisc MRD Managing Research Data Programme 2011–13, www.jisc.ac.uk/whatwedo/programmes/di_researchmanagement/managingresearchdata.aspx.

2   UK Government Digital Service (2013) *Government Service Design Manual*,

  https://www.gov.uk/service-manual.
3 CARDIO, Collaborative Assessment of Research Data Infrastructure and
   Objectives, http://cardio.dcc.ac.uk.
4 KRDS/I2S2 Digital Preservation Benefit Analysis Tools Project, available from
   http://beagrie.com/krds-i2s2.php.
5 DCC Tools and Services Catalogue, Digital Curation Centre,
   www.dcc.ac.uk/resources/external/tools-services.
6 EuroCRIS, *Main Features of CERIF*,
   www.eurocris.org/Index.php?page=featuresCERIF&t=1.
7 ISO 27000 Directory (2008) www.27000.org/index.htm.
8 Data Management Planning for Secure Services (DMP-SS),
   www.ucl.ac.uk/ich/research-ich/mrc-cech/data/projects/dmp_ss.
9 RCUK Common Principles on Data Policy (2011)
   www.rcuk.ac.uk/research/Pages/DataPolicy.aspx.
10 EPSRC Policy Framework on Research Data Expectations (2011),
   www.epsrc.ac.uk/about/standards/researchdata/Pages/expectations.aspx.
11 Data Curation Profiles Toolkit, http://datacurationprofiles.org.
12 MANTRA (2013) MANTRA Research Data Management Training,
   http://datalib.edina.ac.uk/mantra/index.html.
13 Data Curation Profiles Directory, http://docs.lib.purdue.edu/dcp.

7.2 Citations

APARSEN (2012) *D33.1A Report on Peer Review of Digital Repositories*,
   www.alliancepermanentaccess.org/index.php/aparsen/aparsen-deliverables.
Beagrie, N. and Pink, C. (2012) *Benefits from Research Data Management in Universities
   for Industry and Not-for-profit Research Partners*, http://opus.bath.ac.uk/32509.
Becher, T. (1989) *Academic Tribes and Territories: intellectual enquiry and the culture of
   disciplines*, SRHE and Open University Press.
Beitz, A. (2013) Growing an Institution's Research Data Management Capability
   Through Strategic Investments in Infrastructure, *8th International Digital Curation
   Conference*, www.dcc.ac.uk/events/idcc13/programme-presentations.
Bos, N., Zimmerman, A., Olson, J., Yew, J., Yerkie, J., Dahl, E. and Olson, G. (2007)
   From Shared Databases to Communities of Practice: a taxonomy of
   collaboratories, *Journal of Computer-Mediated Communication*, **12** (2), Article 6.
CCSDS (2002) *Reference Model for an Open Archival Information System (OAIS)*,
   CCSDS 650.0-B-1, Blue Book.
Charles Beagrie Ltd (2011) *Benefits from the Infrastructure Projects in the JISC
   Managing Research Data Programme*,

www.jisc.ac.uk/whatwedo/programmes/mrd/outputs/benefitsreport.aspx.

Cockburn, A. (2001) *Writing Effective Use Cases*, Vol. 1, Addison-Wesley, http://alistair.cockburn.us/get/2465.

Cohn, M. (2004) *User Stories Applied: for agile software development*, Addison-Wesley Professional.

Cragin, M. and Shankar, K. (2006) Scientific Data Collections and Distributed Collective Practice, *Computer Supported Cooperative Work (CSCW)*, **15** (2–3), 204, 185.

Cragin, M. H., Palmer, C. L., Carlson, J. R. and Witt, M. (2010) Data Sharing, Small Science and Institutional Repositories, *Philosophical Transactions of the Royal Society, A: Mathematical, Physical and Engineering Sciences*, 368 (1926), 4023–38, doi: 10.1098/rsta.2010.0165.

Crowston, K. and Qin, J. (2010) *A Capability Maturity Model for Scientific Data Management*, http://crowston.syr.edu/content/capability-maturity-model-scientific-data-management-0.

Currall, J. and McKinney, P. (2007) *Espida Handbook*, University of Glasgow, http://hdl.handle.net/1905/691.

Darlington, M., Ball, A., Howard, T., Culley, S. and McMahon, C. (2011) *RAID Associative Tool Requirements Specification*, http://opus.bath.ac.uk/22811.

De Roure, D., Bechhofer, S., Goble, C. and Newman, D. (2011) Scientific Social Objects: the social objects and multidimensional network of the myExperiment website, *1st International Workshop on Social Object Networks*, http://eprints.soton.ac.uk/272747.

Design Council (2011) *Design Methods for Developing Services*, https://connect.innovateuk.org/web/4949575/articles/-/blogs/design-methods-for-developing-services.

Edwards, P. N. (2010) *A Vast Machine: computer models, climate data, and the politics of global warming*, MIT Press.

Faniel, I. M. and Zimmerman, A. (2011) Beyond the Data Deluge: a research agenda for large-scale data shaping and reuse, *International Journal of Digital Curation*, **6** (1), 58–69, doi: 10.2218/ijdc.v6i1.172.

Fry, J. (2006) Scholarly Research and Information Practices: a domain analytic approach, *Information Processing & Management*, **42** (1), 299–316, doi:10.1016/j.ipm.2004.09.004.

Hartswood, M., Procter, R., Taylor, P., Blot, L., Anderson, S., Rouncefield, M. and Slack, R. (2012) Problems of Data Mobility and Reuse in the Provision of Computer-based Training for Screening Mammography. In *Proceedings of the 2012 ACM Annual Conference on Human Factors in Computing Systems* (909–918), ACM, doi:10.1145/2208516.2208533.

Hess, C. and Ostrom, E. (2005) *A Framework for Analyzing the Knowledge Commons: a chapter from understanding knowledge as a commons: from theory to practice*, http://surface.syr.edu/sul/21.

Higgins, S. (2008) The DCC Curation Lifecycle Model, *International Journal of Digital Curation*, **3** (1), 134–40.

Jones, S. (2009) *Data Asset Framework Implementation Guide*, University of Glasgow, Humanities Advanced Technology and Information Institute, www.data-audit.eu/docs/DAF_Implementation_Guide.pdf.

Kettinger, W. J., Teng, J. T. C. and Guha, S. (1997) Business Process Change: a study of methodologies, techniques, and tools, *MIS Quarterly*, **21** (1), 55–80, doi:10.2307/249742.

Lyon, L., Rusbridge, C., Neilson, C. and Whyte, A. (2010) *Disciplinary Approaches to Sharing, Curation, Reuse and Preservation: DCC SCARP final report*, Digital Curation Centre, www.dcc.ac.uk/sites/default/files/documents/scarp/ SCARP-FinalReport-Final-SENT.pdf.

Michener, W. K., Allard, S., Budden, A., Cook, R. B., Douglass, K., Frame, M. and Vieglais, D. A. (2012) Participatory Design of DataONE – Enabling Cyberinfrastructure for the Biological and Environmental Sciences, *Ecological Informatics*, **11**, 5–15, doi:10.1016/j.ecoinf.2011.08.007.

Natural and Environmental Research Council (2012) *Data Value Checklist*, www.nerc.ac.uk/research/sites/data/dmp.asp.

PARSE Insight (2010) *Insight Report*, www.parse-insight.eu/publications.php#d3-6.

Pryor, G. (2012) *Managing Research Data*, Facet Publishing.

Royal Society (2012) *Science as an Open Enterprise*, http://royalsociety.org/policy/projects/science-public-enterprise/report.

Taylor, S. (2011) *Service Intelligence: improving your bottom line with the power of IT service management*, www.informit.com/store/product.aspx?isbn=0132692074.

Tenopir, C., Allard, S., Douglass, K., Aydinoglu, A. U., Wu, L., Read, E. and Frame, M. (2011) Data Sharing by Scientists: practices and perceptions, *PLOS ONE*, **6** (6), e21101, doi:10.1371/journal.pone.0021101.

Van den Eynden, V. (2013) Data Review at the UK Data Archive, paper delivered at workshop 'Data Publishing, Peer Review and Repository Accreditation: everyone a winner?', *8th International Digital Curation Conference*, www.dcc.ac.uk/events/idcc13/workshops.

Whyte, A. (2012) Emerging Infrastructure and Services for Research Data Management and Curation in the UK And Europe. In Pryor, G. (ed.) *Managing Research Data*, Facet Publishing.

Whyte, A. and Wilson, A. (2010) How to Appraise and Select Research Data for Curation, Digital Curation Centre, www.dcc.ac.uk/resources/how-guides.

Whyte, A., Molloy, L., Beagrie, N. and Houghton, J. (2014) What to Measure? Towards metrics for research data management. In Ray, J. (ed.) *Research Data Management: practical strategies for information professionals*, Purdue University Press (to be published).

Williamson, L. (2013) *ADMIRe RDM service models*, http://admire.jiscinvolve.org/wp/2013/03/29/jisc-managing-research-data-programme-workshop.

Wilson, J. A., Martinez-Uribe, L., Fraser, M. A. and Jeffreys, P. (2011) An Institutional Approach to Developing Research Data Management Infrastructure, *International Journal of Digital Curation*, **6** (2), 274–87.

Witt, M., Carlson, J., Brandt, D. S. and Cragin, M. H. (2009) Constructing Data Curation Profiles, *International Journal of Digital Curation*, **4** (3), 93–103.

Wuchty, S., Jones, B. F. and Uzzi, B. (2007) The Increasing Dominance of Teams in Production of Knowledge, *Science*, **316** (5827), 1036–9, doi:10.1126/science.1136099.

CHAPTER 5

The range and components of RDM infrastructure and services

Sarah Jones

1. Introduction

This chapter describes the range of infrastructure and services that institutions may wish to develop to support research data management (RDM). It draws primarily on work from the Jisc Managing Research Data programmes[1] and the Digital Curation Centre's institutional engagements with UK universities.[2] Some examples from Australia, Europe and the USA are also included. As a series of practical steps, this chapter amplifies the introduction to roles and responsibilities given in Chapter 3 and the process of developing services covered by Chapter 4, while at the same time setting the context for the case studies to follow.

2. An outline of potential infrastructure and support

A range of services are needed to support the creation, management and sharing of research data. Figure 5.1 visualizes the different aspects to be addressed. These fall broadly into three categories:

1　An overarching governance framework to shape the delivery of services.
2　Specific infrastructure and services provided at key points in the data lifecycle.
3　Assistance from support staff to aid the uptake and use of services.

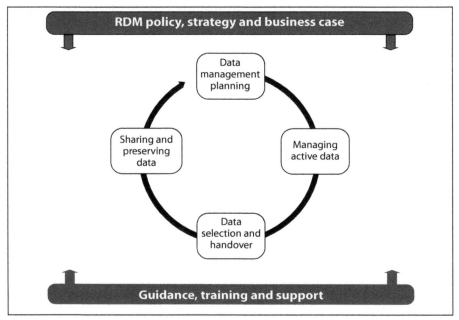

Figure 5.1 Components of RDM support services (*adapted from How to Develop Research Data Management Services – a guide for HEIs (Jones, Pryor & Whyte, 2013), by permission of the Digital Curation Centre*)

Overarching elements of policy, strategy and business case are needed to set the framework in which RDM services will be delivered. These elements will help in defining an institution's approach, in planning the programme of work and ensuring that the proposed infrastructure and support services will be sustainable.

A range of infrastructure and support services is needed at key points in the data lifecycle. Many institutions and research funders require data management plans (DMPs), so guidance, templates, tools and consultancy services may be offered to support this initial activity in the lifecycle. Infrastructure and services are also needed to manage data during the active phase of research, namely data storage and the appropriate tools to facilitate access and collaboration. Not all data will need to be preserved and shared. Processes for data selection and handover will help to identify which data has long-term value and pass this on to appropriate services for long-term curation. Data catalogues and repository services are also needed to preserve data and promote reuse. It is unlikely that an institution will provide all of these components by itself, as there is a wealth of existing infrastructure and services at disciplinary, national and international level.

A very necessary foundation of guidance, training and support should underpin the RDM infrastructure and services. Support may include the provision of websites containing advice and assistance, helpdesk services, training for different audiences and tailored consultancy. The importance of 'human' support (i.e., people who can advise and support researchers to use the infrastructure and tools in place) should not be underestimated.

3. Policy, strategy and business case

The increasing importance of data management in an academic context has caused many universities to develop policies, strategies and business cases as the first steps towards delivering RDM support services. Most have started by undertaking requirements-gathering exercises, surveying researchers' practices and existing infrastructure to support RDM. Armed with an understanding of their current position, institutions can then map out a programme of activity to deliver infrastructure and services. A policy will help to define the institution's core RDM principles and set the framework in which support is to be delivered, while the business case will define how infrastructure and support services will be resourced and make the case for investment. Together these elements will shape the development, implementation and sustainability of RDM support services.

As discussed in Chapter 1, the EPSRC *Policy Framework on Research Data* (EPSRC, 2011) has been an important driver in the UK context, as it requires institutions to produce a 'roadmap' to align their policies and processes with EPSRC's expectations. However, even without this impetus institutions such as the University of Edinburgh and Monash University in Australia have made significant headway. The University of Edinburgh *Research Data Management Policy* (University of Edinburgh, 2011) and Monash University's *Research Data Management Strategy and Strategic Plan 2012–2015* (Beitz, Dharmawardena and Searle, 2012) are seminal examples, much replicated by other institutions when defining their approach.

Where to begin in terms of establishing the overarching governance framework will depend on your organizational context. For a number of universities, the creation of an RDM policy has been selected as the first step. Policies provide clarity on what is expected and who is responsible for which activities. They can also provide leverage to unlock resources for infrastructure development, making implementation more feasible. However, fears have been expressed that approving a policy prior to the development of infrastructure and support may lead to an eventual gulf between aspiration and service implementation. Be mindful of your institutional culture to determine the best approach to take.

3.1 Developing a policy

Extensive consultation is critical when developing a policy. You need to be aware of the roles that different stakeholders play and what their issues and needs are, so that the policy is desirable and realistic. Eliciting feedback and involvement throughout the development process will ensure that the policy is fit for purpose. Remember to keep things simple and use clear language and concepts that speak to the people who will be expected to apply and support the policy.

Existing examples can provide pointers as to what to include. The DCC collates a list of UK institutional RDM policies.[3] High-level guidelines, such as the UK Research Integrity Office's *Code of Practice for Research* (UKRIO, 2009), also provide a useful base, as they outline common expectations for the collection, use, storage and retention of research data. The DCC has produced a policy briefing,[4] which outlines UK funder requirements, the approaches taken by different UK universities and considerations to make when developing institutional RDM policy. There are also a number of RDM policies from universities in Australia and the USA.[5] The University of Melbourne released one of the earliest examples and inspired work at the University of Oxford.[6]

Once you have developed a first draft, review this with a small pilot group to make sure it is understandable and covers the key points. The policy will then need to be ratified by the university's governing bodies, a process that will likely require several iterations and may take considerable time. For this reason, it is useful to keep the policy brief, focusing on high-level principles. Accompanying guidance is essential to aid implementation; however, this is likely to be more fluid, needing to be updated regularly as the supporting services develop, and so it can be useful to maintain this separately.

The most challenging task will be implementing the policy, once approved, as this is likely to imply significant modification or development of infrastructure as well as changes in working practice. The approach being taken at the University of Edinburgh is to run pilot studies that trial implementation in a number of areas, using these as examples to roll out the emerging practice more widely. Finding ways to incentivize adoption – through linking the process to career progression, for example – may prove to be especially worthwhile.

3.2 Developing a strategy

Having a clear strategy is essential to ensure that RDM services develop coherently. It should outline key objectives and the stages of work planned over a set period in order to realize them. There are three key steps to defining your strategy:

1 Understand your current position.
2 Define where you want to be in the future.
3 Map out a programme of activity to make this transition.

Requirements analysis exercises are a critical step in defining your strategy. In order to take stock of the current situation, you need to be aware of the context in which you are working. For instance, what internal and external factors influence research data management and sharing, and which have the greatest implications for you? These could include codes of conduct for research, funder policies, national and international legislation, and collaborative agreements that necessitate the sharing of data across institutional boundaries. Check your institution's mission statement so that you can map RDM activities and benefits to it as a means of garnering support. Also assess the existing support that you have in place to identify gaps and plan the additional services that need to be delivered.

Existing examples can provide pointers to help you get started. Monash University has shared its RDM strategy under a Creative Commons licence for reuse, and the DCC collates a list of EPSRC roadmaps and RDM strategies from UK universities.[7] UK universities are advised to think more broadly than the goal of achieving EPSRC compliance, since most research funders have similar expectations in terms of RDM. The University of Edinburgh roadmap (University of Edinburgh, 2012) organizes planned work under four key areas: data management planning; active data infrastructure; data stewardship; and data management support. A number of objectives are listed under each area of work, together with concrete actions, deliverables and target dates.

3.3 Developing a business case

High-level commitment and investment of resource is critical for service development and sustainability. Many UK universities have made some headway with external funding, particularly from the Jisc Managing Research Data (MRD) programmes; however, to transition to fully embedded services a commitment is ultimately needed from the institution. Many UK universities are beginning to develop business cases for RDM and there are a few notable examples of success. Two principal examples, already introduced in Chapter 2, are the University of Bristol and the University of Edinburgh.[8]

The University of Bristol has been developing pilot RDM services via the Jisc-funded data.bris project.[9] They have built on a separate £2 million institutional investment in a Research Data Storage Facility, around which RDM services are being layered. Towards the end of the data.bris project the team developed a business case for a research data service to be piloted in the period 2013–15. Given the existing investment in storage, non-staff costs in the business case were fortuitously marginal. Approved institutional funding supports five staff: one service director, three research data librarians and one technical support post. These staff will support researchers in the creation of DMPs, provide training and validate datasets being deposited in the data repository. In contrast, the £2 million investment planned at the University of Edinburgh over the same period will be split equally between technical infrastructure and staffing. Additional storage will be purchased to provide circa 1Tb per researcher to be allocated on a group basis, whilst library, IT and research office personnel will be reskilled to support researchers in applying RDM.

In order to make a persuasive case, your business plan should reflect the institutional mission and describe what returns on investment are predicted. At the University of Bristol it was found that potential research benefits, such as greater collaboration and impact, carried more weight with senior management than the need to achieve compliance with regulatory mandates. Offering different levels of provision (e.g., from do nothing, do little, preferred, to gold-plated) can also help to ensure that proposals are not immediately discounted. Similarly, a phased approach with plans stepped over three, five and ten years would allow you to start small and plan for growth. Finally, it is worth considering whether any costs can be recouped by charging for services or reduced by collaborating with other organizations to provide shared services.

4. Data management planning

4.1 Requirements for data management plans

Requirements for data management and sharing plans are prevalent in the UK. As a consequence, a plethora of templates, tools and support is emerging. Six of the seven UK Research Councils and several key health charities require DMPs as an integral component of research grant applications (Jones, 2012). Moreover, the vast majority of institutional RDM policies released by UK universities (15 out of 17 released by February 2013) require or encourage the creation of DMPs as the procedure by which researchers should comply with university expectations.[3]

In North America, the National Science Foundation and National Institutes of Health are the most high-profile examples of research funders that require the submission of DMPs. Others such as Genome Canada and the Gordon and Betty Moore Foundation also require data sharing plans.[10] The demand for DMPs in continental Europe is minimal by comparison. For example, the German Research Foundation issued *Recommendations for the Secure Storage and Availability of Digital Primary Research Data* (Deutsche Forschungsgemeinshaft, 2009) and expects researchers to consider how data will be managed and shared. More portentously, it is likely that a requirement for DMPs will be introduced by the European Commission under its Horizon 2020 programme. Somewhat surprisingly, given the national focus on research data, funders in Australia do not require the creation of DMPs, although some institutions are encouraging the practice.

As we have already intimated, compliance with the policies of funders and institutions, whilst important, is not the sole reason to encourage data management planning. There are many benefits that researchers should gain from the process. Planning saves time and effort in the medium-to-long term. It enables researchers to make informed decisions so that problems such as data loss can be anticipated and avoided. By considering what data will be created, and how, researchers can also check that they will have the necessary support in place. DMPs can also be very useful to institutions: they provide an opportunity to gather details on expected data volumes to assist in capacity planning; help to identify datasets to be recorded in institutional catalogues; and allow early engagement of data management experts to validate the appropriateness of proposed approaches.

4.2 DMP guidance, training and support

Where institutions require DMPs, they should provide templates or guidance on what to include in plans. Various universities give an overview of expected coverage in their policies. The University of Hertfordshire, for example, provides a data planning checklist as an appendix to its policy (University of Hertfordshire, 2011). This lists seven themes that should be covered and a number of useful questions as pointers to what to address. Others have developed templates for specific audiences. The Research360 project at the University of Bath, for example, has developed a very popular template for postgraduate students.[11] There are also several useful examples from the USA, such as the *What's Your Data Plan?* guide from the University of Wisconsin-Madison[12] and the MIT Libraries *Data Planning Checklist*.[13] The revised DCC *Checklist for a Data Management Plan* may also prove useful. This synthesizes the main funder requirements into a short set of questions with accompanying guidance.

Guidance on appropriate methods should also be provided. Indeed, institutions may wish to prescribe a handful of recommended approaches for certain areas of work, such as storage and back-up. Researchers are often unfamiliar with the support available to them, so providing associated guidance that raises awareness and provides links to support is invaluable. Requests for worked examples are also prevalent. The ICPSR, a social science data archive in the USA, provides a very useful *Framework for Creating a Data Management Plan*, which couples basic guidance with worked examples.[14] Some institutions have also considered compiling libraries of successful DMPs for researchers to learn from and reuse.

Training in data management planning and more in-depth consultancy services may also be required. The University of Edinburgh has developed an online learning unit covering DMPs as part of the Research Data MANTRA training resource.[15] This includes generic guidance, videos and interactive exercises. Tailored assistance via one-to-one consultations could also be provided to help researchers define their plans. The University of Virginia Library, for example, offers a Data Management Consulting Group.[16] Anecdotal evidence suggests that consultancy services may be required more by researchers in the arts and humanities than in the sciences.

4.3 Data management planning tools

There are two main tools that provide support on data management planning. The DCC has developed a web-based tool called DMPonline[17] to help researchers create and maintain DMPs. This is in use across the UK and is being trialled in Australia. In addition, a large consortium of research institutions has developed DMPTool[18] to provide a similar service in the USA. Both tools help researchers to write DMPs that meet specific funder requirements and provide features such as custom guidance, boilerplate text, sharing and exporting plans. Most significantly, both tools can be customized by institutions. This is critical, as researchers may not be aware of local support and services within their institution and are often unsure of existing best practice and standards that they can adopt.

The history of the two DMP tools is outlined in a paper by Sallans and Donnelly (2012). The first version of DMPonline was launched in April 2010 at the Jisc conference in London. A second iteration with increased functionality was released in March 2011, then, as a result of developments with the DMPTool team and projects in the Jisc MRD programme, a full redesign took place with version 3.0, released in March 2012. The DCC undertook an in-depth evaluation of the tool in autumn 2012 and concluded that major architectural changes were also needed. The fundamental change concerned how the DCC Checklist was used in the tool: rather than mapping requirements to the checklist and presenting these, questions from research funders or institutions are now asked directly. Progress in the development of version 4.0 was reported to the community via the DCC blog,[19] culminating with its release in autumn 2013.

The DMPTool consortium grew out of discussions at the International Digital Curation Conference held in Chicago in December 2010. DMPTool arrived in beta form in August 2011, with the first public version being released in November 2011. Extensive user engagement was undertaken to test concepts and guide development. As reported by Sallans and Donnelly (2012), over the first seven months of activity the DMPTool saw an overwhelming community response. During this period the tool had over 2000 unique users, enrolled over 50 institutions with single sign-on capacity via Shibboleth integration, and 19 of those institutions took the extra step of providing localized institutional guidance. The Consortium was awarded a grant from the Alfred P. Sloan Foundation in early 2013 to support further development. This grant will fund improvements that include expanded functionality, training modules, documentation and the creation of an open-source community to sustain DMPTool in the future.

5. Managing active data

Two primary concerns when delivering services to support the management of data during the active phase of research are the provision of:

- sufficient volumes of research data storage to ensure broad uptake and use
- relevant applications that offer the flexibility and functionality required

by researchers to store, access and share their data during the research process.

5.1 Research data storage

If you are not aware of the quantity of research data being created within your institution, or if you do not know where it is held and whether it is backed up, a preliminary study to understand the scale of the problem is worthwhile. Requirements-gathering exercises have uncovered numerous incidences of hand-crafted approaches to research data storage, often referred to informally as DUDs – Data centres Under Desks. These are typically the consequence of internal institutional policy. Quite simply, faced with substantial charges from IT services for additional managed storage, research groups have opted to buy cheap storage and to run their own systems. However, while the upfront costs may be only a fraction of those quoted by central services, the risk of data loss and security breaches are significantly higher, potentially leading to far greater costs in the long run.

Responding to this challenge, many universities are now providing much greater capacities of research data storage free of charge. A strong business case is crucial to securing the additional investment to allow this provision but, once funding has been committed, there are a number of storage options that can be pursued. Some universities are utilizing their High Performance Computing (HPC) facilities while others are extending the capacity of existing file stores or exploring secure cloud storage options. Regardless of which route is taken, engagement with end-users is critical to ensure that the proposed option will meet their needs.

Procedures also need to be developed to allocate and manage the storage. The model developed by the data.bris project[9] is of use here. At Bristol, researchers are required to sign up as a data steward to be allocated 5Tb of storage, and are then responsible for controlling who has access and how long the data should be kept. Above 5Tb the cost of storage is priced on a 'pay once store forever' basis, where 'forever' is defined as 20 years. Principal investigators (PIs) anticipating a need for more than 5Tb of disk storage are advised to include a request for funding in their grant applications.

Cloud services may be considered as an option to reduce capital investment and avoid the need for expertise to establish services in-house. They may also offer a means of meeting the flexibility of access that researchers frequently demand, whereby they and any collaborators can access and use the data regardless of their location. However, maintaining data security does become more of a challenge when data is distributed globally over a large number of devices that are being shared by a diverse community of unrelated users. The selection of cloud services for data storage is therefore a matter of judging the balance of risk to your data that may be acceptable when compared to the advantages from cost containment and ease of access. The DCC has provided a white paper on curation in the cloud to help with such decisions (Aitken et al., 2012). The UK's JANET Brokerage[20] is one route that the DCC recommends, since it aims to establish relationships between suppliers and the higher education sector, with the objective of developing a community cloud of dynamically available resources. Work is in progress towards a sector-wide deal with Microsoft and others are anticipated for Amazon Web Services, Google, Dropbox and Microsoft Azure.

5.2 Developing RDM systems

The common requirements that seem to be emerging in terms of data storage and access are for a globally accessible cross-platform file store that provides all collaborators with access to the data, regardless of where they are based. Routine back-up, long-term archiving and data sharing should always be addressed, and options for back-up and synchronization of data on mobile devices could also be considered. To ensure uptake, appropriate volumes of storage need to be provided and the systems need also to be sufficiently flexible, most notably in terms of access, to fit with the broad range of researchers' working practices.

As previously intimated, researchers regularly use Dropbox, since it allows them to access and work on their data from multiple devices, automatically synching back to a central copy. This is often far easier for remote working and collaboration than operating via centrally managed networked storage, particularly when collaborators are based in other organizations. However, due to the perceived security and legal risks of using third-party services, many universities have been investigating options for running services that can be kept firmly under their own control. The Universities of Lincoln and Edinburgh have both piloted OwnCloud, an open-source alternative to Dropbox, although neither found it sufficiently developed for non-technical users to implement it without ongoing support.[21] Elsewhere, the University of Oxford has developed DataStage,[22] a tool to allow research groups to share their data and collaborate.

Complete research data management systems may also be developed. At the University of Manchester the MaDAM project[23] has developed a prototype system in collaboration with biomedical researchers. Several other examples of disciplinary systems are also available, such as OMERO[24] and BRISSkit.[25] OMERO is a tool for microscope images. It handles hundreds of image formats, allowing researchers to gather all their images in a secure central repository where they can view, organize, analyse and share the data from anywhere via internet access. The BRISSkit project, meanwhile, is designing a national shared service brokered by JANET to host, implement and deploy biomedical research database applications that support the management and integration of tissue samples with clinical data and electronic patient records.

The RDM platforms section of the DCC's Monash University case study is particularly instructive (Jones, 2013). Monash has adopted a mantra to 'adopt, adapt, develop'. If a research community already has a solution (or there is an emerging one), they adopt this and, where necessary, adapt it to suit the needs of researchers at Monash. Only as a last resort will an entirely new solution be developed. Developing a new product may be expensive and costly to support, and could split researchers from their community. This approach acknowledges that researchers' loyalty to their discipline is often stronger than to their institution, and that close engagement with researchers is critical when designing RDM systems to ensure their applicability and uptake. The Monash approach is described in more detail in Chapter 8.

6. Data selection and handover

6.1 Selecting which data to keep

It is impractical and undesirable to keep everything. While there is a cost to selecting data for retention, this is minimal in comparison with the costs of managing data effectively in the long term so that it can continue to be retrieved and understood. The UK Research Councils expect data with 'acknowledged long-term value' to be preserved and remain accessible and usable for future research (RCUK, 2011). Moreover, they require that data management activities are both efficient and cost-effective in the use of public funds. If institutions are to ensure the appropriate use of public funds, a selection process is essential in order to prioritize data for long-term curation.

A first step in establishing a selection process is to determine the broad categories of data that are aligned with your institutional mission. First on the list will be data that you are legally obliged to retain, generally for contractual or regulatory reasons. The DCC's *How to Appraise and Select Research Data for Curation* (Whyte and Wilson, 2010) proposes the seven criteria outlined below:

1 **Relevance to mission**: the resource content fits any priorities stated in the institution's mission, or funding body policy, including any legal requirement to retain the data beyond its immediate use.
2 **Scientific or historical value**: is the data scientifically, socially, or culturally significant? Assessing this involves inferring anticipated future use, from evidence of current research and educational value.
3 **Uniqueness**: the extent to which the resource is the only or most complete source of the information that can be derived from it, and whether it is at risk of loss if not accepted, or may be preserved elsewhere.
4 **Potential for redistribution**: the reliability, integrity, and usability of the data files may be determined; these are received in formats that meet designated technical criteria; and intellectual property or human subjects issues are addressed.
5 **Non-replicability**: it would not be feasible to replicate the data/resource or doing so would not be financially viable.
6 **Economic case**: costs may be estimated for managing and preserving the resource, and are justifiable when assessed against evidence of potential future benefits; funding has been secured where appropriate.
7 **Full documentation**: the information necessary to facilitate future discovery, access, and reuse is comprehensive and correct; including metadata on the resource's provenance and the context of its creation and use.

There are also a number of useful data selection tools. The Natural Environment Research Council (NERC) has developed a data value checklist to help identify which data should be deposited in its environmental data centres.[26] The checklist is a weighted list of criteria, phrased as questions, to help determine which data is of long-term value. Elsewhere, the UK Data Service is developing a data appraisal kitemark, which similarly uses a set of scales to determine which data should be prioritized for selection.[27] In North America, the US Geological Survey provides a records appraisal tool to determine which data to keep.[28]

A selection process may take time to set up and operate, but should pay off in terms of the ability to forecast preservation and storage costs. It also minimizes risks to the institution, such as the reputational damage from exposing dirty, confidential or undocumented data that has been retained long after the researchers who created it have moved on.

6.2 Data handover: managing the transition to data repositories

Research data is often managed by different groups during the active phase of research and subsequent long-term curation. As can be seen in Figure 5.1 (p. 90), the handover phase sits between these two periods in the lifecycle. This is typically when data is transferred to respository services. In some cases data may continue to be held in the active research data store over the long term; however, this is not ideal, as there is much greater risk of inadvertent change, data corruption or deletion. Data which has been selected for long-term preservation and sharing should be placed in a separate, properly managed environment.

Data repositories should be clear about what services they offer. Guidelines should clarify which data falls within the repository's remit, what kinds of data will be accepted and which are the priority areas. It should also be clear what range of outcomes is envisaged, as different levels of curatorial care may be applied. At a minimum, it is likely that metadata will be assigned and recorded to aid discoverability. In cases where data cannot be shared but must be retained for a certain period, the repository may opt for basic archiving (i.e. storing, backing-up and performing periodic integrity checks). When data can be shared, increasing degrees of processing may be applied, depending upon the condition of the dataset and the anticipated level of reuse. Different levels of access may be provided, ranging from closed or embargoed access, through various levels of restricted access (e.g., to registered users or certain approved communities), to open, public access. Such conditions need to be negotiated with data creators at the time of deposit.

Researchers also need to know what is expected of them during the handover process. Deposit agreements, metadata guidelines and data transfer forms will help to clarify the process and ease the provision of information. A deposit agreement sets out terms and conditions to communicate the responsibilities of depositor and service provider. The agreement should give the repository rights to manipulate the data, as preservation may require migration to new formats. It should also allow the repository to reserve the right to withdraw the data for legal or other reasons. Examples of deposit guidelines[29] and deposit agreements[30] are available via the UK Data Service and Edinburgh DataShare repositories.

The provision of tools to ease deposit is also critical. In the UK Jisc has supported the development of various tools to facilitate repository deposit. The DataFlow[31] and SWORD-ARM[32] projects, for example, both make use of the SWORD2 protocol to ease the deposit process. Several deposit scenarios are outlined on the SWORD blog.[33] Other tools such as DepositMOre[34] and DataUp[35] make use of widely used software (Microsoft Word and Excel respectively) by embedding options to deposit directly. DataUp also aims to ease the creation of metadata, which is often the hurdle that puts researchers off deposit. Consulting researchers to define deposit workflows that fit their practices should also pay off in achieving better uptake.

7. Sharing and preserving data

7.1 Data repositories

There are a number of existing data repository services and so it is likely that any provision within the higher education sector will be part of a hybrid environment. Certainly, by default, researchers are likely to use a mix of institutional and external repository services. Many repositories are discipline-specific or community-based, some are linked to publishers, others have grown out of small start-ups, while yet more are large international initiatives such as the World Data Centre. The number of repositories is growing. One of the more recent significant additions is Zenodo, a free cross-disciplinary repository designed with the aim of sharing all scientific research outputs across Europe.[36]

A useful list of research data repositories from around the world is available via Databib,[37] which shows the subject areas supported by each repository and outlines any restrictions on data access, licence agreements and the identifiers used. However, this list does not include any quality assurances. As such, institutions may wish to approve certain repositories or state a preference for those that have achieved an acknowledged repository standard, such as the Data Seal of Approval.[38]

The immediate benefit of using an established data repository is the access it provides to a ready-made and expert infrastructure, not only for storing data but also for enabling discovery and access. Some research funders directly support facilities to curate the data generated from the research they have sponsored. Although there is an onus on researchers to offer data for deposit, designated data centres such as those provided by the

UK Data Service and NERC nonetheless apply strict criteria to determine whether data will be accepted. There may also be a cost. The Archaeology Data Service, for example, expects to recover the cost of archiving from the body funding the archaeological investigation, in the form of a one-off payment collected at the time of deposit. Before deciding how to incorporate the data centres into any research data management strategy, it is essential to understand the rules of engagement for each of them.

Institutional repositories have typically been created to store research publications rather than data, but their technical infrastructure can be extended to enable the curation of data without the development or purchase of an entirely new software platform. If you plan to use your existing repository to manage data, we recommend that you seek advice from another institution using the same repository software. The Universities of Cambridge and Edinburgh both run DSpace repositories for research data[39] and several institutions are exploring the use of CKAN to catalogue and store data.[40] If you use an EPrints platform you might want to investigate the ReCollect plug-in[41] produced by the UK Data Archive and the University of Essex. This transforms a conventional EPrints installation into a research data repository with an expanded metadata profile for describing research data (based on DataCite, INSPIRE and DDI standards) and a redesigned data catalogue for presenting complex collections. Long-term, archive storage can also be outsourced to external contractors such as Arkivum.[42] A number of institutions in the USA and Australia also offer data repositories. The California Digital Library, for example, offers Merritt,[43] a repository built from a number of microservices. Interestingly, individual services such as EZID,[44] a tool for persistent identification, are offered to the community to build into their own services. This is a model worth investigating if you are establishing your own data repository.

7.2 Data catalogues

Research data needs to be properly described if it is to be discovered and reused. In the UK there are clear drivers in this area from the research councils: research organizations are expected to have a record of the research data they hold and to make this metadata available online to support data discoverability and reuse (RCUK, 2011). Requirements also cover the need for persistent identifiers. The work of the international DataCite consortium[45] is of interest here. By working with data centres, DataCite assigns digital object identifiers (DOIs) to datasets and is developing an infrastructure to support simple and effective methods of data citation, discovery, and access. Useful content is available via the British Library, which ran a series of five workshops between 2012 and 2013 to support research organizations in the implementation of DOIs.[46]

One of the most advanced initiatives in this area emerged from Australia. Research Data Australia (RDA) is a national catalogue describing, and where possible linking to, Australian research data collections.[47] RDA is delivered by the Australian National Data Service (ANDS) in collaboration with Australian universities. A number of metadata stores have been supported via the ANDS 'Seeding the Commons' funding programme and this content is harvested into the national RDA register (ANDS, 2012). Options for collating metadata at a national level are also being explored by Jisc and the DCC in the UK, using a number of comparative pilot studies to draw out lessons for the wider community and subsequently inform the development of a national data registry. Community initiatives also seek to raise awareness of existing data: DataHub[48] is a data registry and repository maintained by the non-profit Open Knowledge Foundation using its open-source data hub software, CKAN.

A number of UK universities have been engaged in work to define what metadata is required to describe datasets. At the University of Oxford, the DaMaRO project,[49] referred to in Chapter 2, has been instrumental in developing the DataFinder tool, applying a three-tier metadata approach comprising:

- mandatory minimal metadata – a set of 12 fields extended from DataCite metadata
- mandatory administrative information – e.g. funder details and grant number
- optional, discipline-specific metadata to enable reuse.

The University of Essex is adopting a similar three-tier approach. Their schema (available via the ReCollect EPrints plug-in) is a combination of generic metadata schema and specific disciplinary standards used for social science data. Another group of universities involved in the C4D project[50] is exploring options to create an extension to the CERIF standard to describe datasets. The use of accepted standards is key to enhance discoverability and to comply with global metadata harvesting initiatives such as that provided by OpenAIRE.[51]

The primary concerns for HEIs are to collect metadata in a seamless way, integrating systems wherever possible to avoid placing additional administrative burdens on researchers, and to ensure that standards are followed wherever possible to enable export into any national systems as they develop. When considering how metadata can be captured, opportunities to automatically harvest data from related systems to avoid re-entry should be explored. Different options can also be considered for where to store the metadata: existing repositories or research information management systems could potentially be extended or specialized metadata stores could be employed, as in the ANDS model.

8. Guidance, training and support

Underpinning the individual services that are provided at each stage of the data lifecycle, one expects to find a wealth of guidance materials, training and support. Various levels of provision may be needed; some generic advice, provided, for example, via institutional RDM webpages, could be complemented with more tailored individual or team support. One-to-one consultancy sessions may be required to help researchers define relevant approaches for creating, managing and sharing their data. A range of options is likely to be needed to engage different groups, so think broadly about what provision will be the most advantageous to your research community.

8.1 Guidance and helpdesks

Basic guidance is required on all aspects of data management. Several universities have produced websites that collate best practice and direct researchers to local support.[52] These tend to cover the whole research lifecycle from applying for funding, through creating and managing data, to long-term preservation and reuse. Guidance is typically pragmatic and gives basic advice such as how to structure, name and version data, control access, and identify relevant data centres. There are a number of excellent sources of best practice that you can reuse when developing such guidance, such as the UKDA guide on managing and sharing data (Van den Eynden et al., 2011).

RDM websites are usually put together following an internal review of existing support. Relevant content can be searched for using common RDM-related terms, such as IPR, data ownership, repository, storage, back-up and research computing. Once preliminary material has been collated, some form of engagement with the established support services can lead to additional content being identified. When drafting new content, general guidance can be copied and customized from existing websites, many of which are Creative Commons licensed.

Help desk services may also be required. Several universities have set up generic e-mail addresses to filter RDM queries. Existing help desk systems could be used to save resources, with schema of typical questions developed to assist in routing enquiries. It is also worth bearing in mind that some studies have identified a desire for named contacts in preference to generic help desks (Freiman et al., 2010, 20). Making contact details more visible, or introducing support staff on training courses to raise awareness of local contacts, may help researchers to get the most out of the RDM services on offer.

8.2 Training for researchers

Training in data management techniques for researchers is best developed in partnership with academic staff or disciplinary data experts (such as those employed by data centres) to ensure that content is both relevant and meaningful. Good practice can also be embedded in their routines by working with researchers from early in their careers; one obvious and low cost approach is the incorporation of RDM messages into existing induction programmes or PhD core skills courses. Two examples of how this can be achieved are the Open Exeter project,[53] which has involved PhD students in the development of their training programme, and the DataTrain initiative,[54] which brought together researchers and data centre staff.

A large body of training materials is already available for reuse. In the UK the Jisc MRD programmes have included strands that supported RDM training projects. A key focus within these has been the provision of discipline-specific training. The materials produced cover a range of subject areas, including archaeology, geoscience, psychology, health and the creative arts. One particularly useful resource is MANTRA,[15] a set of online learning units and software tutorials used to introduce PhD students to research data management. Excellent training materials are also available from Australia and the USA. To highlight a few examples: the University of Wisconsin-Madison provides data management essentials in its *Escaping Datageddon* presentation,[55] MIT Libraries provide a 101 crash course via a case study of how one dataset is managed[56] and the Australian National University provides a comprehensive data management manual (Australian National University, 2013).

Given the availability of training materials, institutional effort is often wisely focused on repurposing existing content and embedding provision in current programmes. A continuing trend has been to add RDM training into existing core curricula aimed at captive communities, such as those who pass through doctoral training centres. This approach has been trialled by the University of Bath, which views the doctoral training centres as catalysts for change.[57] By training each year's cohort of interdisciplinary students they hope to connect with a range of academic staff and students across the institution and influence the overall culture within the graduate school. Other institutions, such as the University of Northumbria, have secured the insertion of data management into core PhD skills courses. Targeting researchers early on in their careers can be useful, since good RDM practice can become embedded before less rigorous habits are formed. Also, if you can build training into existing programmes there will be an even greater chance of sustainability, which makes it a better route to follow than offering one-off courses.

8.3 Consultancy services

In some cases, researchers may require more hands-on, tailored support, for example to check the appropriateness of their data management plans. Several universities, particularly in the USA, provide short consultations in this vein to help researchers to develop data management plans. A brief discussion about the research and proposed methods to create, manage and share data is likely to uncover areas where further guidance or pointers to local services would be useful. It also allows the institution to check the appropriateness of plans and that relevant support and infrastructure are included in the cost projections.

More in-depth support may also be needed during the active phase of a research project, particularly in terms of delivering technical aspects such as database design. In some institutions, researchers have requested that IT services provide a dedicated pool of research support staff that could be included in grant proposals as an identifiable cost for technical support. A small-scale example of this is provided by the College of Arts at the University of Glasgow, where several members of technical staff are available to consult during bid development and are frequently costed in as technical partners.[58]

8.4 Providing RDM support – reskilling support staff

In order to provide support, existing staff may need training to acquire new skills and build confidence in assisting researchers with RDM. As noted in Chapter 3, the main groups engaged in supporting RDM in a higher education context are university libraries, IT services and research administrators. We have already remarked how librarians often play a leading role in supporting RDM. In the USA, in particular, there is a strong culture of data librarianship, and in the UK the number of programmes that focus on upskilling liaison librarians has been on the ascendant. Cox, Verbaan and Sen (2012) explore the reasons that librarians are well positioned to support RDM, reflecting on librarians' existing networks within institutions, their understanding of generic information management principles that can potentially be applied to data management and their complementary roles in promoting open access.

Over the past decade a growing body of training materials has emerged to assist in the reskilling of support staff, particularly librarians.[59] If using such materials, do bear in mind that different messages may be needed for librarians, IT services and the staff of the research office, since each group will approach the subject from a different professional perspective. Content should therefore be tailored to focus on each group's particular skills and needs. Research administrators, for example, may be primarily involved at the grant application stage and hence most interested in supporting data management plans. It is also useful to add details that explain the wider institutional context so that staff can know what is being provided by others in the organization. In that way, training serves a second purpose of raising awareness about what is already in place, which knowledge is often lacking.

9. Putting it all together

There are many services that an institution could provide to support RDM. While these may be led by different groups or functions within the organization, it is important to maintain a coherent vision across the services as they develop. The move to integrate systems and workflows is also key; many universities are attempting to join up research information systems with repositories, or to support data management planning through the inclusion of flags in grant application systems. Co-ordination of RDM service development with these parallel activities is crucial to avoiding wasted effort and to embed services in the broader research support environment.

The key to getting started is to identify your current position and understanding what is required to prioritize action. Service development can then be approached incrementally, with each component addressed as a manageable task whilst keeping an eye on the co-ordination of individual components. Input from a wide range of researchers, colleagues and senior management is crucial to achieve your aims and ensure that services are relevant, sustainable and well embedded.

Numerous references and examples have been provided throughout this chapter and more detailed examples are given in the case studies that follow. The DCC is also committed to the development of a series of case studies to accompany its guide to developing RDM services.[60] They will not provide you with a fully functioning bespoke service but using these existing models and resources will undoubtedly help you to get started.

10. References

10.1 Websites

1 Jisc Managing Research Data programme 2011–13: www.jisc.ac.uk/whatwedo/programmes/di_researchmanagement/ managingresearchdata.aspx; Jisc Managing Research Data programme 2009–11: www.jisc.ac.uk/whatwedo/programmes/mrd.aspx.

2 DCC institutional engagements: www.dcc.ac.uk/community/institutional-engagements.

3 List of UK institutional RDM policies: www.dcc.ac.uk/resources/policy-and-legal/institutional-data-policies.

4 DCC *Research Data Policy Briefing*, www.dcc.ac.uk/webfm_send/705.

5 Examples of RDM policies from institutions in the USA and Australia can be seen at: www.dcc.ac.uk/resources/policy-and-legal/policy-tools-and-guidance/policy-tools-and-guidance.

6 Details of the collaboration between Oxford and Melbourne can be seen in the workshop report from the Institutional Policy and Guidance for Research Data event: http://eidcsr.oucs.ox.ac.uk/policy_workshop.xml.

7 List of UK institutional RDM roadmaps or strategies: www.dcc.ac.uk/resources/policy-and-legal/epsrc-institutional-roadmaps.

8 Neither business case has been made public. However, information has been shared in presentations at the DCC Research Data Management Forum on funding research data management, www.dcc.ac.uk/events/research-data-management-forum-rdmf/rdmf-special-event-funding-research-data-management, and at the Jisc MRD closing conference session 2B on business

cases and plans for sustainability (slides linked to in programme), www.jisc.ac.uk/whatwedo/programmes/di_researchmanagement/ managingresearchdata/events/jiscmanagingresearchingdataacrworkshop.aspx.

9   Data.bris project: https://data.blogs.ilrt.org.

10 A summary of funder requirements for DMPs in the USA is available via DMPTool: https://dmp.cdlib.org/pages/funder_requirements.

11 Research360 *Postgraduate Data Management Plan Template* is downloadable from http://blogs.bath.ac.uk/research360/2012/03/postgraduate-dmp-template-first-draft.

12 *What's Your Data Plan?* is downloadable from: http://researchdata.wisc.edu/make-a-plan/data-plans.

13 MIT *Data Planning Checklist*: http://libraries.mit.edu/guides/subjects/ data-management/checklist.html.

14 ICPSR *Framework for Creating a Data Management Plan*: www.icpsr.umich.edu/icpsrweb/content/datamanagement/dmp/framework.html.

15 Research Data MANTRA training course: http://datalib.edina.ac.uk/mantra.

16 University of Virginia Library Data Management Consulting Group: http://dmconsult.library.virginia.edu.

17 DMPonline: https://dmponline.dcc.ac.uk.

18 DMPTool: https://dmp.cdlib.org.

19 DMPonline current status (March 2013): www.dcc.ac.uk/blog/ dmponline-current-status.

20 JANET brokerage: https://www.ja.net/products-services/janet-cloud-services.

21 See, for example, the blog post by Joss Winn of the Orbital project: http://orbital.blogs.lincoln.ac.uk/2012/08/06/owncloud-an-academic-dropbox.

22 DataStage: www.dataflow.ox.ac.uk/index.php/datastage/ds-about.

23 MaDAM project: www.library.manchester.ac.uk/aboutus/projects/madam.

24 OMERO: www.openmicroscopy.org/site/products/omero.

25 BRISSkit: www.brisskit.le.ac.uk.

26 NERC data value checklist: www.nerc.ac.uk/research/sites/data/dmp.asp.

27 Draft appraisal criteria are given in the presentation *Data Review at the UK Data Archive* by Veerle v. d. Eynden at IDCC '13 Workshop 'Data Publishing, Peer Review and Repository Accreditation: everyone a winner?', www.dcc.ac.uk/events/idcc13/workshops#Datapub.

28 US Geological Survey, Earth Resources Observation and Science Appraisal Tool: http://eros.usgs.gov/government/ratool/view_questions.php.

29 UK Data Service deposit guidelines: http://ukdataservice.ac.uk/deposit-data/ how-to/regular/regular-depositors.aspx.

30 Edinburgh DataShare depositor agreement:

www.ed.ac.uk/schools-departments/information-services/services/research-support/data-library/data-repository/depositor-agreement.

31 DataFlow project: www.dataflow.ox.ac.uk.

32 SWORD-ARM project: http://archaeologydataservice.ac.uk/research/swordarm.

33 SWORD blog: http://swordapp.org/2012/07/data-deposit-scenarios.

34 DepositMOre blog: http://blog.soton.ac.uk/depositmo.

35 DataUp: http://dataup.cdlib.org.

36 Zenodo: http://zenodo.org/features.

37 Databib list of repositories: http://databib.org.

38 Data Seal of Approval: http://datasealofapproval.org.

39 DSpace@Cambridge: www.dspace.cam.ac.uk and Edinburgh DataShare; and http://datashare.is.ed.ac.uk.

40 See for example, *Choosing CKAN for Research Data Management*, a blog post by Joss Winn of the Orbital project: http://orbital.blogs.lincoln.ac.uk/2012/09/06/choosing-ckan-for-research-data-management.

41 ReCollect: http://bazaar.eprints.org/280.

42 Arkivum: www.arkivum.com.

43 Merritt repository: www.cdlib.org/services/uc3/merritt/index.html.

44 EZID: www.cdlib.org/services/uc3/ezid.

45 DataCite: www.datacite.org.

46 DataCite workshops: www.bl.uk/aboutus/stratpolprog/digi/datasets/workshoparchive/archive.html.

47 Research Data Australia: http://researchdata.ands.org.au.

48 DataHub: http://datahub.io.

49 DaMaRO project: http://damaro.oucs.ox.ac.uk.

50 C4D project blog: http://cerif4datasets.wordpress.com.

51 OpenAIRE: www.openaire.eu.

52 List of RDM guidance websites produced by UK universities: www.dcc.ac.uk/resources/policy-and-legal/rdm-guidance-webpages/rdm-guidance-webpages. ARL list of US research library websites on data management planning: www.arl.org/focus-areas/e-research/data-access-management-and-sharing/nsf-data-sharing-policy/243-resources-for-data-management-planning.

53 Open Exeter project: http://as.exeter.ac.uk/library/resources/openaccess/openexeter.

54 DataTrain project: www.lib.cam.ac.uk/preservation/datatrain.

55 *Escaping Datageddon* presentation, downloadable at: http://researchdata.wisc.edu/make-a-plan/data-plans.

56 MIT libraries, *The Lifecycle of a Dataset* presentation:
    http://libraries.mit.edu/guides/subjects/data-management/Managing%20
    Research%20Data%20101.pdf.
57 See details in the *Doctoral Training Centres as Catalysts for Research Data
    Management*, blog post by Jez Cope:
    http://blogs.bath.ac.uk/research360/2011/12/doctoral-training-centres-as-
    catalysts.
58 Technical and data management support in the College of Arts:
    www.gla.ac.uk/services/datamanagement/whocanhelp/
    resourcedevelopmentofficers.
59 Examples of RDM training for librarians:
    www.dcc.ac.uk/training/rdm-librarians.
60 The DCC how-to guide and accompanying case studies on developing RDM
    services are available at: www.dcc.ac.uk/resources/developing-rdm-services.

10.2 Citations

Aitken, B., McCann, P., McHugh, A. and Miller, K. (2012) *Digital Curation and the
    Cloud*, Digital Curation Centre,
    www.jisc.ac.uk/whatwedo/programmes/preservation/CurationCloud.aspx.
ANDS (2012) *Metadata Stores Solutions*,
    www.ands.org.au/guides/metadata-stores-solutions.html.
Australian National University (2013) *ANU Data Management Manual V.6*,
    http://anulib.anu.edu.au/_resources/training-and-resources/guides/
    DataManagement.pdf.
Beitz, A., Dharmawardena, K. and Searle, S. (2012) *Monash University Research Data
    Management Strategy and Strategic Plan 2012–2015*, https://confluence-vre.its.
    monash.edu.au/download/attachments/39752006/Monash+University+
    Research+Data+Management+Strategy-publicrelease.pdf?version=1.
Cox, A., Verbaan, E. and Sen, B. (2012) Upskilling Liaison Librarians for Research
    Data Management, *Ariadne*, **70**, www.ariadne.ac.uk/issue70/cox-et-al.
Deutsche Forschungsgemeinshaft (2009) *Recommendations for Secure Storage and
    Availability of Digital Primary Research Data*,
    www.dfg.de/download/pdf/foerderung/programme/lis/ua_inf_empfehlungen_
    200901_en.pdf.
EPSRC (2011) *Policy Framework on Research Data*,
    www.epsrc.ac.uk/about/standards/researchdata/Pages/policyframework.aspx.
Freiman, L., Ward, C., Jones, S., Molloy, L. and Snow, K. (2010) *Incremental: scoping
    study and pilot implementation plan*, www.lib.cam.ac.uk/preservation/

incremental/documents/Incremental_Scoping_Report_170910.pdf.

Jones, S. (2012) *Summary of Research Funders' Expectations for Data Management and Sharing Plans V. 4.4*, DCC, www.dcc.ac.uk/webfm_send/358.

Jones, S. (2013) *Bringing It All Together: a case study on the improvement of research data management at Monash University*, DCC RDM services case studies, www.dcc.ac.uk/resources/developing-rdm-services.

Jones, S., Pryor, G. and Whyte, A. (2013) *How to Develop Research Data Management Services – a guide for HEIs*, Digital Curation Centre, www.dcc.ac.uk/resources/how-guides.

RCUK (2011) *Common Principles on Data Policy*, www.rcuk.ac.uk/research/Pages/DataPolicy.aspx.

Sallans, A. and Donnelly, M. (2012) DMP Online and DMPTool: different strategies towards a shared goal, *International Journal of Digital Curation*, 7 (2), doi:10.2218/ijdc.v7i2.235.

UKRIO (2009) *Code of Practice for Research: promoting good practice and preventing misconduct*, www.ukrio.org/what-we-do/code-of-practice-for-research.

University of Edinburgh (2011) *Research Data Management Policy*, www.ed.ac.uk/is/research-data-policy.

University of Edinburgh (2012) *Research Data Management (RDM) Roadmap August 2012–January 2014*, www.ed.ac.uk/schools-departments/information-services/about/strategy-planning/rdm-roadmap.

University of Hertfordshire (2011) *University Guide to Research Data Management*, http://sitem.herts.ac.uk/secreg/upr/pdf/IM12-apx%20III-University%20Guide%20to%20Research%20Data%20Management-v03%201.pdf.

Van den Eynden, V., Corti, L., Woollard, M., Bishop, L. and Horton, L. (2011) *Managing and Sharing Data: best practice for researchers*, 3rd edn, UK Data Archive, http://data-archive.ac.uk/media/2894/managingsharing.pdf.

Whyte, A. and Wilson, A. (2010) *How to Appraise and Select Research Data for Curation*, Digital Curation Centre, www.dcc.ac.uk/resources/how-guides.

CHAPTER 6

Case study 1: Johns Hopkins University Data Management Services

G. Sayeed Choudhury

1. Introduction

This case study describes the development of the Johns Hopkins University Data Management Services (JHUDMS),[1] with an emphasis on lessons learned. While many individuals – noting that only some of them are mentioned in this chapter – are responsible for the development of JHUDMS, this account is written in a chronological sense from the perspective of the individual who was involved in every aspect of the development. Every effort has been made to describe this case study accurately but any errors in understanding or recollection are solely the author's.

The launch of JHUDMS represented the culmination of over a decade of research and development, prototyping, needs assessment, capacity building and sustainability planning. Beginning with the archiving and preservation of the Sloan Digital Sky Survey (SDSS)[2] and advancing through the work of the Data Conservancy,[3] described in section 3, the Sheridan Libraries at Johns Hopkins University (JHU) developed substantial expertise and initial infrastructure for data management that contributed directly to the development of the JHUDMS.

Fundamentally, the JHUDMS represents an important step in an overall, long-term data infrastructure development programme led by the Sheridan Libraries. The Sheridan Libraries at JHU include two unique departments –

an R&D group known as the Digital Research and Curation Center and a business unit known as the Entrepreneurial Library Program – that were instrumental in the development of JHUDMS. However, several lessons that were learned should be applicable or useful to other institutions as they plan for and implement research data management services.

The origins of the data management program at JHU can be traced back to an initial exchange between two individuals. Professor Alexander Szalay (Department of Physics and Astronomy at JHU) was the principal investigator for the 'National Virtual Observatory' award from the US National Science Foundation. Shortly after the announcement of the award, I contacted Szalay to inquire about their data management plans. This seemingly simple exchange led to a long-term collaboration that has greatly influenced the data management program at JHU. While systematic and organizational approaches are essential for comprehensive, sustainable data management services, JHU's experience provides evidence regarding the importance of individuals in initiating appropriate dialogue. Institutions seeking to develop research data management services might consider identifying a faculty champion who can advocate its importance and an administrator who can appreciate and channel this faculty champion's viewpoint.

Following a series of exchanges subsequent to our initial dialogue, Szalay approached me to discuss the archiving and preservation of the SDSS-I and SDSS-II data. The Sheridan Libraries signed a memorandum of understanding (MOU) with the Astrophysical Research Consortium (ARC) for a five-year agreement related to SDSS data archiving and preservation. As part of this MOU, the Sheridan Libraries acquired and studied SDSS data releases to gain greater awareness. This experience led to a greater understanding regarding different types and levels of data, databases and data-processing pipelines. Through grants from the US Institute of Museum and Libraries and Microsoft Research, the Sheridan Libraries worked with the National Virtual Observatory (which evolved into the Virtual Astronomical Observatory) and the American Astronomical Society to develop a modelling framework for connecting data and publications. Additionally, the Sheridan Libraries submitted a successful grant application to the US National Science Foundation's DataNet program to launch the Data Conservancy. These events mark key milestones that led to development of the JHUDMS.

2. Sloan Digital Sky Survey

As mentioned on its website, SDSS is

> one of the most ambitious and influential surveys in the history of astronomy. Over eight years of operations (SDSS-I, 2000-2005; SDSS-II, 2005-2008), it obtained deep, multi-color images covering more than a quarter of the sky and created 3-dimensional maps containing more than 930,000 galaxies and more than 120,000 quasars.
>
> (www.sdss.org)

In many ways, SDSS is a quintessential data-intensive scientific project. SDSS has been called the 'cosmic genome project.' Its influence is significant in both scholarly and public realms. SDSS data have been cited in hundreds of publications. There are apparently about 10,000 professional astronomers in the world yet almost a million registered users of the SDSS Skyserver.

As SDSS-II was reaching its conclusion, the Sheridan Libraries engaged Richard Kron (Department of Astronomy and Astrophysics, University of Chicago) and William Boroski (Fermilab) to discuss archiving and preservation of SDSS data. Both individuals had been involved in the development of SDSS's data processing system. This interaction was one of the first – if not the first – exchanges between a research library and a community-based scientific project focused on data transfer, archiving and preservation. Over the course of these exchanges, the development and signing of the MOU and eventual transfer of a copy of the SDSS data, the Sheridan Libraries gained a tremendous amount of knowledge regarding scientific data and sustainability planning. Additionally, the Sheridan Libraries learned a great deal about technical issues related to the nature of the data, which are being tracked at a 'lessons learned' wiki.[4]

2.1 Levels of data

The most fundamental lesson learned regarding the nature of scientific data was that even for a single-instrument, community-based 'big science' project, the data is tremendously diverse. Figure 6.1 depicts the levels of SDSS data, ranging from 'Level 0' – raw, unprocessed data from the telescope (upper left corner) – to 'Level 3', in the form of calibrated, processed data releases within a database (bottom right corner).

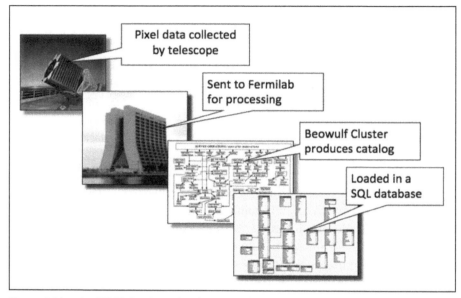

Figure 6.1 Levels of SDSS data (*reproduced courtesy of Alexander Szalay*)

As the data moves from Level 0 to Level 3, it becomes more refined or processed, offering more accessibility to greater numbers of individuals. Eventually, the data releases that are available through SkyServer on the SDSS website are accessible enough for amateur astronomers.[5] Examination of the SDSS data also highlighted the importance of software, particularly as it relates to provenance. The SDSS team developed software to collect the data, to process the data between levels, to load data from the Data Archive Server (DAS) into the Catalog Archive Server (CAS) databases, to query the databases and to interface with SkyServer. Tim DiLauro (Chief IT Architect and digital preservation lead at Sheridan Libraries) was responsible for the substantial effort to develop a complete inventory of SDSS data and software and the connections between them.

It became clear that even for a well funded, community-based project with a single instrument and substantial information technology capacity, there were fundamental issues to address related to the preservation of databases (in addition to flat files) and software. These issues were not immediately apparent to Kron and Boroski, who assumed they had been preserving the SDSS data by storing and backing up the data. This exchange represented the first time that the Sheridan Libraries recognized the lack of clarity regarding what constitutes preservation. As the dialogue continued,

Kron and Boroski acknowledged the more complex facets of preservation and recognized that additional work was necessary. Perhaps more importantly, they also recognized that funding would be required.

2.2 Memorandum of understanding

Kron and Boroski worked with Choudhury and DiLauro to define the scientific and technical aspects related to an agreement for SDSS archiving and preservation. At this point, Barbara Pralle (Head of Entrepreneurial Library Program at Sheridan Libraries) became involved to incorporate sustainability planning into the discussions. As mentioned on its website,[6] the Entrepreneurial Library Program (ELP)

> creates a wide range of customized library and information services for clients in the academic, corporate, allied-health, non-profit and other sectors. For more than 10 years we have worked collaboratively with partners to develop customized services and online libraries. ELP offers tailored consulting related to online libraries; existing physical libraries; companies; and other organizations.

The ELP has experience with developing fee-based services and creating associated agreements that clearly outline expectations, service levels, delineation of roles, legal matters, etc. In their final report, the Blue Ribbon Task Force on Sustainable Digital Preservation and Access (BRTF-SPDA, 2010) noted that such formal agreements represent an important component of sustainability, particularly regarding post-agreement decisions such as the renewal or transfer of data. The SDSS MOU provided an exemplar for the BRTF-SPDA to consider in this regard.

Pralle's prior experience and expertise was invaluable in enriching the academic conversation with a business conversation between the Sheridan Libraries and ARC, which manages SDSS on behalf of the participating institutions. Eventually, Michael Evans, ARC Business Manager, agreed to an MOU that included funding for the Sheridan Libraries toward the archiving and preservation of SDSS data. Given the understanding of the various types of data and different requirements, the MOU outlined the full range of data for archiving and preservation:

- final version of the Data Archive Server (DAS)
- all of the incremental Catalog Archive Server (CAS) releases (EDR through DR7)

- all of the software used to collect the data
- all of the software used to process and calibrate the data
- the interface code for the SkyServer interface
- the raw data in binary format.

It should be noted that ARC allocated funds from the 'sunset' funds for SDSS-II. Given the various demands on these funds, it is noteworthy indeed that they chose to allocate a portion of funding toward archiving and preservation. There is little doubt that the approach of examining and understanding the scientific data and needs, of explaining carefully the specific requirements for archiving and preservation and of making a business case through a clearly defined MOU was critical in persuading SDSS principals (Kron and Boroski) and ARC of the value of their investment.

The MOU was a scoping document that outlined specific tasks and associated service levels. The Sheridan Libraries realized that such scoping would also be important in terms of next steps from a technology development perspective. As part of the scoping, the Sheridan Libraries received one of the SDSS data releases to become directly familiar with astronomy data. While this direct experience with scientific data was invaluable, it also prompted the Sheridan Libraries to consider how to generalize the findings from the engagement with SDSS in an extensible and tractable manner. Robert Hanisch (Senior Scientist at the Space Telescope Science Institute and Director of the US Virtual Astronomical Observatory) provided the inspiration for a relevant idea. Hanisch explained that in addition to the three levels of data of SDSS that result in public data releases, there is an additional Level 4 of derived data based on queries against these releases. This derived Level 4 data is cited directly within publications. Based on subsequent conversations with the American Astronomical Association and the University of Chicago Press, the Sheridan Libraries developed two successful proposals to the US Institute of Museum and Library Services and Microsoft Research (informally named 'DataPub') to develop a prototype framework for integrating data and publications in a persistent manner (Choudhury et al., 2007).

One of the main outcomes from DataPub was the development of an Open Archives Initiative – Object Reuse and Exchange (OAI-ORE) model for data and publications. Figure 6.2 depicts one of the Resource Maps (ReMs) that was generated from DataPub.

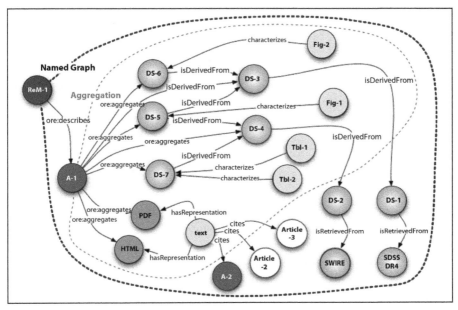

Figure 6.2 Open Archives Initiative Object Reuse and Exchange (OAI-ORE) Resource Map (ReM)
(*reproduced courtesy of Timothy DiLauro*)

This ReM includes an aggregation of a publication (node A-1) with a figure
(node Fig-1) that cites data (e.g., nodes DS-5). Furthermore, the ReM also
depicts that the data represented by node DS-5 was derived from underlying
data represented in nodes DS-3 and DS-1, which were ultimately derived
from an SDSS data release (node SDSS DR4). This graph-based view of data
and publications that encompasses critical scientific and preservation
concepts such as levels of data, compound objects and provenance was
based on astronomy but also represented a useful framework for modelling
other scientific data. The experience with SDSS offered the Sheridan
Libraries an opportunity to conduct a deep examination of data-intensive
science within a mature scientific community in terms of data-sharing
practices and standards. The MOU and DataPub model represented
formalized mechanisms for extending the lessons learned from dealing with
SDSS data. Those lessons learned formed the foundation for the Data
Conservancy.

3. Data Conservancy

The Sheridan Libraries led a successful proposal called Data Conservancy

(DC) for the first round of the US National Science Foundation's (NSF) DataNet program. The proposal incorporated ideas inspired by working with SDSS and the recommendations from the BRTF-SPDA. DC was also informed by the report *Understanding Infrastructure: dynamics, tensions, and design* (Edwards et al., 2007). As the former Director of NSF's Office of Cyberinfrastructure, Daniel Atkins cited this report as one of the influences for the DataNet program. Perhaps the most important finding described within the report is that successful infrastructure development does not proceed according to a rigid road map but follows principles of navigation that account for social dimensions (in addition to technical dimensions) over time. Relying upon principles of navigation also mitigates the possibility of 'path dependence' – described as the tendency to become fixed on a particular pathway or trajectory, despite evidence of rising costs or inability to address evolving requirements.

DC's principles of navigation included an emphasis on preservation, a specific focus on cross-disciplinary science as it relates to grand research challenges, capacity building and sustainability planning from its inception. DC was designed to address the multi-dimensional aspects of data management across domains, including technical, scientific, education and business requirements. Four teams were established to focus on each of these sets of requirements: infrastructure research and development (IRD), information science (IS), broader impacts (BI) and sustainability.

Given the experience with SDSS data, DC realized that re-engineering institutional repositories or using other document management systems would not be sufficient. Consider that even if it were possible to deposit all of the SDSS Level 0 data into an institutional repository, only a few astronomers in the world would be able to work the data and perhaps no one could properly interpret it without information about the processing pipeline from telescope to storage system. To understand, reproduce and build on the underlying science, data management must move beyond the model of depositing data for subsequent downloading. Data management is a means rather than an end.

DC recognized the importance of addressing all levels of data (including databases), provenance and queries against properties of the data. For these reasons, the DC IRD team designed and developed a new form of infrastructure focused on research data as primary, compound objects. DC's open, modular, flexible approach to infrastructure design and its interoperability demonstration with multiple services including the International Virtual Astronomical Observatory (IVAO), the National Snow and Ice Data Center

(NSIDC)'s glacier photo service, arXiv.org, Sakai and Google Earth are described further in Treloar, Choudhury and Michener, 2012.

At the core of DC is its data model that was inspired by the European Planets Project, illustrated in Figure 6.3.

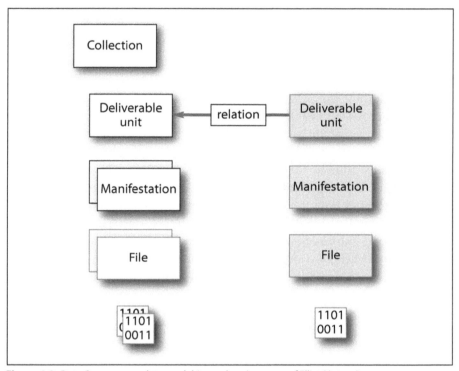

Figure 6.3 Data Conservancy data model (*reproduced courtesy of Elliot Metsger*)

Deliverable units represent the object of scientific interest for search and query (e.g. rock samples); manifestations are cases of deliverable units (e.g. images); and files are specific representations of manifestations (e.g. jpeg). This data model possesses four important features. First, it emphasizes and supports preservation. Second, it reflects the granularity of data highlighted within SDSS and other data-intensive science projects. Third, it supports the graph-based view of the OAI-ORE ReM from DataPub. Fourth, it generalizes across scientific domains. DC successfully applied this data model to data from astronomy, geology and oceanography. As part of its initial plans, DC proposed to deploy an alpha release of its software after three years of its initial award. Despite NSF's continuously changing requirements and personnel during the first three years of the DataNet program, DC successfully launched its alpha release in September 2012.

The IS team conducted research toward better understanding of scientific requirements based on an interlinked, comprehensive set of programmes at the University of California at Los Angeles (UCLA), the University of Illinois at Urbana (Illinois) and Cornell University. Christine Borgman (Graduate School of Education and Information Studies) led a team at UCLA that examined deeply the social aspects of SDSS and other astronomy projects through ethnographic techniques as they relate to decision and consensus making, including the SDSS and ARC choice to work with the Sheridan Libraries. Carole Palmer (Graduate School of Library and Information Science) led a team at Illinois organized into two groups – Data Practices and Data Concepts – to explore practices that facilitate or inhibit data sharing and to identify fundamental characteristics that define or describe data. UCLA led a deep exploration of an exemplar scientific community and Illinois considered how the dimensions that led to successful data sharing might be applied to other scientific communities. Carl Lagoze (formerly Department of Information Science at Cornell and currently School of Information at Michigan) led a team at Cornell that studied the concept of an observation as a semantic or ontological framework across scientific domains, particularly related to concepts of space, time and name. DC's technical framework includes support for spatial, temporal and taxonomic queries through a feature extraction framework that atomizes data into constituent features and a general query model that exploits the features for indexing and searching.

It is unfortunate that this rich, unprecedented research programme did not have an opportunity to reach its fruition. In a fundamental sense, DC's IS teams were developing a theoretical framework for data curation. Arguably, digital libraries have suffered a lack of definition and coherence because of the absence of such a theoretical framework. NSF's DataNet programme originally included a major emphasis on this type of social and information science research but ultimately changed toward more technical development. It remains to be seen what will happen, given that the social dimensions are not receiving the same level of attention. However, DC managed to learn a great deal with this early experience and continues to work with colleagues at UCLA and Illinois through grants from the Alfred P. Sloan Foundation and the US Institute of Museum and Library Services.

One of the most important findings from this IS research is that developing cross-disciplinary scientific requirements is a challenge in itself.

While the process for identifying such requirements remains a work in progress, DC realized that preservation requirements represent an important and useful framework for early technical development. By mapping the initial DC architecture to the Open Archival Information System (OAIS) reference model, the DC IRD team developed a set of initial requirements. Additionally, DC also realized that the actions required to prepare data and to develop software for preservation represent highly useful actions for reuse of data. Ruth Duerr (National Snow and Ice Data Center) developed DC's working definition of data preservation:

> Data preservation involves providing enough representation information, context, metadata, fixity, etc. such that someone other than the original data producer can use and interpret the data.
>
> (R. Duerr, personal communication, 2011)

The BI team carried this message forward as one of DC's core principles of navigation. It is worth noting that the BI team led DC's professional branding effort by working with the Social Design Department at the Maryland Institute, College of Art (MICA). This branding effort clarified and reinforced DC's sense of community, approach and message. The BI team also broadened DC's reach and influence through a series of targeted, strategic partnerships. In particular, DC became an important voice and resource within the academic research library community through participation in programmes such as the Association of Research Libraries' eScience Institute. This capacity building has profound implications in terms of both service delivery and sustainability for data management. Academic libraries represent a natural organizational home for data management services, assuming that they are able to reallocate resources and reconceive their organizations accordingly.

DC's BI team made significant contributions to development of new educational courses, programmes and tutorials, thereby raising awareness for current professionals and training a next generation of data managers. UCLA developed new courses. Illinois augmented their data curation concentration and offered summer institutes for scientists and librarians. Ruth Duerr led the development of data management training tutorials that have been well received and reviewed at the American Geophysical Union annual conference. Even students and interns from outside the immediate team contributed significantly to DC's programme.

Within JHU, DC benefited from a series of analyses by capstone team[7] students at the Carey Business School. Over the course of two years, DC's Sustainability team worked with five different teams, which progressively conducted a total cost of ownership for JHU's existing storage system and developed a framework for analysing vendor proposals for a new storage system. These capstone teams incorporated feedback from the technical lessons learned from working with SDSS data. This comprehensive business analysis represented a critical component of the sustainability plan for JHUDMS.

Other ways through which DC infused sustainability planning from its inception to the launch of JHUDMS include the incorporation of rigorous software development practices from Tessella Inc., an examination of the operational production environment at Portico and an initial market analysis of possible fee-based services. Finally, DC ensured that its programme was well aligned with the needs of researchers, particularly at JHU through the participation of seven faculty members from its Krieger School of Arts and Sciences, Whiting School of Engineering and School of Medicine. This alignment of DC's programme with stakeholder needs – another important recommendation from the BRTF-SPDA – laid down the foundation for the launch of JHUDMS.

4. Johns Hopkins University Data Management Services (JHUDMS)

In May 2010, NSF announced that they would require all proposals, effective January 2011, to include a two-page data management plan. Perhaps not surprisingly, faculty members at JHU inquired about the possibility of support from the Sheridan Libraries, given its leadership of DC. Eventually, a combination of department chairs, deans and the Provost's office contacted the Sheridan Libraries regarding data management support for faculty submitting NSF proposals.

The Sheridan Libraries had gained relevant experience through working with SDSS data in an R&D capacity. DC's social and information science research and education or training expertise was relevant in this regard. The total cost of ownership and analysis of storage systems represented an important business analysis for a data management service. Finally, DC's planned launch of its alpha software represented an obvious component of an overall data management service. Each of these components comprised a foundation for a business plan but additional analysis remained to be conducted.

Given this foundation and the potential demand for a data management service, the Sheridan Libraries began a comprehensive analysis of the specific environment and needs within JHU. Even before the January 2011 implementation of the NSF data management plan mandate, the Sheridan Libraries started to work with faculty members on developing data management plans. These early consultations provided information regarding the nature of skills that would be necessary from a staffing perspective.

In addition to these faculty consultations, the Sheridan Libraries also conducted a survey of all JHU NSF principal investigators (PIs) for the past five years. The Provost's office at JHU supported this survey by identifying the PIs, supplying the e-mail addresses and authorizing the Sheridan Libraries to contact them. The Vice-Provost for Research sent the survey on behalf of the Sheridan Libraries. The survey was intentionally brief. It focused on questions related to storage needs, current practices, roles and potential retention periods. The survey was not intended to be research-oriented but rather information-gathering and awareness-raising. The Sheridan Libraries also determined the overall number of NSF proposals and success rate for the five years preceding 2010.

As part of this overall analysis, the Sheridan Libraries reviewed existing data management plans and best practices and developed a questionnaire that was designed to guide the consultation process with PIs. This initial questionnaire has evolved over time with greater experience and feedback from PIs, but continues to represent the core framework for data management plan consultations.

Pralle led the effort to combine all of the inputs from this analysis into a business plan that was submitted to the JHU administration. The proposed costs and services reflected support for NSF proposals only but could be extrapolated to other funding agencies or types of data management needs. The proposed costs were allocated according to the distribution of NSF proposals submitted among the JHU schools based on a three-year average. Additional scoping characteristics included the amount of storage per proposal, retention periods according to the existing JHU data policy, and initial support for unencumbered data only. The proposed budget included all costs such as storage, staffing, and overheads, and made assumptions about the total amount of data managed and impact of the complexity of data on ingest preparation. The DC software was proposed as the underlying technology, which was to be branded as the JHU Data Archive.

The JHU administration approved the business plan and the JHUDMS was launched officially in July 2011. It is worth noting that the Sheridan

Libraries conducted its analysis, developed its business plan and launched the service within six months. It is unlikely that JHU would have designed and launched such a fully fledged service in a relatively short time within an academic environment without the prior experience and expertise within the Sheridan Libraries. One of the key lessons learned during this process was that it is important for administrators to consider choices in terms of support for a data management service. Rather than begin with an *a priori* assertion of a funding model (e.g. indirect cost), the JHUDMS business plan outlined costs, trade-offs, options, etc., that the university administration assessed and incorporated into their final decision. This direct engagement with university administration and faculty led to the JHUDMS being viewed as a research support service delivered by the libraries, rather than a library service *per se*. JHUDMS continues to rely on the extensive network of research support systems and personal contacts within JHU for ongoing engagement, marketing, education, etc.

Pralle (2012) outlines the three facets of sustainability – financial, human and technical – that aligned in the planning and launching of the JHUDMS and the comprehensive scope of the service, which spans both pre-proposal planning and post-award data management. The JHU administration chose to fund the pre-proposal consultation directly so that this service is free to faculty. If faculty chooses to use the JHU Data Archive for data management, it is required to include funds within its proposals as a percentage of the modified total direct costs. JHUDMS will eventually develop customized estimates of costs for use of the JHU Data Archive once sufficient experience has been gained. It should be noted that neither the pre-proposal consultation nor the post-award use of the JHU Data Archive are a requirement for JHU faculty. When available and appropriate, JHUDMS consultants will inform PIs of alternatives (e.g. domain repository) and discuss the relative pros and cons of such alternatives.

From Pralle (2012), the JHUDMS pre-proposal data management planning scope includes:

- understand all data products
- review operational data management
- use questionnaire as basis for consultation
- discuss archival data management needs and options
- review domain repository options
- provide JHU Data Archive information
- clarify language and help researcher iterate a two-page plan.

In cases where PIs choose to use the JHU Data Archive for post-award data management, the JHUDMS adopts the following approach:

- prepare an in-depth data management plan (above and beyond the NSF proposal two-page plan)
- recommend metadata standards
- transfer data into JHU Data Archive
- manage data for researcher so he/she can find, access and use data
- archive conducts integrity checking
- archive tracks provenance and lineage
- archive will conduct format migration and enable tools such as feature extraction in the future software releases.

Pralle also describes what is not currently within scope for the JHUDMS or JHU Data Archive:

- unlimited archiving of data indefinitely
- operational data management
- in-depth curation of the data
- boilerplate language for data management plans
- written data management plans for researchers to edit
- data management solutions for encumbered data (e.g. IRB or HIPAA restricted).

Some of these currently out-of-scope elements will change over time as DC develops additional software releases. For example, subsequent releases of the DC software will offer additional curation capabilities such as feature extraction and will probably deal with encumbered data. However, some aspects of scope will probably remain the same. JHUDMS data retention policies reflect the existing JHU data policy that calls for data retention of five years beyond the end of project. Furthermore, JHUDMS's business analysis highlighted that long-term data management entails costs that are not captured by the initial funding. Offering unlimited data retention in such circumstances could easily lead to long-term sustainability issues.

JHUDMS also believes that a customized approach for data management planning fosters the greatest prospects for data sharing, access and preservation. It is probably easier to generate a data management plan through a template but the data management plan represents the beginning of the journey. As indicated earlier, JHUDMS develops an additional, in-depth data management plan for successful awards because a two-page plan rarely, if ever, provides enough context, background, detail, etc., to fully understand the data and associated requirements for sharing, access and preservation. A reasonable analogy is the reference interview. A researcher may begin with the approach: 'I am looking for this article.' However, a successful reference interview not only reveals additional, relevant resources but also the underlying research questions and methods. In this manner, JHUDMS focuses on what researchers are trying to accomplish with their data rather than meeting the goals of a funding agency requirement.

The JHUDMS approach has also highlighted important inconsistencies or confusion regarding terms related to data management. Specifically, researchers use the terms storage, archiving, preservation and curation interchangeably and inappropriately. For example, when researchers state that they are 'preserving' their data, they may be referring to storing their data on a hard drive, hopefully (though not always) with back-up and restore. In this case, it is not surprising that a researcher may wonder why there are additional costs associated with preservation.

To provide clarity and consistency regarding these terms, Choudhury et al. (2013) developed the data management layer stack model 'Levels of Services and Curation for High Functioning Data.' This model specifically describes storage, archiving, preservation and curation as a series of hierarchical layers that build upon each other.[8] Storage is necessary but not sufficient for archiving. In turn, archiving is necessary but not sufficient for preservation, and so on. This model has been helpful during consultations with PIs to explain the full range of current and future functionality for DC software. Both DC software and the JHUDMS intend to eventually cover the entire range of functionality described with each of the layers of this stack model. However, not every institution needs to support all of these functions. JHU has considerable experience with and commitment to data management. If an institution chooses to focus on a subset of functions within this data management layer stack model, then it is important that they acknowledge the other layers and realize the interdependency between the layers. An institution may choose to begin by providing a storage service for their researchers. This is perfectly reasonable and useful. However, if this institution then claims it is providing a full data management service, it could lead to false expectations. Furthermore, if it stores its data in a manner that complicates or perhaps even inhibits archiving, preservation and curation, it could lead to future problems and sustainability issues.

Other libraries and universities have contacted JHUDMS for advice and guidance regarding data management services. In an effort to provide a systematic, comprehensive feedback in this regard, JHUDMS developed the notion of a Data Conservancy instance. Mayernik et al. describe the Data Conservancy instance as:

> an implementation of infrastructure and organizational services for data collection, storage, preservation, archiving, curation, and sharing. While comparable to institutional repository systems and disciplinary data repositories in some aspects, the DC Instance is distinguished by featuring a data-centric architecture, discipline-agnostic data model, and a data feature extraction framework that facilitates data integration and cross-disciplinary queries. The Data Conservancy Instance is intended to support, and be supported by, a skilled data curation staff, and to facilitate technical, financial, and human sustainability of organizational data curation services.
>
> Mayernik et al. (2013)

The DC instance can be thought of as a blueprint for comprehensive data management services that includes hardware, software, policies, context and business plan. While DC technology represents the software component, all of the other components can be considered more generally. As with any blueprint, it is important to note that it represents a plan or framework, not a specific set of instructions. Each institutional context or set of goals will influence which elements of the blueprint are most relevant or appropriate.

5. Conclusions

These considerations will become even more important in the US context, given the executive memorandum of 22 February 2013 from the White House Office of Science and Technology Policy.[9] As this memorandum outlines, US Federal agencies with a research and development budget of over $100 million will be required to respond and develop a plan for data management within six months after the release of the memo. The memo also places greater emphasis on data sharing, access and preservation through data management plans and core components of infrastructure such as identifiers. Initial feedback through various forums, including the National Academies Board on Research Data and Information, indicate that most US federal agencies are now considering data management plan requirements or mandates.

In addition to this OSTP memo, the US Congress has expressed greater interest in data management. On 5 March 2013, I testified as an expert witness at a hearing of the Research Subcommittee of the Committee for Science, Space and Technology on scientific integrity and transparency. During this hearing – referring back to ideas from the 'Understanding Infrastructure' report – I presented the case that data management represents a new form of infrastructure development that includes both social and technical dimensions.[10]

These developments cast data management within the greater context of US economic activity and competitiveness. That is, data management is no longer viewed as only an academic or scientific concern. In this light, it seems reasonable to assert that institutional data management programs need to deal directly not only with data, but also with those who produce the data. More specifically, data management programmes will need to influence – perhaps even change – the culture associated with data sharing, access, and preservation.

Such culture change does not occur through technology alone. When the institutional repository movement gained momentum within research libraries, there were predictions of major changes in the scholarly communication landscape. While there are encouraging signs in terms of new open-access journals and publications, those changes arguably occurred because of raising awareness amongst researchers regarding issues such as copyright agreements, rising subscription costs, etc. – the social dimensions – rather than the option of depositing pre-publications into institutional repositories. Similarly, comprehensive data management will require more than depositing data into repositories. It will require an understanding of the overall context regarding data, engagement with the researchers who produce the data and the provision of services that account for data as primary, compound objects within a broader scholarly communication landscape. The JHUDMS represents an important step within a longer-term effort to develop data infrastructure that will ultimately not only store, archive, preserve and curate data but also change the culture of data sharing, access, and preservation.

6. References

6.1 Websites and explanatory notes

1   http://dmp.data.jhu.edu.

2   www.sdss.org.

3   http://dataconservancy.org.

4   https://wiki.library.jhu.edu/x/eY1XAQ.
5   This concept of levels of data and processing applies to other domains as well. For example, consider the NASA levels of processing: http://science.nasa.gov/ earth-science/earth-science-data/data-processing-levels-for-eosdis-data-products.
6   http://elp.library.jhu.edu.
7   A 'capstone team' is a group of people who work together on a project at the end of specific developmental programmes. This team typically meets after a programme to evaluate and discuss findings and results.
8   This stack model is also described in the YouTube video: www.youtube.com/watch?v=F6iYXNvCRO4.
9   www.whitehouse.gov/sites/default/files/microsites/ostp/ostp_public_access_memo_2013.pdf.
10   http://dataconservancy.org/congressional-hearing-testimony.

6.2 Citations

BRTF-SPDA (2010) *Sustainable Economics for a Digital Planet: ensuring long-term access to digital information*, http://brtf.sdsc.edu.
Choudhury, G. S., DiLauro, T., Szalay A., Vishniac E., Hanisch, R., Steffen, J., Milkey, R., Ehling, T. and Plante, R. (2007) Digital Data Preservation for Scholarly Publications in Astronomy, *International Journal of Digital Curation*, **2** (2), 20–30, www.ijdc.net/index.php/ijdc/article/view/41/26.
Choudhury, G. S., Palmer, C., Baker, K. and DiLauro, T. (2013) Levels of Services and Curation for High Functioning Data, *8th International Digital Curation Conference*, www.dcc.ac.uk/sites/default/files/documents/idcc13posters/Poster192.pdf.
Edwards, P. N., Jackson, S. J., Bowker, G. C. and Knobel, C.P. (2007) *Understanding Infrastructure: dynamics, tensions, and design*, http://hdl.handle.net/2027.42/49353.
Mayernik, M. S., Choudhury, G. S., DiLauro, T., Metsger, E., Pralle, B., Rippin, M. and Duerr, R. (2013) The Data Conservancy Instance: infrastructure and organizational services for research data curation, *D-Lib Magazine*, **18** (9/10), www.dlib.org/dlib/september12/mayernik/09mayernik.html.
Pralle, B. (2012) Data Curation Services Models: Johns Hopkins University, *Research Data Access & Preservation Summit*, www.slideshare.net/asist_org/data-curation-models-jhu-barbara-pralle-rdap12.
Treloar, A., Choudhury, G. S. and Michener, W. (2012) Contrasting National Research Data Strategies: Australia and the USA. In Pryor, G. (ed.), *Managing Research Data*, Facet Publishing.

CHAPTER 7

Case study 2: University of Southampton – a partnership approach to research data management

Mark L. Brown and Wendy White

1. Introduction

By 2009 researchers at the University of Southampton had been working for some time with the issues around e-Science and the challenges posed by integrating research data with publication (Heery et al., 2004). Individual researchers were already engaged in national collaborations, but it was the experience of collaboration around the UK Research Data Service (UKRDS) feasibility project in 2008–9 that acted as the catalyst for initiatives to support researchers across the institution in managing their research data.[1] UKRDS was a sector-wide initiative to investigate how the UK could respond to the increasing pressure on institutions to manage their researchers' data. It initiated a corpus of work on the complexities of storage, retrieval, preservation and reuse and, if the proposal for a national framework did not go forward, the knowledge gained on the issues for the successful management of research data provided the background for the next phase of development.[2] UKRDS was built on a partnership between the librarians, heads of computing services and leading researchers in the major research universities who, together with Jisc and HEFCE, set out a programme to respond to the needs of the research community. It was this collaborative approach that was taken forward in the next phase of development.

The University of Southampton is a major research-led university with a broad spread of disciplines and receives a significant level of research income. In line with the major commitment to science and engineering, the university had since 2000 been investing considerable resource in high-performance computing with the consequent increase in data output. In terms of managing research data, at the outset of the project there were some disciplines for which the deposit of data for the purposes of archiving and sharing was well established, but for the majority of research areas there was no corresponding facility.

UKRDS estimated that 21% of UK researchers used a national or international facility, and that there was an increasing level of data sharing.[3] At Southampton this was reflected in the deposit of data in the national data centres, such as those provided by NERC, ESRC, UKDA or the Rutherford-Appleton Laboratory, but there were important areas left without a model for data deposit and archiving, and little provision to match the level of interdisciplinary and trans-institutional research being conducted. One of the aims of UKRDS had been to address the issue of archiving for those disciplines without a data centre, and there was disappointment that the proposal for a national approach did not go forward. The withdrawal of funding from the Arts and Humanities Data Service (AHDS) in 2008–9 also highlighted potential vulnerabilities for a university with a strong commitment to the humanities.

Southampton has a long tradition of supporting open access for research outputs. The two core academic support services, the University Library and the University Computing Service (iSolutions), were partners in these developments, and it was a natural step to consider the role of data within the open access environment. The university had a strong track record of working on Jisc-funded projects and welcomed the positioning of Research Libraries UK, the Russell Group IT Directors Group and Jisc in pushing forward the agenda and providing opportunities to engage with initiatives at a national level. Within the university a community of shared interest evolved as a partnership between the two services and major research groups in engineering, archaeology, computer science and chemistry.

This community approach underpinned the partnership established through the Institutional Data Management Blueprint (IDMB) project, part-funded by Jisc under the Managing Research Data (JiscMRD) programme, which ran from October 2009 to September 2011.[4] The Jisc programme dovetailed with the final report of UKRDS, which appeared in May 2010. A second phase of the programme part-funded DataPool,[5] a follow-on project described in section 3, which ran from October 2011 to March 2013.

2. The Institutional Data Management Blueprint project

IDMB (Brown, Parchment and White, 2011) was seen by its supporters as a 'great leap forward' in terms of taking a researcher-led approach to translating research data management principles into effective practice deliverable at institutional level. To achieve this the project team, representing both academic and service champions,[6] set out to engage the university institutionally to secure support for a ten-year roadmap for data management, jointly 'owned' by the Research and Enterprise Advisory Group, responsible for research strategy, and the University Systems Board, responsible for systems strategy.[7]

IDMB was intended to combine two approaches; first a bottom-up approach based on researchers' needs and designed to broaden the adoption of good practice and, second, a top-down approach designed to set out the requirements for institutional policies and infrastructure. UKRDS had identified a great deal of work already under way in the UK, and the Jisc programme was intended to extend these to foster awareness and promote good practice. UKRDS had also heightened awareness of the value of the existing data centres and, given the wide discipline range within the university, IDMB was in a good position to benefit from existing links with those provided by the Natural Environmental Research Council (NERC), the Economic and Social Science Research Council (ESRC), the UK Data Archive (UKDA) and the Archaeology Data Service (ADS). The project also sought to apply the tools being developed nationally by the Digital Curation Centre.[8] This blend of national and local perspectives was important in the success of the project.

2.1 A research-led approach

From the beginning, the team were determined to exploit existing good practice within the institution and to raise awareness of the implications of not managing research data. The serious fire which destroyed the laboratories of the Optoelectronics Research Centre in October 2005 (BBC News, 2005) had already had an effect on the researcher community's awareness of the vulnerability of the research record. Also the debate surrounding climate science data at the University of East Anglia sharpened perceptions of the role of Freedom of Information requests in access to publicly funded research (Times Higher Education, 2010) .

To cement the importance of a research-led approach, the project team ran a 'kick-off workshop' in March 2010, which attracted around 40 attendees.

The profile report identified what participants considered to be current issues of concern, long-term aspirations and 'quick wins'. This was followed up by a data management survey using a questionnaire and selected in-depth interviews and an audit using the Assessing Institutional Digital Assets (AIDA) toolkit to benchmark current capability at departmental and institutional level. In exploring the toolkit the project team were referencing the wider work being funded by Jisc in the Integrated Data Management Planning Toolkit & Support (IDMP) project, intended to support the use of research data management planning tools across the Managing Research Data (MRD) programme.[9]

Taking a research-led and evidence based approach helped to formulate a set of preliminary conclusions as the basis of recommendations to the university. The key conclusions were:

• There was a need from researchers to share data, both locally and globally.
• Data management was carried out on an ad-hoc basis in many cases.
• Researchers' demand for storage was significant, and outstripped supply.
• Researchers resorted to their own best efforts in many cases to overcome lack of central support.
• Back-up practices were not consistent, with users seeking a higher level of support.
• Researchers wanted to keep their data for a long time.
• Data curation and preservation was poorly supported.
• Data management capabilities varied widely across the different schools within the university.

From these stemmed a number of institutional challenges. Although there was evidence of good practice, there was no coherent approach to data management across disciplines, and the current business model for curation and preservation was neither scalable nor sustainable in terms of future demands. The audit revealed that researchers were becoming more conscious of the requirements from funders and there was a need to consider issues around IPR, sharing data and the protection of the university's digital assets. Elements of a service infrastructure were in place, but they lacked capacity and coherence; training and guidance was rudimentary.

2.2 Institutional challenges

Encouraging the university to adopt an institutional approach to developing policy and infrastructure faced barriers. The university has a very broad discipline spread and a strong culture of autonomy, which did not fit easily with a centralized approach. On the other hand, in an institution with a highly collaborative research culture, many researchers were aware of debates over managing research data and Southampton's long-standing commitment to open access extended naturally into the realm of open data.[10] Extensive work with research and learning repositories had orientated researchers to the principles and benefits of the central deposit of research outputs, but delivering an effective technical and service infrastructure was clearly beyond the capacity of individual academic units. The services therefore saw it as their role to explore the idea of a set of centrally delivered services that would be flexible and responsive to local needs. Here there were a number of assets within the pattern of existing practice. Although there was still a mixed economy in IT, there had already been a partial centralization, and the university had set up mechanisms for the central evaluation and procurement for IT investment. The library service successfully runs as a centralized service, and had well embedded partnerships with academic groups across disciplines as well as a culture of collaboration with both iSolutions[11] and Research and Innovation Services (RIS). The high profile of the UK research libraries in UKRDS and their position in many of the Jisc-funded projects emphasized the importance of the role of libraries in the data management landscape and the university library emerged as a service lead.

From an institutional perspective, funder policies were shifting perceptions of the significance of data management as a strategic issue. In the course of the project RCUK published guidance setting out seven core principles on data policy, which highlighted the principle that publicly funded research data should be generally made as widely and freely available as possible in a timely and responsible manner, though with appropriate safeguards for the inappropriate release of data (RCUK, 2011). For the university, as a significant holder of EPSRC funding, the EPSRC framework on research data, which was under discussion during 2010 and adopted by the Council in March 2011 (EPSRC, 2011), held particular importance.

In contradistinction to practice by research councils such as NERC, which provided a national data centre, EPSRC clearly placed responsibility for policy and compliance on research institutions.[12] For the project team, these developments posed the issue of achieving an appropriate balance between assuming voluntary adherence to good practice and an element of compliance based on institutional policy. Policy alone, however, would not be sufficient to create a change in the assumptions behind research practice in key areas. The audit provided evidence that researchers were open to new practice as long as it was researcher-led, integrated into research workflow, reflective of discipline distinctions and supported by advice and training. Clarity over policy and responsive service support were essential to gaining their commitment to incorporating good practice into workflow.

The roadmap was designed to set out a staged approach over a ten-year period, during which it was accepted that policy and technical opportunities would inevitably shift. The accompanying Blueprint was built around the concept of a multifunctional team, which could bring together the knowledge and expertise of both professionals and researchers within a flexible technical and service framework. The message to the university was that IDMB was not a set of solutions imposed on researchers, but a pragmatic and iterative process, flexible enough to meet the needs of a multi-disciplinary research institution. This implied an approach based on promoting cultural and political change.

Senior representatives of the University Executive Group (UEG)[13] were involved with the project from the beginning as members of the project steering group. Reports to Senate were made through the Research and Enterprise Advisory Group (REAG), which included the Associate Deans (Research and Enterprise) and senior representatives from the research support services. This forum provided governance for the project and a forum for discussing future proposals. In terms of taking forward the principles in the Blueprint, the project identified three priorities: the formulation and agreement of an institutional policy, an advocacy and training programme for the research community, and a strategy for the storage and security of data. Each of these priorities posed significant issues.

2.3 Shaping a data management policy

The team considered it important to link discussion of data management policy to the earlier debates on open access at Southampton. The work to build support for the institutional repository had helped shape researchers' response to the central deposit of publications, and had created a momentum for making research outputs more visible, whilst recognizing the concerns over sharing data. This experience of long-term engagement was seen as important in winning support for the data management policy, which needed to be seen as part of the wider policy framework for research, and to appeal to researchers in terms of their needs. Data management, however, raises additional implications in terms of organization, technology and resource. The policy had to set the context within which the institution could make decisions about investment and service support without introducing a set of requirements that would inevitably be perceived as an unjustifiable additional burden on research time.

In line with this thinking, the team adopted a dual approach. At institutional level the policy sets out the university's assumptions on roles and responsibilities, provides guidance on what is expected and sets the framework for decision making and governance. It also provides a link to other institutional policies such as IPR Policy. For researchers it provides guidance on policy and governance and provides a framework for them to feel supported in responding to both internal priorities and external requirements. In terms of the researchers' perspectives it sets a framework around the implications of changing funder mandates, the management of data workflow, the access, retrieval and security of data, and the facilitation of collaborative work with internal or external partners. By attaching ownership of the Blueprint jointly to the Research and Enterprise Advisory Group, responsible for university research strategy, and the University Systems Board, responsible for overarching strategic decisions on university systems, it was intended that the policy would be embedded within university governance structures.[14]

Having set out a draft policy it was important to put in place processes to support researchers in adhering to the base precepts. Researchers are working in a complex funder economy, in which some research councils provide a national data centre and others assume institutional data management structures. In both cases, however, the issues of integrated workflow, data sharing, technical support and training for good practice would benefit from an institutional approach. The two priorities emerged as storage, security, curation and preservation of the data on the one hand, and advice and support to the researchers in managing their data on the other. Progress on the second element turned out to be easier than the first, not least because there was already a degree of good practice that could be used to extend support across disciplines.

2.4 Integrated workflow: storage, security and archiving

The Data Management Policy identifies the importance of the proper recording, maintenance, storage and security of research data, compliance with relevant regulations, including appropriate access and retrieval, and places the onus for achieving this on researchers. This reflected the consensus in the audit that individual researchers had to be responsible for management of their project data.

The choice made by researchers in their approach to storage was less consistent than might be assumed from the policies that funders were requiring of institutions. In the audit researchers identified a wide array of data storage locations, with 24% using their local computer, 34.9% using CD/DVD, USB flash drive or external hard disk, and only 24.3% using a file server either at the university or off-site.[15] A significant number of respondents calculated that they held more than 100 GB of data, and 45.9% stated they kept their data forever. It was assumed from the return that a significant number of users managed this locally on a PC, CD/DVD, external hard drives or USB flash drives. More than 50% also indicated that they had experienced storage constraints, and overall the tracking of existing data was variable and often relied on paper logs.

When researchers were asked how the university could make data management and storage easier, the main requirements cited were the need for more storage space, archiving, automated back-up, security for sensitive data, a registry function and integrated guidance and training. Some researchers in electronics and computer science, engineering sciences and archaeology also requested 'e-Prints for data', reflecting the familiarity with the processes around the use of the research outputs repository. In terms of archiving, only 10% deposited data with another external service, an average stretching between 28.6% in psychology and social sciences and 9% in geography.[16]

This kaleidoscope of current practice revealed a potential mismatch between the way in which researchers were managing their data and the implications of the requirements from funders, most importantly for the university the EPSRC.[17] In the expectations set out by the EPSRC emphasis was given to the provision of 'appropriately structured metadata describing the research data held which would be freely accessible on the internet, and that EPSRC-funded research data is securely preserved for a minimum of 10 years from the date that any researcher "privileged access" period expires or, if others have accessed the data, from last date on which access to the data was requested by a third party'. These provisions made an assumption about institutional infrastructure and set a date, 1 April 2015, by which it was expected to be operable. One response to this was to put in place the policy; a second was to set in motion a debate on the deliverability of a suitable infrastructure.

In response to the debate on infrastructure the IDMB team produced an outline business model based on the assumption that the university would provide a secure and sustainable repository capable of hosting the university's entire digital assets. Not surprisingly, the university had no detailed knowledge of the quantity of research data held, nor of its likely growth over a specific timeframe, and the model had to be constructed on the basis of the indicative data from the audit and estimates from the current mid-scale research storage platform. The estimates indicated a current total of the order of 0.8–1.2 Pb, rising to between 11.2 Pb and 21.2 Pb by 2016/17. The high-level architectural design which was used to inform the cost model included three layers: an active storage layer, a metadata layer and an archive storage layer. The model also considered staffing and facilities support as well as operating costs, and made assumptions about the costs of storage over time. This allowed some scenarios to be constructed with options for the university to consider investment on a phased basis.[18]

Although this work was speculative, it did provide a very useful baseline for assessing potential investment. This in turn had an effect on perceptions at senior university level of the pressures resulting from the combination of the growing size of institutional research data output and the requirements by funders for its management and accessibility. The knowledge and expertise being developed by the IDMB team was increasingly seen as an institutional asset. This was useful in the work being taken forward to design a metadata layer for a registry function.

2.5 Integrated workflow: metadata models

In approaching this issue the IDMB team explored how a relatively straightforward metadata structure could be defined as a means of encouraging researchers to adopt external standards within an institution-wide registry. It was accepted that disciplines approached the value of metadata from different perspectives. Some used metadata just to identify and retrieve files, whereas others, archaeology researchers for example, were accustomed to providing detailed metadata as part of their workflow and as preparation for deposit in the Archaeology Data Service.[19] Some of the detailed analytical models at discipline level were seen to be too complex for researchers, so the model was developed around a practical approach to encouraging researchers to submit baseline data.

The core metadata structure that evolved was based on Dublin Core, a standard already in use for data by the National Crystallography Centre at Southampton[20] and which built on the basic data deposit work undertaken in the DataShare project.[21] The three-level structure (project, discipline and core) was devised to be as straightforward as possible and to be supported by usable tools for metadata assignment and import. Figure 7.1 shows the three-level metadata structure applied by archaeology, the pilot discipline, to a project exemplar.

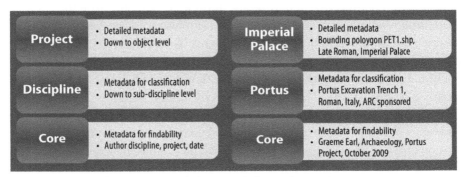

Figure 7.1 A three-layer metadata model for research data, with example

The option for the inclusion of additional, more complex, metadata to be added as xml files at discipline-specific level was also included in the specification, and work began on designing an ingest system. The initial scoping informed discussions over achieving an appropriate balance between a central, local and distributed technical infrastructure and was carried forward in the second Jisc-funded project, DataPool.

2.6 Integrated workflow: training and support

In terms of training and support, it was clear from the audit that researchers needed a wide-ranging and flexible service model which would dovetail the separate services from the university library, the computing service (iSolutions), Research and Innovation Services (RIS) and Legal Services. These services had a good track record of collaborative working and the experience of partnership in the IDMB project highlighted the value of closer integration. The team wanted to consider the need for support across the whole research cycle, encompassing the spectrum of research careers from the PhD student and the early-career researchers to the mature research group engaged in large-scale national and international collaborations.

As an initial pilot the IDMB team ran a training programme for archaeology PhD students. Training took the form of workshops where participants worked through a specific example, looking at issues of storage and curation, and discussed potential solutions and the roles of different stakeholders in managing the data. Students were introduced to the three-layer metadata model and encouraged to think about how this would apply to their data collected in the course of fieldwork. Although this was a small pilot, it showed the value of integrating training into a broader programme of research skills training. The workshop approach was designed to test a template for implementation across other disciplines and from the feedback it was possible to determine priorities for the next phase of development, which would incorporate desk-side training and more tailored one-stop-shop guidance with further workshops (Earl, White and Wake, 2011). In the course of the pilot, reference was also made to the other projects within the Jisc programme, to help reinforce the design.

2.7 The impact of IDMB

IDMB was intended to be the first phase of an iterative, dynamic model for supporting data management. The roadmap which emerged from the project identified three phases of development:

Short-term (1–3 years)

This phase was centred on the building of a core infrastructure, including an integrated approach to policy, technical infrastructure and support which could meet the demands of the growth in the level and complexity of research data, the requirements by funders and the need for the institution to manage its digital assets effectively.

The core components for this phase were:

- a robust institutional policy framework agreed and implemented by the institution
- an agreed scalable and sustainable business model for storage, based on the three components of active data, descriptive metadata and archive storage
- a working institutional data repository which could satisfy researchers' data management requirements for ingest, metadata creation and retrieval. It had to have sufficient capacity to attract users and offset the

incentive to procure local solutions
- a one-stop shop for data management advice and guidance to provide information on policy and legal issues to support the creation of data management plans, access to advice on technical capability, funder requirements and the benefits of managing data to exploit and share.

Medium-term (3–6 years)

During this phase it was assumed that the demands for the management of very large amounts of data of greater sophistication and complexity would increase, and that some disciplines would require potentially higher levels of data management input than can be managed within one institution. Although the cost of storage was likely to continue to decline, the management process itself would increase demand on staff skills. There would also be a higher profile for open and shared data and the value of pooling and sharing between institutions would be explored through specific exemplars.

The core components for this phase were:

- an extensible research information management framework to respond to the variations in discipline needs
- a comprehensive and affordable back-up service for all, based on the cost benefits of backing up different classes of data
- an effective data management repository model able to manage the potential full range of data deposit
- building an infrastructure to respond to a commitment to open research data with a model for data publication
- based on the cost-benefit analysis for backing up different classes of data, comprehensive solutions for managing research data across its whole lifecycle
- embedding data management training and support across the disciplines through partnership working between services and researchers
- pilots with consortia to manage data collectively using standard infrastructure applications, including cloud computing, and supported by shared staff knowledge and expertise.

Longer-term (6–10 years)

Long-term aspirations would focus on providing significant benefits realization across the whole university and a stable foundation for the future. The institution would have policies and infrastructure in place to make strategic judgements on how to manage its digital assets, and would have moved to a mixed mode of data management within consortia or national frameworks. There would be a higher level of partnership between funders, organizations, local consortia and national facilities. Data management processes would be embedded throughout the research data lifecycle, and the infrastructure would fully support researchers, with supply meeting demand via an easy-to-use data management service. This would significantly improve research productivity, allowing them to concentrate on their research, rather than worrying about data management logistics. The core components for this phase were envisaged as follows:

- coherent and flexible data management support across all disciplines and across the whole data management lifecycle
- agile business plans for continual improvement in response to changing requirements
- commitment to innovation in open data publication and the infrastructure to support this across the institution
- active participation in consortia and national framework agreements, contributing capacity and skills to building overall capability.

In promoting a debate over the role of policy and infrastructure in determining effective data management practice and institutional compliance with funder requirements, IDMB set the context for an institutional approach to research data management and defined the core elements in the framework for technological and organizational support. If compliance with funder requirements was a catalyst, it was not in itself a sufficient incentive for an institutional approach. The audit and the work undertaken with specific disciplines had engaged researchers in the issues underlying the management of their data; researchers had shown a very strong interest in adopting improved data management practice, and were open to working with the services to support their needs. It was clear, however, that any major investment would not be forthcoming without further evidence of value and impact.

3. Initiating Phase 1 of the Blueprint: the DataPool project

The DataPool continuation project provided the opportunity to progress and extend the first phase of that roadmap.[22] Taking as a starting point the principles outlined in IDMB, the intention was to promote the framework across a full range of disciplines and to assess its adaptability to the more complex issues surrounding multi-disciplinary research.[23] One of the challenges was to create sufficient impetus to engagement by both the researcher community and the university to take the issues beyond a project approach into a sustainable service infrastructure. IDMB had provided the framework and had established a network of senior managers, disciplinary leaders, faculty contacts and data producers; it was the role of DataPool to create the infrastructure needed to realize it. As with IDMB, DataPool was therefore as much about cultural as technical change.

DataPool set out six key objectives designed to blend policy and infrastructure with local discipline perspectives. These were:

- Implement the draft institutional research data management policy with an associated one-stop-shop of web guidance and data management planning advice.
- Develop flexible support services and guidance for researchers extending across the research lifecycle.
- Create and embed a range of training materials and workshops for postgraduates and early career researchers.
- Enhance repository infrastructure to create comprehensive records of data outputs.
- Scope options for storage and archiving including institutional structures, locally managed storage of small-scale outputs and a platform for sharing data.
- Develop a suite of case studies to investigate multidisciplinary issues in depth, including gathering granular evidence for cost analysis.

These strands were interdependent and were pursued in parallel to maximize the benefits of cross-fertilization and to embed previous pilots into sustainable institutional services. The data management community was extended by embracing existing informal networks such as the multi-disciplinary University Strategic Research Groups (USRGs) and by engaging existing communication routes for research support between professional services and the academic community. The links with external sector providers were also extended through the involvement of senior academic co-investigators and the project steering group, which had the benefit of advice from representatives from the University of Oxford, the British Oceanographic Data Centre, the DCC and the UK Data Archive.[24]

3.1 Sustaining the research-led approach

Although compliance with funder policies had been a significant driver in engaging senior management, the team were conscious that researchers were most concerned with enhancing their research practice and heightening research impact. This posed issues for the team in terms of the variety of perspectives across the institution, and required close engagement with a wide range of researchers and nuanced disciplinary perspectives. This was particularly evident when drafts of the research data management policy were discussed. In the course of their liaison with colleagues, the nominated faculty champions raised a variety of issues relating to the implementation of the policy across the data lifecycle, appraising data for long-term retention, data security and sharing and the different roles and responsibilities in decision making. Given the importance of open access for the university, there were also discussions on the role of open data as a concept in data management practice.

In the light of these discussions the draft policy that had been drawn up under IDMB was modified and then presented to Senate in February 2012, with associated web guidance.[25] It was emphasized in discussions at Senate that the policy was intended to be iterative and that the guidance would develop in response to feedback with relevant amendments being made on the basis of the experience. This was in part a response to the body of opinion that remained sceptical as to the financial implications and cost-benefit of implementing policy at an institutional level, and confirmed the team's view that aside from funder requirements the emphasis should be on the embedding of good practice. The policy having been passed by Senate, the DataPool team were able to focus on developing the service infrastructure (White and Brown, 2013).

3.2 Integrated workflow: storage, security and archiving – Phase 2

IDMB had highlighted the complexities facing researchers over storage and archiving. The DataPool project team recognized that without development in this area researcher engagement would be limited. The cost modelling undertaken as part of the IDMB project set out options, but did not provide fully scoped business models which could convince the university to undertake large-scale investment. Attention therefore focused on options for developing one of the infrastructure components, a registry function for the deposit and tracking of data. The archaeology pilot had confirmed that even where a discipline had access to a national repository for the archiving and sharing of data, there was a need for local infrastructure to deposit and describe data.

In approaching this issue the team understood that a 'one size fits all' approach was unlikely to be successful. From the audit it was clear that researchers had preferences about how they gathered and explored their data and in some cases this required high levels of security, which made them sceptical towards central networked solutions. The point at which a researcher decides to deposit data in a registry would differ between disciplines; some researchers would welcome a workflow management system similar to that offered in a virtual research environment (VRE) while others would only want to deposit final data at the end of the project. In terms of ingest the audit indicated that researchers in some disciplines had a preference for depositing data through the existing ePrints research repository, whereas in terms of longer-term infrastructure developments ePrints might not be able to sustain storage across all disciplines. As the university was engaged in a pilot to evaluate SharePoint 2010, it was decided to explore both ePrints and SharePoint as potential registry systems using the three-layer metadata model. As part of this evaluation it was hoped that some data might be interfaced directly from other corporate systems, thereby easing the burden on researchers in adding data.

The SharePoint application was ambitious. The first phase of a model was developed which provided researchers with a facility to deposit, manage and share data with colleagues during the lifecycle of a project, and potentially to export data to an external repository. With input from a group of PhD students and researchers in a range of disciplines, an initial working demonstrator was designed, but further work was dependent on a university decision over the university SharePoint 2010 evaluation. Due to delays in this process further work on implementation has not proceeded as planned, and the business case for the next phase is still being assessed. SharePoint proved to be potentially flexible and to offer the prospect of importing relevant data from other corporate systems such as HR and finance, but despite the success of the initial pilot, the level of knowledge and expertise needed to develop the software outstripped the resources of the project. The work with SharePoint underlined the tension between embedding research data management requirements into a large-scale institutional strategic IT deployment and the flexibility to respond quickly to researcher feedback. It is clear from the Jisc programme as a whole that seamless technical workflow through the stages of the research lifecycle across all disciplines at scale is a sector-wide challenge.

Attention therefore turned to the option to extend the ePrints research repository to encompass the function of a registry for data linked primarily to research papers. Whereas SharePoint was perceived as a possible 'front door' for both managing working data and final secure deposit, the ePrints model is being developed for deposit and access to research findings supporting published research. This approach meets the requirement of funders to identify how research findings can be accessed.[26]

ePrints has the advantage of being familiar to researchers across the institution, and has a community of common interest across the sector. Although ePrints is not able to handle the storage of 'big data', it can act as a registry and facilitate the deposit of data in significant discipline areas. In pursuing this option Southampton was also able to benefit from the work taken forward on metadata modelling by the University of Essex in the ReCollect EPrints data app,[27] and from the discussions between the Universities of Essex, Southampton, Glasgow and Leeds and EPrints Services on standards and field mapping. There was agreement that local implementations should keep core metadata such as that required for DataCite and INSPIRE in common and to register a commitment to engage as an EPrints community on future developments in this area. The ReCollect app is now integrated into the live service at Southampton and we anticipate that use of this service will provide additional feedback to inform service enhancements.

Using ePrints to facilitate data management requirements showed the advantage of enhancing at relatively low cost an existing service with a broad user base. The 'innovation to service' model was associated with a parallel development, the use of automated tools to support minting of DataCite DOIs that have been developed by researchers in the Chemistry department. Building on the existing UK National Crystallography Service repository, where there is already expertise in using DOIs to link to publications, this has created momentum to explore options for a multidisciplinary approach to the use of identifiers with DataCite. Work undertaken by Chemistry in relation to the LabTrove notebooks has also investigated potential granularity of DOI links. This includes modelling how a landing page might work within the dynamic notebook environment while at the same time providing a snapshot to support a publication.[28]

As DataCite is specifically set up for data and has a growing researcher-led engagement and sector support through the British Library, there is a commitment to move to the DataCite Service. The disciplinary activity with Crystallography has evolved a generic app to automate DOI minting in EPrints. This is now being implemented in the central ePrints Soton repository and we are starting to explore policy implications. Whilst there is perceived institutional risk in assigning a DOI inappropriately, there is strong steer from senior researchers to take a pragmatic view to development, working with trusted frequent users and those with datasets underpinning publications as early adopters, whilst less clear-cut and more unusual cases are discussed.

3.3 Integrated workflow: multidisciplinary case studies

If there were advantages in building on existing services and extending their application across disciplines, the DataPool case studies highlighted the need to think through the implications for specific areas where such a generic approach might not meet researcher needs.[29] In the report on imaging, for example, it was confirmed that there existed extensive guidance on the effective management of raster and 3D data, but this was unevenly distributed across disciplines. It was also shown that there was insufficient entry-level guidance and insufficient resources were available to assist researchers in applying general principles to their own work (Beale and Pagi, 2013).

The Integrated Modelling of European Migration (IMEM) database case study created a database and visualization tool that could be applied across disciplines, which explored the characteristics of probability distributions (Wisniowski, Chivers and Whitton, 2013), and the Tweeting study investigated various approaches to capturing and archiving tweets (Hitchcock, 2013a). These studies provided evidence of where service and institutional support could provide benefits to the researcher, and emphasized the potential complications facing researchers in providing evidence to funders of their impact and archiving strategies.

The case studies have revealed some relatively 'quick wins' to promote change in practice: for example, the addition of raster and 3D equipment to the cross-institutional EPSRC-funded national equipment registry that is being set up to share resources across institutions. They have also provided a level of detail on storage requirements that can feed into business planning and create a narrative around investment and value. Also of value to business modelling was work on the potential of shared and third-party services. Of particular significance was the development of an app linking EPrints to Arkivum's A-Stor archiving service.[30] This could be a component of a range of business models, including the potential to link with the DataCite implementation and the emerging service model for LabTrove electronic notebooks. The Jisc programme has inspired much discussion of possible shared-services solutions and this is an area we will be continuing to explore.

3.4 The data management planning service

Evidence from the case studies was fed into a new data management planning (DMP) service. Given the range and complexity of research proposals, providing a generic advice service for specific discipline requirements poses particular issues for the building of a trusted partnership. Our approach has been to provide web-based guidance to help interpret funders' requirements, to offer desk-side consultation and to refer specific issues to specialists in the discipline or data area. Raising awareness of the service across the university has been important as a means to bring together knowledge and expertise and provide the best advice. Key roles in this area are those of the faculty business relationship managers for the central IT services (iSolutions), academic liaison staff in the library supporting specific disciplines, collaboration managers, bid managers and research support officers in Research and Innovation Services who, due to their involvement with the bid process, can contribute to specific areas such as intellectual property.

The DMP service is also proving important for engaging more experienced researchers who are time-pressured and can be harder to reach. Awareness of policy requirements among this group can sometimes be limited and the need to complete a DMP is a spur to engagement. In the Faculties of Medicine, Health Sciences and Natural and Environmental Sciences this has led to requests for training for principal investigators on research data management plans, which has in turn provided examples for the training DataPool has been developing for PhD researchers. Researchers have sometimes started out looking for a template solution, but the feedback from the face-to-face support is a positive way of enhancing the programme and providing links across projects to such exemplars, as business-cases for more specialist data management.

3.5 Developing a training programme

IDMB had piloted an initial training template based on a workshop approach for archaeology research students. The DMP service has led to direct requests for specific DMP training for all staff from early-career researchers to PIs. Figure 7.2 illustrates the approach taken to engage with the various groups involved with research data management from the new postgraduate researcher to the experienced principal investigator. It shows how events are channelled through existing structures reflecting lifecycle, format and audience with co-delivery in each case between professional services and researchers.

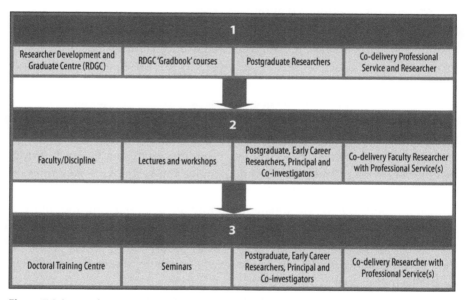

Figure 7.2 Approach to engagement and co-delivery of services (from Byatt et al., 2013a)

In developing the training programme, reference is being made to the VITAE Researcher Development Framework and parallel work in other Jisc programme projects and the DCC that is broadening understanding of how training can play an important role in supporting researchers. Co-delivery of training has been very effective, particularly in sessions aimed at postgraduate or early-career researchers, and PhD students have been involved in developing the supporting guidance and disciplinary case studies as well as co-delivering training.

Implementing the programme has revealed a number of important issues in balancing generic and specialized content, positioning the audience in terms of their knowledge and experience, and identifying the appropriate length and format of the workshops. For generic sessions, for example, feedback indicates that it would be productive to provide more time for discussion on different aspects of data management, to enhance thinking of how practices might be changed. It would also be useful to signpost level and content more clearly so that researchers gain the most from their attendance. Extending the range of training in terms of the research lifecycle, training at masters' level has been piloted, and data management has been embedded in a new MSc in Instrumental Analytical Chemistry, which has data management as one of the modules.

An evolving programme of training for professional services staff has been designed which will be further developed by incorporating the results of a survey exploring levels of staff confidence in various research data management areas and knowledge of referral options. The survey has also been completed by staff in the University of Oxford, which provides useful comparative data and opportunities for joint/regional training (Byatt et al., 2013b). This partnership between services and academic groups which are often focused on quite specific issues for their research is particularly valuable for engaging with the issues of multidisciplinary research, but it also raises issues about the breadth of knowledge and expertise which can be accrued by those offering training within the professional support services. The current survey to assess the needs of library and computing professional service staff, and how these can be supported, will facilitate further reflection and iteration. As researchers' level of engagement and expectations rise, there can be significant issues for the services in being able to respond effectively at the different levels required. The investigation will therefore be reviewing both the capacity and the scope for using a wider variety of approaches.

4. Reflections on current progress

The DataPool project came to an end in March 2013. In terms of building institutional capacity within the framework laid out in the first phase of the IDMB roadmap, it had signalled some of the major challenges and showed how some solutions might be put in place. It had taken these forward to the next stage of development and significantly extended institutional and researcher engagement. Of the four key components outlined in the roadmap, three had been delivered to a point where they were poised to be recognized in policy and practice. An institutional policy framework had been agreed and implemented, the basis for a working institutional data registry had been scoped within ePrints, and a one-stop shop for data management advice and guidance to provide information on policy, legal issues and guidance had been put in place. The gap remains the development of an agreed, scalable, and sustainable business model for storage based on the three components of active data, descriptive metadata and archive storage. Scoping work has taken place, but as this developed it was clear that the financial and systems investment would be considerable. The university recognizes the issues involved, but has to be convinced that a single, standalone institutional solution can be realistically funded and implemented. At the point of writing thinking is now pointing towards collaborative shared services.

The IDMB and DataPool projects provided a focus for the university to address the question of how Southampton should design and deliver its research data management strategy. If some of what was presented in the IDMB roadmap was too far in the future to be embraced with certainty, the concept of a gradual and iterative process embodying good practice was established in institutional thinking and some key milestones defined. The progress made under IDMB set the scene for the programme of work in DataPool, which began the process of embedding policy into services that could support researchers. The continuity between the two phases was reinforced by the existence of a common core project team who acted as change agents. Both projects were essentially about cultural change, which was to be nurtured through a combination of a top-down and a bottom-up approach.

In terms of the top-down element, there is no doubt that a formal university policy on research data management was very important in achieving visibility for a collective approach across the university. The team was careful to work through a process of consultation before the policy was formally put to Senate, and that process made the policy more acceptable in the eyes of the research community. The team was also aware that without a responsive approach to some of the key concerns of researchers it would not be an effective mechanism to take forward the agenda. Through the common governance structure for both IDMB and DataPool, the DVC Research and Enterprise, the Provost and the Associate Deans (Research) were all associated with the investigations and outcomes. Senior university management was therefore well informed about the issues, and the same governance model is being taken forward in the post-project phase, emphasizing the long-term approach set out under IDMB. The team hopes that this will act as the political mainspring for future infrastructure investment; up until now convincing evidence for a return on investment is lacking. The next phase is to work alongside specific externally funded projects with each faculty to strengthen disciplinary narratives and provide more granular evidence.

Although top-down policy and support was important, the development of low-cost, low-overhead solutions to some of the challenges facing researchers as a result of institutional or funder requirements was a major incentive for cultural change. The researcher-led approach was taken forward in a number of ways. The project group itself was forged through collaboration between academics across a variety of disciplines and the leading academic support services. PhD students and research fellows have been significant contributors, offering knowledge of specialist data needs and contributing to training. This peer engagement has meant that they have also acted as key change agents, often bridging gaps between research groups across disciplines. They have led project activity through the case studies, contributed to testing the SharePoint and ePrints developments, designed training material and led workshops, often in conjunction with colleagues from the services. They have also contributed specific technical expertise as part of service development. For PhD and research Fellows the informal networks have played a key role in developing and engaging with communities of practice.

PhD researchers, Research Fellows and technical experts have led strands of the project that aim to promote an 'innovation to service' approach that ties in with the mid-phase of the institutional roadmap. The multi-disciplinary case studies on imaging requirements and data visualization for impact both provided evidence of innovation that can be embedded in services. The technical work which has provided EPrints bazaar apps to automate DataCite DOI minting and link EPrints to Arkivum storage gives us an opportunity for community implementation and service refinement. Further proof of concept work with DOI minting for Labtrove electronic notebooks and data transfer to Arkivum pave the way for possible shared services approaches with roles for third-party providers.

Reflecting on the progress since 2009, it is clear that the issues surrounding research data management are becoming more complex rather than less. We now understand much more about the range of data to be managed, its size and sophistication and the expectations of researchers to manage workflows and share data. We also know that at institutional level the requirements of government and funders are placing potentially significant financial costs on institutions which they are finding challenging to bear in the present financial climate. Our approach has been to build a partnership around discipline needs, researcher workflow, low-cost technological applications and training support, and this will be integral to the way in which we continue with the implementation of the IDMB roadmap.

5. References

5.1 Web resources and explanatory notes

1 The UKRDS feasibility study was in part a response to the Office of Science and Innovation report (OSI, 2007), on developing the UK's e-infrastructure for science and innovation and led to funding by HEFCE for a shared services programme.

2 UKRDS (http://web.archive.org/web/*/http://www.ukrds.ac.uk) was perceived as a centre of excellence, as a standards-guiding body and as a source of expertise and information about data management and repositories, commissioning additional capacity and building on current best practice and facilities.

3 Only 12% of researchers surveyed did not make their data available in any way, according to the UKRDS Final Proposal, p.13, http://web.archive.org/web/*/http://www.ukrds.ac.uk/resources.

4 Jisc Managing Research Data programme, www.jisc.ac.uk/whatwedo/programmes/mrd.aspx.

5 DataPool Project, www.jisc.ac.uk/whatwedo/programmes/di_researchmanagement/ managingresearchdata/infrastructure/datapool.aspx.

6 Kenji Takeda (Engineering Sciences), Mark Brown (University Librarian), Wendy White (Head of Scholarly Communication), Simon Coles (Chemistry), Les Carr (Electronics and Computer Science, Eprints), Jeremy Frey (Chemistry), Peter Hancock (iSolutions), Graeme Earl (Archaeology).

7 See Southampton Data Management, www.southamptondata.org.

8 The DCC (www.dcc.ac.uk) focuses on building capacity, capability and skills for research data management across the UK's higher education research community, and was a key partner in the Jisc-funded projects.

9 IDMP, Integrated Data Management Planning Toolkit & Support, ran from January 2010 to March 2011, wwwjisc.ac.uk/whatwedo/programmes/mrd/ supportprojects/idmpsupport.aspx.

10 See, for example, the early work of Jeremy Frey in Chemistry at Southampton,

http://eprints.soton.ac.uk/38009/2/www2006_panel.pdf.

11   iSolutions is the name given to the University of Southampton Computing Service.

12   Section iii of the EPSRC policy (EPSRC, 2011) states 'Each research organisation will have specific policies and associated processes to maintain effective internal awareness of their publicly-funded research data holdings and of requests by third parties to access such data; all of their researchers or research students funded by EPSRC will be required to comply with research organisation policies in this area or, in exceptional circumstances, to provide justification of why this is not possible.'

13   Specifically the Deputy Vice-Chancellor for Research and Enterprise, the Provost and the Registrar and Chief Operating Officer.

14   The Research Data Management Policy was agreed by Senate in February 2012 and published in the University Calendar, www.calendar.soton.ac.uk/sectionIV/research-data-management.html.

15   Data management questionnaire results: IDMB Project (Whitton and Takeda, 2011). The disciplines represented in the audit were electronics and computer science, engineering sciences, geography, humanities, maths, psychology and social sciences.

16   There were a number of significant deposits outside the framework of the Research Councils' data centres, including the Africa Centre for Health and Population Studies, the Max Planck Institute for Demographic Research and TPTP (Thousands of Problems for Theorem Provers).

17   In the EPSRC policy (EPSRC, 2011) there was an expectation that there would be 'appropriately structured metadata describing the research data held which would be freely accessible on the internet, and that EPSRC-funded research data is securely preserved for a minimum of 10-years from the date that any researcher "privileged access" period expires or, if others have accessed the data, from last date on which access to the data was requested by a third party', www.epsrc.ac.uk/about/standards/researchdata/Pages/policyframework.aspx.

18   The Business Model forms Appendix B of the IDBM itself (Brown, Parchment and White, 2011), http://eprints.soton.ac.uk/196241.

19   Archaeology Data Service Guidelines for Depositors, http://archaeologydataservice.ac.uk/advice/guidelinesForDepositors.

20   Welcome to eCrystals, http://ecrystals.chem.soton.ac.uk.

21   DataShare Project, www.jisc.ac.uk/whatwedo/programmes/reppres/sue/datashare.aspx.

22   The DataPool website contains links to the reports and the blog maintained by

Steve Hitchcock, joint project manager, throughout the project, Document1, http://datapool.soton.ac.uk.

23 The DataPool team was the same as that for IDMB except that with the departure of Kenji Takeda the role of principal investigator was placed with the University Library.

24 Steering Group: Louise Corti (Associate Director, UK Data Archive), Graham Pryor (Associate Director, Digital Curation Centre), Sally Rumsey (Digital Research Manager at The Bodleian Libraries, University of Oxford), Helen Snaith (National Oceanography Centre, Southampton), Philip Nelson (Pro-Vice-Chancellor Research), Adam Wheeler (Provost and Deputy Vice-Chancellor), Mylene Ployart (Associate Director, Research and Innovation Services) and the project investigators.

25 The policy was published in the University Calendar with links to four guidance sheets on topics which the research community had prioritized in the discussions on the policy: Storage Options, Guidance on Retention Periods, Recommended Practices for Destruction of Data and Restricting Access to Research Data, www.calendar.soton.ac.uk/sectionIV/research-data-management.html.

26 This requirement is contained within the RCUK open access policy released in 2012. The current guidance confirms that each publication must include a statement on access to the underlying research materials, www.rcuk.ac.uk/documents/documents/RCUKOpenAccessPolicy.pdf.

27 See UK Data Service, www.data-archive.ac.uk/media/395364/rde_march2013_repositoryoutputs.pdf.

28 See http://datapool.soton.ac.uk/2012/12/18/trialling-datacite-for-chemistry-lab-notebooks-and-repository-data-services.

29 Datapool carried out three case studies based around multidisciplinary imaging, data visualization and impact, and tweeting, and produced a cost-benefit analysis (Hitchcock, 2013b) built around the management of significant-sized data and the value of an institutional approach. This report included the Open Data Service at Southampton.

30 Arkivum A-Stor Storage Backend plug-in, http://bazaar.eprints.org/285.

5.2 Citations

BBC News (2005) 'Fire destroys top research centre', 31 October, http://news.bbc.co.uk/1/hi/england/hampshire/4390048.stm.
Beale, G. and Pagi, H. (2013) *DataPool Imaging Case Study: final report*, University of Southampton, http://eprints.soton.ac.uk/id/eprint/350738.

Brown, M., Parchment, O. and White, W. (2011) *Institutional Data Management Blueprint*, University of Southampton, http://eprints.soton.ac.uk/196241.

Byatt, D., Scott, M., Beale, G., Cox, S. J. and White, W. (2013a) *Developing Researcher Skills in Research Data Management: training for the future – a DataPool project report*, University of Southampton, http://eprints.soton.ac.uk/id/eprint/351026.

Byatt, D., De Luca, F., Gibbs, H., Patrick, M., Rumsey, S. and White, W. (2013b), *Supporting Researchers with their Research Data Management: professional service training requirements – a DataPool project report*, University of Southampton, http://eprints.soton.ac.uk/352107.

Earl, G., White, W. and Wake, P. (2011) *IDMB Archaeology Case Study: summary*, University of Southampton, http://eprints.soton.ac.uk/196237.

EPSRC (Engineering and Physical Sciences Research Council) (2011) www.epsrc.ac.uk/about/standards/researchdata/Pages/policyframework.aspx.

Heery, R., Duke, M., Day, M., Lyon, L., Hursthouse, M. B., Frey, J., Coles, S. J., Gutteridge, C. and Carr, L. A. (2004) *Integrating Research Data into the Publication Workflow: the eBank UK experience*, University of Southampton, http://eprints.soton.ac.uk/9705/1/PV2004-heery.pdf.

Hitchcock, S. (2013a) *Collecting and Archiving Tweets: a DataPool case study*, University of Southampton, http://eprints.soton.ac.uk/id/eprint/350646.

Hitchcock, S. (2013b) *Cost Benefit Analysis Experience of Southampton Research Data Producers*, http://datapool.soton.ac.uk/2013/03/21/cost-benefit-analysis-experience-of-southampton-research-data-producers.

OSI (Office of Science and Innovation) e-Infrastructure Working Group (2007) *Developing the UK's E-infrastructure for Science and Innovation*, www.nesc.ac.uk/documents/OSI.

RCUK (Research Councils UK) (2011) *Common Principles on Data Policy*, www.rcuk.ac.uk/research/Pages/DataPolicy.aspx.

Times Higher Education (2010) 'There's More to a Story Than Facts and Figures', 25 November, www.timeshighereducation.co.uk/414350.article.

White, W. and Brown, M. (2013) *DataPool: engaging with our Research Data Management Policy*, University of Southampton, http://eprints.soton.ac.uk/id/eprint/351945.

Whitton, M. and Takeda, K. (2011) *Data Management Questionnaire Results: IDMB project*, University of Southampton, http://eprints.soton.ac.uk/196243.

Wisniowski, A., Chivers, M. and Whitton, M. (2013) *Integrated Modelling of European Migration Database Case Study*, University of Southampton, http://eprints.soton.ac.uk/id/eprint/350672.

CHAPTER 8

Case study 3: Monash University, a strategic approach

Anthony Beitz, David Groenewegen, Cathrine Harboe-Ree, Wilna Macmillan and Sam Searle

1. Introduction

Monash University recognizes that if research data is better managed, more discoverable, available for reuse and exposed to relevant communities it will contribute to increased research impact, enhanced research practice (including collaboration) and improved education outcomes.

Monash has taken on the challenge of developing research data management (RDM) using a multifaceted, multilevel and strategic approach. This has included leadership and participation in large Australian Federal Government initiatives at the same time as using 'little steps' approaches within the institution. Monash has led national projects to prototype and develop RDM infrastructure, assumed responsibility as the lead agency of the government-funded Australian National Data Service (ANDS), formed an institutional structure for RDM governance, established a Strategy and Strategic Plan for 2012–15 and an RDM policy with associated procedures and guidelines, delivered programmes for RDM skills development, established a petabyte data store and developed and deployed a range of discipline-specific and versatile solutions for the management of research data and associated metadata.

The university continues to identify RDM as critically significant to its research performance and to the fulfilment of compliance requirements and community expectations. All members of the Monash community share responsibility to improve RDM in a co-ordinated and integrated way; to support this, the university has made ongoing appointments into research data management roles while also seconding librarians and information technology staff into shorter-term positions to build capability and expertise.

This chapter explores the university's work in the period from 2006 to 2013 and examines the issues and challenges to be resolved when planning and implementing effective RDM. It describes in some detail the characteristics of Monash's organizational approach to RDM, explores both the non-technical and technical components of Monash's RDM infrastructure, looks at what developments are anticipated and outlines Monash's strategy to promote sustainable RDM infrastructure.

2. Background

2.1 Monash University's research environment and history in research data management

Monash University was established in 1958 and comprises ten faculties on six Australian campuses. It also has campuses in Malaysia and South Africa as well as centres in Italy, India and China. The student body numbers around 63,000, from more than 100 countries (7.1% of these are higher degree by research students). The university has approximately 3800 academic staff and received over $AU282 million in externally funded research income in 2011.

Although Monash conducts research across numerous fields of study – over 150 in all – it has a particular focus on a number of specializations, described internally as 'leading capabilities'. These capabilities fall into four categories, aligned closely with the Australian Commonwealth Government's National Research Priorities and its National Collaborative Research Infrastructure Strategy. They are:

- Health and wellbeing (accident, injury and trauma, cancer, health, wellbeing and social change, infection and immunity, neuroscience)
- New therapeutics (public health, stem cells and regenerative medicine and women's, children's and reproductive health)
- New industries and productivity (advanced manufacturing, aerospace, energy-related materials, nanomaterials)
- Sustainable environments (climate change and weather, energy, green chemistry, sustainability and urban water) and resilient cultures and communities (development economics, economic modelling, education, mental health law).

Monash's journey towards more effective RDM began with the release of its information management strategy in 2006, the establishment of a Research Data Management Subcommittee, and the subsequent creation of a dedicated organization-wide Data Management Coordinator role based within the library. Monash's decision to provide centrally funded digital research data storage for all researchers, including higher-degree research students (HDRs), was a great incentive for researchers to think about their research data and how it might be better managed. This was a significant practical expression of the university's intention and commitment to improve RDM.

With the release of the *Australian Code for the Responsible Conduct of Research* in 2007 (see below), Monash established a Research Governance Implementation Committee (RGIC). This provided the context and a process for the development and endorsement of the RDM policy and procedures for staff, adjuncts and visitors as part of a full review of all research-related policies and procedures. The iterative process of developing these policies was used as a communication and awareness-raising activity in its own right. At Monash, all policies are required to have associated procedures and guidelines. In order to provide practical guidelines on data management issues for researchers a data management website was launched, developed by the Data Management Coordinator.

Well into the development of the policy and procedures for staff, Monash's Research Graduate School (now known as the Monash Institute of Graduate Research) indicated that it wanted to develop procedures targeted specifically for HDRs, to parallel those for staff. The RDM policy and staff procedures were endorsed by the Academic Board in 2010 and the separate but related HDR procedures in early 2011. The RDM strategy and strategic plan were endorsed in 2012.

These activities have led to new research outcomes, better research practices and facilitated collaborative research. For instance, the Biomedical Data Platform data capture solution, MyTARDIS, is a multi-institutional collaborative venture. It facilitates the archiving and sharing of data and metadata collected at major facilities such as the Australian Synchrotron and Australian Nuclear Science Technology Organisation, and within Monash University and other institutions (see section 5.1 for more detail). Monash is now investing in an extended programme of co-ordinated RDM activities that holistically address technology, professional development and cultural change. Monash began trialling a faculty-wide approach to improving RDM with a small faculty, Pharmacy and Pharmaceutical Science. The outcomes of this trial are discussed in section 4.1.

2.2 The Australian research environment

One critical aspect of the Australian research landscape is the *Australian Code for the Responsible Conduct of Research* (NHMRC et al., 2007), a guide to good research practice and research integrity, which details areas such as authorship, collaboration, research training and broader research practice. It also covers the management of research data and primary materials, outlining the responsibilities of researchers and their institutions. As a result, it has provided guidance for much of the RDM effort to date in Australia. In regard to RDM, the *Code* is aspirational. All Australian universities have formally agreed to be guided by it; however, at the time of writing, there are currently no audit processes associated with the RDM sections. Monash has focused on improvements rather than compliance, while using the document to provide context and to raise awareness.

Within the *Code*, RDM is expressed as a joint responsibility, requiring researchers to manage their data well and their institutions to provide tools, advice and processes to enable them to achieve this. As part of the institutional commitment to shared responsibility noted in the *Code*, Monash took a critical first step by offering a large-scale institutionally managed digital research data store, with essentially unlimited storage for researchers and HDRs. Monash was the first Australian university to provide this service. The storage is paid for centrally, so it can be offered at no direct cost to researchers. The barriers to adopting this solution are thereby reduced, as is the need for researchers to purchase less persistent and lower-quality storage from elsewhere, which was a key consideration in its design. Storage is of course only a part of data management, but its ready availability facilitates conversations around other aspects.

Australia has two main government funding councils for publicly funded research, the Australian Research Council (ARC) and the National Health and Medical Research Council (NHMRC). Policies introduced by both require publications from funded research projects to be made available on open access within 12 months of publication, but they do not mandate the deposit of data into repositories. Unlike in the UK, there is no history of disciplinary archives in Australia, with the exception of the Australian Social Science Data Archive (now the Australian Data Archive), so the funding bodies have been less inclined to mandate the deposit of data. There is, however, a strong institutional repositories community, due to the provision of significant government start-up funding – much of which has been directed to university libraries – and the central role of repositories in Excellence in Research Australia (ERA), a government research quality assessment exercise. This means that libraries across the country have been well placed to become involved in institutional RDM developments. It is worth noting that data management plans are not promoted in the *Code* or local research funder guidelines, although the requirement to maintain registries or inventories is; as a result, Monash does not actively require researchers to lodge plans, focusing instead on improving practice through the provision of documentation relevant to particular projects.

The Australian government further supported development in this area through the National Collaborative Research Infrastructure Strategy Program (NCRIS) and the Education Investment Fund (EIF) Super Science Initiative. Of particular relevance to data management have been the $AU75 million investment in capability building and infrastructure for data reuse in the form of the Australian National Data Service (ANDS), the AU$50 million investment in national research data storage called Research Data Storage Infrastructure (RDSI)[1] and the $AU47 million investment in collaborative research infrastructure known as National e-Research Collaboration Tools and Resources (NeCTAR).[2] These projects have injected large sums into research institutions across the country to pursue projects in this area.

As Monash is the lead agent for the ANDS project it has been particularly closely involved with ANDS' work. ANDS has established several national services in research data management, has helped to publish data collections that are managed, connected, discoverable and reusable, has partnered with institutions to establish coherent institutional research data infrastructure and has improved the ability of the Australian research system to exploit its research data using tools, policy and human capability.

ANDS partners with research organizations and government agencies to build a cross-connected data environment called the Australian Research Data Commons.[3] This environment can be accessed through Research Data Australia[4] which, as the Australian national research data collection, provides a window onto the commons. This portal publishes information on research data collections, the parties that generate them, the projects that used them and the services that enable access to the data or that exploit the data. ANDS has adopted this collections-focused approach to data because it is not possible to make a national cross-discipline portal that is optimized to all of the different types of data; for example, time series data is best accessed in very different ways to spatial data, and is different again to image collections that might be collected from a telescope or a microscope. Research Data Australia focuses rather on the national visibility of data collections within their richest possible research context by including related people, organizations, research projects, journal articles, access services, facilities, instruments, etc. While Research Data Australia enables discovery, access to the data is delivered through local institutional repositories and domain-specific access portals.

Funding from ANDS has had a significant impact on the range of services and projects undertaken at Monash, while also leading to the development of staff capability. Some of these activities are described below. Monash has made a number of collections available through Research Data Australia, and will continue to use its infrastructure to do so.

3. Organizational support for research data management

At Monash RDM is a shared responsibility, as is expected in the *Australian Code for the Responsible Conduct of Research*. The Provost, in association with senior managers, has been a staunch advocate for improving the management of research data, recognizing its potential for improved research practice with increased research impact, reuse and communication. Rather than using compliance with regulation to justify improvements in RDM, she advocates improvement as a means of increasing the value of the data, especially by making it more accessible as and when appropriate. Monash is fortunate to have this kind of understanding and commitment expressed at a high level, making it a key university objective.

Governance has changed from time to time, and now the Research Data Management Sub-Committee reports to the Academic Board through the Monash Research Committee. An RDM advisory group with a practitioner focus has also been established, with representatives from all faculties and other key areas. Leadership of the work to be undertaken is shared between the library, the Monash e-Research Centre (MeRC) and eSolutions (the university's information technology division), who work with the Research Office, the Monash Institute of Graduate Research and, of course, the researchers, research managers, research assistants, faculties, academic units and centres.

Through the efforts of the University Librarian the library is recognized as the chief steward of RDM at Monash. It co-ordinated the development of policy and strategy and provides leadership of the governance groups. It is also responsible for the co-ordination, development and implementation of RDM capability building and skills development for both researchers and professional staff, by providing advice to researchers directly and through the RDM website, leading the ongoing development of data management planning, curating strategically important data collections, and managing the Monash University Research Repository. The library has an ongoing professional development programme to equip subject librarians to participate actively in RDM advocacy across the university.

MeRC provides a bridge between the researchers and eSolutions, leads technical innovation in RDM infrastructure and provides RDM advice that is mainly technical in nature to researchers. eSolutions provides platforms-as-a-service, software-as-a-service, software development capabilities and technical support for technical RDM infrastructure.

4. Overview of Monash University's non-technical research data management infrastructure

Monash has spent time considering the breadth of possibilities in non-technical RDM infrastructure activities and subsequently divided activities into themes or groups. These themes have evolved over time and at the time of writing are:

- governance, policy and strategy
- information and advice
- knowledge and skills.

When Monash decided on its initial approach it was referred to as 'little steps', for even small steps in the right direction were recognized as significant improvements.

4.1 Governance, policy and strategy

The first iterations of the current Monash RDM policy were long, quite descriptive and experimented with organizing the information in different ways – for example, by responsibility or by stakeholder. The separation of content relating to higher-level policy principles and that relating to procedures enabled the fine-tuning of the policy, and provided a better understanding of the potential role of the procedures. The policy defines researchers, data management and research data and identifies stakeholders and their roles and responsibilities. Further refinement involved extensive consultation, which proved to be an effective outreach activity in its own right. To be effective it required an understanding of the researchers and the roles they play, as well as the need to establish partnerships between the university's areas of responsibility for policy, risk and audit, legal matters, research management, records and archives, commercialization, copyright/ intellectual property, ethics and research training, so that all could contribute to improving the policy and helping with harmonization.

Monash policies extend to all campuses, including those in Malaysia and South Africa, and wherever possible the RDM Policy is linked to related documents, policies and legislation, of which there are many. This process exposed the interconnections between RDM and other university policies, including those relating to intellectual property, ethics and record keeping.

The initial process of engagement focused on looking for early adopters across faculties by choosing research groups and approaching them about their RDM needs. It was notable that all researchers who were spoken with wanted to improve their data management and welcomed advice and assistance. This process was not intended to focus on HDRs, but discussions with senior researchers led to a focus on this cohort because fostering best practice amongst HDRs is more likely to change the overall environment in the long run, as they are the future of research practice.

One of the first faculties to adopt the new Monash RDM Policy was the Faculty of Pharmacy & Pharmaceutical Sciences (PPS), a discipline that produces and values raw data. The Associate Dean of Research was a member of both the Monash Research Committee and the Research Governance Implementation Committee and consequently was prepared to take the lead in promoting the objectives of the new policy within the faculty while developing practical processes to improve the management of their research data.

PPS was a very useful area in which to begin at Monash, because it is a small single-campus research-active faculty with a culture of discoverable records for drug development. Some groups within this faculty have been early adopters of electronic laboratory notebooks, which offer interesting challenges. Laboratory notebooks have long been a key source of data about research and replicating their unique attributes in the digital form for the long term has proven difficult, not least because of the cost of implementation. The outcomes of engagement with PPS have been:

- establishment of a faculty subcommittee, led by the Associate Dean of Research, that includes researchers, faculty information technology staff, the Research Manager and representatives from MeRC and the library
- connection of the faculty's local central data storage to the university's large institutional research data store, enabling nightly archival transfers

- mandated network storage for honours students with agreed file directory structures and naming protocols for funded projects (although persuading the students to adhere to this has been an ongoing challenge)
- new hardcopy laboratory notebook protocols (with electronic ones to be addressed in future)
- faculty leadership in training and cultural change in the area of RDM.

This project has also been a useful demonstration of the way that diverse sections of the university can work together to achieve aims in RDM. The Associate Dean of Research provides an introduction to honours and HDR students in association with library staff on campus, who follow up after induction. In the project the library has taken on the role of encouraging and marking progress through the 'little steps' approach, while MeRC and eSolutions contribute to and facilitate technical solutions.

This faculty recognized the benefits of improved research practices and the promotion of cultural change. Professor Chris Porter, the Associate Dean of Research, when asked for an impression of the experience and progress in mid-2011, responded by saying:

> Forcing ourselves to get in early with addressing the challenges of research data management has been very valuable. 'Wins' – such as central storage that is easily accessible by all staff – are proving to be much more powerful than perhaps we first thought. These systems are starting to focus attention on behaviours, and in many respects are changing the way data is viewed, shared, accessed, etc. So a physical solution is actually changing the way we work – which in the long run will be a more useful benefit than safe storage.
>
> (C. Porter, personal communication, 2011)

This illustrates the importance of both technical solutions and the role of people in order to achieve a long-term impact. While of course there is more to do, the shared responsibility approach is working and will continue to bring improvements.

4.2 Information and advice

The RDM website (a component of the library's website) is the main focus of the information and advice theme. Figure 8.1 shows the RDM website's introductory page. It raises researchers' awareness of RDM and provides

Figure 8.1 Screenshot of Monash University's research data management website

guidelines in dealing with common RDM issues. The website contains current information about:

- planning, ownership, copyright, ethics and consent, storage and back-up
- case studies
- training seminars and material
- relevant resources (such as Monash's RDM strategy and policy documents).

RDM information and advice are also available through a range of introductory printed materials and a strong focus on interpersonal communication.

4.3 Knowledge and skills

Much work is taking place in the area of skills development. In particular, new HDR students are made aware of data management through a range of events including induction sessions, presentations, consultations with groups and individuals, attendance at special events such as the annual Monash e-Research e-XPO and extended sessions run by learning skills advisors and subject librarians.

Librarians, frequently in collaboration with MeRC and faculty staff, have contributed to a range of local programmes, campus research days and HDR activities. The library has also developed programmes that include RDM, such as the Focus series of workshops that run at least twice yearly for HDRs in medicine, nursing and health sciences. Working with the Monash Institute of Graduate Research, the library has contributed RDM content to inductions and supervisor training and has been running two-hour data management planning workshops for new HDR students. More formal procedures may emerge in future, for example tying confirmation of candidature to some form of data plan or asking HDR students to deposit data associated with theses. The Monash Institute of Graduate Research has been developing a more formal training and coursework programme for HDR students and early adopting faculties began some of these programmes in 2012. The library has been working with the institute and with faculties to provide RDM and other discipline-tailored skills development opportunities.

While policies and procedures are about best practice, it is possible and desirable to frame RDM in different ways when talking to researchers. After much engagement with its researchers, Monash has evolved communication strategies that focus on benefits and ask researchers to imagine a future in which better RDM has made a real difference to everyone's day-to-day working life. In the belief that in the long run carrots are more effective than sticks, Monash tries to take a 'what's in it for you' approach to RDM training.

4.4 Sustainability of non-technical research data management infrastructure

In order to sustain non-technical RDM infrastructure activities, Monash is seeking to integrate them into the wider outreach and teaching roles of the university so that RDM is seen as an overall part of good research practice rather than an exceptional or special activity. To achieve this, the role of Data Management Coordinator is expected to develop into that of a 'broker', one that provides input and advice into a broad range of university engagement with researchers.

5. Monash University's technical research data management infrastructure

Research institutions are increasingly aware of the need to ensure that their approach to RDM contributes to their institutional research strategies and goals and to this end they require fit-for-purpose RDM infrastructure to enable leading-edge research, increase research outcomes and impact, validate research, reduce legal risk and attract the best researchers and additional research income. All this must be within a clearly promulgated institutional context to ensure that funds invested in infrastructure are not wasted.

Researchers need RDM infrastructure to achieve new research outcomes and higher research impact, to safeguard their data and deal with the data deluge, to facilitate collaboration, enable data reuse and validate their research. They also need to conform to funding body requirements, institutional policies, legal obligations, codes of conduct and cultural norms. Researchers themselves are generally focused on research outcomes, have goals that may change over time, and may be more loyal to their research community than their institution. As a result, if research institutions deploy RDM infrastructure that does not serve researchers' needs, researchers are likely to deploy their own, engage with external RDM infrastructure or move to a research institution that they perceive will provide for their needs.

Researcher and institutional needs can, therefore, be markedly different even though both recognize that research data and its associated metadata are critical to achieving their goals. Monash has considered these issues in the selection, development and deployment of RDM infrastructure and in the ongoing work to make RDM sustainable, and the resulting experience is now being used to develop the next generation of RDM infrastructure.

5.1 Enhancing research by integrating research data management infrastructure into the research workflow

Research workflow can be modelled in various ways, some more sophisticated than others. In order to demonstrate where research data management infrastructure fits into the research process, the workflow can be modelled as a simple linear sequence of activities, as shown in Figure 8.2.

This model demonstrates that the relationship between the research process, RDM principles and practical data management starts at the concept stage and continues beyond publication to the ongoing dissemination of findings. RDM and its associated platforms span the total lifecycle of research data by supporting the gathering and production of

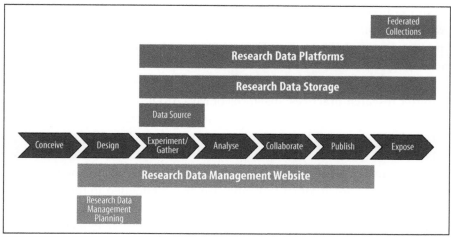

Stage	Description
Conceive	Conceiving a hypothesis to test.
Design	Designing a number of experiments to test the hypothesis.
Experiment/ Gather	For the sciences, conducting the experiments and collecting the results. For the arts, gathering research material.
Analyse	Analysing the results of the experiments and determining their findings.
Collaborate	Sharing findings with colleagues in order to gain different perspectives and to promote discussion.
Publish	Describing findings and making them publicly available.
Expose	Maximizing research impact by disseminating the findings to key target communities.

Figure 8.2 Associating research data management infrastructure with the research process

digital research data, analysis and sharing of results and publication of outcomes, and by ensuring ongoing impact of the research through discovery and reuse of the data by others. Publicly available research data needs to be well curated, its metadata harvestable in major formats, the data source registered with key repositories (such as institutional, national, and community portals) and references to the research data placed in key electronic journals. Underlying the research data platforms is research data storage. Recognition of the extent of the confluence between the research process and RDM has led Monash to implement RDM infrastructure which is either tailored to specific disciplines or else has enough flexibility to be adapted or repurposed to ensure that it supports the whole research process. Adoption of these platforms has led to better research practices, new research outcomes and facilitated collaborative research.

An example of an RDM platform that not only supports research at the project level but also provides broader benefits is the MyTARDIS platform for protein crystallography. This platform, developed by Monash, is facilitating:

- **Better research practices:** Instances of MyTARDIS now exist at the Australian Synchrotron and at many universities around Australia. As raw data is captured by the Synchrotron's Protein Crystallography beamlines, metadata is automatically extracted. If the owner of the data belongs to a university with a local instance of MyTARDIS, the metadata and raw data are automatically shipped and catalogued in the researcher's local instance of MyTARDIS.
- **New research outcomes:** Monash's instance of MyTARDIS has been collecting raw datasets for a number of years. Researchers analyse the raw datasets in order to solve the crystal's atomic structure but not all structures can be solved. However, new analysis techniques are now solving atomic structures that were previously unsolvable. These new techniques are now being applied to earlier unsolved raw datasets stored in MyTARDIS. This recently led to the resolution of the PlyC atomic structure. PlyC is a potential replacement for antibiotics and its discovery is a significant research outcome.
- **Collaborative research:** Data collections in MyTARDIS can be kept private, shared with other researchers, or made public. Data collections in MyTARDIS can also be registered in Research Data Australia – or with TARDIS, The Australian Repositories for Diffraction ImageS.[5]

5.2 High-level overview of research data management infrastructure

To provide a different perspective on the Monash RDM infrastructure, it can be split into six major categories, as shown in Figure 8.3.

This entire infrastructure need not be provided by an individual research institution; some elements may be provided by a state, national, international or commercial service provider. Monash has sought to identify a variety of options where appropriate.

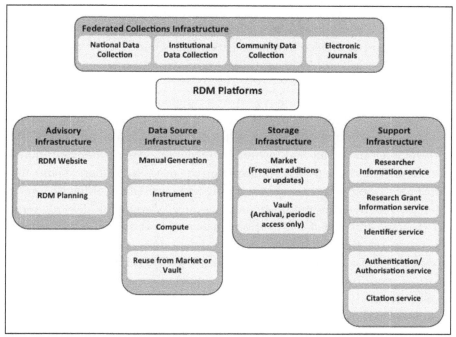

Category	Description
Federated Collections	Components in this category facilitate the federation, discovery, and reuse of data.
RDM Platforms	RDM platforms facilitate the capture, curation, organization, analysis, sharing, discovery, and reuse of data.
Advisory	Raises awareness in RDM and includes institutional RDM policies, strategies, practices, and tools and encourages RDM planning.
Data Source	The source of the digital research data, be it either manually generated, from an instrument, from a compute node or reused data.
Storage	Provides the fundamental storage for the research data. This can generally take two forms: Market, which is frequently accessed or updated; and Vault, which is archival, with only periodic access.
Support	This category contains various components which enrich the research data collection's metadata, provide persistent identifiers, enable authentication and authorization, and facilitate citation.

Figure 8.3 Overview of research data management infrastructure

5.3 Strategies in selecting, developing and deploying research data management infrastructure

Selection strategy

Researchers predominantly engage with an RDM platform. For this platform to be effective and have high utility it must fit with researchers' tools, workflows, instrumentation, methodologies, environment and, most importantly, culture. As most of these vary from discipline to discipline, it is unrealistic to believe that a single RDM platform will consistently meet researchers' needs. Indeed, research institutions should expect that a range of RDM platforms will be required in order to accommodate their researchers.

Researchers frequently have strong allegiances to their research community, sometimes in preference to their institution. Consequently, researchers may be inclined to choose to adopt a research community RDM platform over an established institutional solution, even if the institutional solution and service is technically superior; the need to collaborate with and contribute to their professional community takes precedence. Monash's view is that if a research community already has a well developed RDM platform and strategy, and that if this platform meets the needs of the institution's researchers in the discipline, then the institution should facilitate its adoption by those researchers. In some cases, this might mean re-purposing the RDM platform to meet local needs, requiring some degree of software development.

Monash has many research disciplines, so it is unrealistic for the university to support an RDM platform for every discipline. Therefore, it has sought to strategically select the discipline-specific RDM platforms that it supports. Methods of doing this included filtering on research disciplines that are ready, willing and able to engage and focusing on disciplines that are strategically important to the institution's research impact and funding. Cloud-based services, which alleviate the need for local expertise and support and may also reduce the costs and certain risks in providing these platforms to researchers, have also been considered.

Development strategy

Monash's philosophy is that given the potentially high development costs and numerous risks and challenges inherent in software development projects, development of new RDM platforms should be a last resort. However, given the uniqueness of some research requirements and environments, the development of new tailored RDM platforms may at times be required.

In the Monash experience, the process of developing software for researchers is often quite different from that required for mainstream business software. Development partnerships between software developers and researchers generally work in an interpretive mode, with characteristics including an iterative process that is open-ended and thrives on ambiguity. Researchers are ultimately focused on the research outcome, and their requirements may change over time. In some cases, therefore, the software solution may only be required in the short term.

When developing RDM platforms for researchers at Monash, the following key principles and methods have been successful:

- Researchers must lead the development of solutions.
- These solutions must be owned by their research community rather than the institution.
- Existing RDM platforms should be adapted to save development time and reduce the risks of green field development.
- Agile software development methodologies should be used.
- Software should be easily deployable at other institutions.
- Support should be provided for researchers in marketing the RDM platform to their research discipline.

Deployment strategy

Federated collections infrastructure: In the context of a research institution, federated data collections may have an internal or broader scope. Monash's view has been that it is preferable for federated collections infrastructure to be hosted and supported outside the institution. This raised the question of whether the university needed a central institutional research data repository. An institutional research data repository has two major uses: to showcase a research institution's data and to track data holdings so that researchers within the institution can discover and reuse accessible collections. Monash has not implemented a comprehensive institutional data repository. Instead, it disseminates metadata to federated collections infrastructure from a range of data tools (such as research data management platforms and the Monash University Research Repository) using various interchange protocols and formats. Research Data Australia federates Australian research data collections and enables each research institution to showcase its own collections. This has been Monash's preferred method for comprehensive discovery.

Research data management platforms: The number of RDM platforms is growing. They can be hosted by research institutions, regional government based service providers, national government-based service providers, international organizations or commercial organizations, and so it is important that research institutions are flexible in their approach to providing and supporting RDM infrastructure. Since a single research institution cannot afford to host and support an RDM platform for every discipline, it can be assumed that many RDM platforms used by its researchers will be hosted externally. The exception to this is in the case of sensitive data, such as that produced from clinical trials, which for legal and/or ethical reasons may need to be hosted on a local RDM platform. Monash assists with hosting RDM platforms by providing virtual machines, a range of popular databases, plenty of freely available research data storage (with good access time) and assistance in deploying the software.

Data storage: The RDSI project noted above is now establishing national research data storage, which will impact on Monash's strategies for its own data storage infrastructure. Monash is acting as a local storage node as part of RDSI, and is considering how to maximize storage opportunities between the node and its own infrastructure. Movement of the data between these two options in order to maximize discovery and reuse is of particular interest. Monash views itself as the primary place for its researchers to store their research data because it has a longevity that exceeds that of regional or project-funded organizations.

5.4 Integration of research data management infrastructure with internal and external systems

Integration between institutional administrative systems and research data management platforms

When registering research data collections associated with a publication and/or to encourage reuse, it is desirable to include metadata about the related researchers, associated grants (including granting bodies) and associated publications. RDM platforms at Monash will increasingly include mechanisms to enable the association between a data collection and the related research administration metadata, the association of a research data collection with a persistent identifier, and the public release of a data collection via publication, syndication and/or harvesting. To achieve this, institutions need to consider techniques for making their research administration information systems accessible by RDM platforms. At Monash, this is provided through a web service that interrogates the central research administration system.

Integration between external systems and research data management platforms

To promote collaboration and the reuse of research data, and to simplify and expedite workflow, RDM platforms need to integrate with a variety of external systems, including such aspects as:

- authentication and authorization
- citation
- dissemination
- the minting and maintenance of persistent identifiers
- appropriate provision of analysis infrastructure (such as high-performance computing).

Since one of the main aspects of RDM is data sharing and as most researchers will have collaborators external to their institution, RDM platforms that support single-sign-on through federated access technologies, such as Shibboleth, will be more convenient to use and are more likely to be adopted. Institutions will need to link their authentication systems with relevant identity providers and Monash has adopted the solutions provided by the Australian Access Federation.[6]

RDM platforms are likely to disseminate metadata describing their research data collections to a range of repositories, including national/institutional catalogues of research data collections, community portals and electronic journals. Metadata may also need to be disseminated in a range of formats and using a variety of techniques. For instance, metadata contributed to Research Data Australia uses RIF-CS[7] to describe the data collection and its associated researchers, grants, and services, and is disseminated using OAI-PMH.

When a research data collection is made available as part of a paper/journal/blog, a persistent identifier is useful in enabling the data collection to be relocated. When selecting an identifier service, institutions should consider the longevity of the identifier provider service, cost in generating an identifier and the extent to which the type of identifier is used within the research community. Monash has chosen to use the Digital Object Identifier (DOI) service provided by ANDS and DataCite[8] to encourage persistent identification of the datasets and facilitate citation and impact tracking.

5.5 Monash's technical research data management infrastructure
Research data storage

Many researchers still store their research data on personal storage devices, such as CDs, USB sticks, portable hard drives and laptops. These kinds of media are easily lost, difficult to collaborate around and are easily corrupted, especially if they are stored under sub-optimal conditions; this approach also results in fragmented research data collections.

In the past many researchers using Monash's enterprise-networked storage found their default quota too small. Increasing the quota was relatively expensive, so researchers began purchasing personal storage devices and/or being forced to make hard decisions about what to keep and what to delete. Monash responded by commissioning a petabyte research data store, known as LaRDS (Large Research Data Store). To reduce the barriers to uptake and to promote the fundamentals of good research data management practice, storage allocation is generous and provided free of charge. Access can also be customized. To enhance performance and reduce intra-university network congestion, some research teams have been provided with a local high speed NAS (network-attached storage), functioning as a staging post, which is synchronized to LaRDS on a regular basis.

As LaRDS retains multiple copies of each data file in order to ensure data integrity and reliability, its total storage capacity is much greater than the effective capacity that can be allocated to users. In April 2013, LaRDS stored 1.489Pb of unique research data and had an effective capacity of 2.14Pb. Figure 8.4 shows the growth in LaRDS use in 2011–13.

Researchers in the long tail of data management often require only a safe place for storing their data, from which they can easily share it with colleagues. Further, researchers in general do not want to spend time thinking about what they keep and what they should throw away. LaRDS provides these researchers with access to very large and reliable research digital data storage.

Research data management planning

Monash provides advice on RDM planning in the form of guidelines posted on its RDM website and through a data planning checklist. This document guides researchers through a comprehensive planning process that addresses all the aspects of data management covered by the *Australian Code for the Responsible Conduct of Research* as well as the Monash University Research Data Management Policy.[9] As the contents of the checklist and

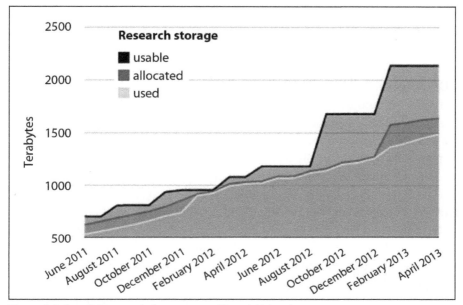

Figure 8.4 Growth in research data storage at Monash University

supporting processes are still being refined and there is currently no requirement in Australia to lodge a data management plan, Monash does not provide software tools to automate data planning.

Monash University Research Repository

The Monash University Research Repository contains content representing Monash's research activity. It was initially put into service as an open-access publications repository but has since been extended to expose research data holdings. The Repository provides a place to securely store and centrally manage selected research data, collections and related publications so that they are globally accessible online. It contains accepted versions of published works such as books, book chapters, journal articles and conference papers; non-published manuscripts and grey literature such as theses, technical reports, working papers and conference posters; and research data holdings, including data sets, image collections, audio and video files. Its primary role has been to host research material not available elsewhere and it contains over 90,000 records. The University Repository's role in RDM is expected to grow.

Discipline-specific research data management platforms

At Monash, a diverse range of discipline-specific RDM platforms is used by researchers. This section provides a sample of them:

CDD (Collaborative Drug Discovery) Vault: CDD Vault[10] offers a web-based solution for managing drug discovery data, primarily around small molecules and associated bio-assay data. Licensing is fee based.

DaRIS: DaRIS is a framework for managing data and metadata. It is primarily used to supply a secure repository for biomedical imaging data and metadata, although there is no actual technical restriction on data types. Licensing is part open-source and part fee-based.

Healthy Food Basket: The Healthy Food Basket[11] was developed by Nutrition and Dietetics researchers at Monash University to measure and monitor the cost and affordability of a healthy basket of food for typical families. Its supporting IT platform facilitates the collection of data from supermarkets using a mobile app, reducing errors in collection and transcription, simplifying the management and reuse of the collected data, and expediting analysis and the production of reports.

Interferome: Interferome[12] assimilates a large number of data sets, including detailed annotation and quantitative data, from the microarray analysis pipeline and makes this available to researchers by providing enhanced search capabilities that allow them to query more than 2000 data points. This platform also has the ability to publish metadata about research data collections to Research Data Australia. The service promotes citations and data reuse and enables new discoveries from old data. It also facilitates comprehensive analyses like tissue expression and regulatory analysis. Licensing is open-source.

MyTARDIS: MyTARDIS[13] began as an automated solution for managing and sharing raw protein crystallography data (see section 5.1 above). Since then, efforts from many independent projects have enhanced and evolved the central MyTARDIS product. New features such as data staging mounts, automated metadata extractors, parameter set creation and high-performance computing task scheduling have been added to meet researcher needs. A diagram showing an implementation of MyTARDIS sourcing research data from beamlines at the Australian Synchrotron is shown in Figure 8.5. Licensing is open-source.

OMERO: Data-intensive research depends on tools that manage multi-dimensional, heterogeneous datasets. Open Microscopy Environment Remote Objects (OMERO)[14] is an open-source software platform that

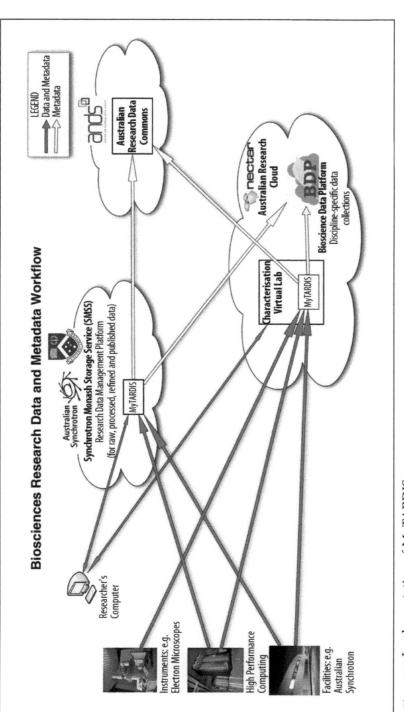

Figure 8.5 Implementation of MyTARDIS

enables access to and use of a wide range of biological data. OMERO uses a server-based middleware application to provide a unified interface for images, matrices and tables. Licensing is open-source.

OzFlux Repository: Ecosystem research in Australia investigates the role of ecosystems in the cycling of water and carbon between biospheric and atmospheric stores and the response of these ecosystems to changes in these cycles. Effective research is hampered by the lack of co-ordination in data collection, archiving and quality control from independently managed measurement stations across remote Australia. The OzFlux Repository[15] standardizes and automates the collection of data, archives and controls the quality of measurements from a network of measurement stations, integrates complementary data streams from different sources into a single data and metadata repository and facilitates the linking of data through Research Data Australia to encourage reuse. The licensing is open-source.

Versatile research data management platforms

Most researchers do not have access to a discipline-specific RDM platform, so research institutions need to provide researchers with access to one or more versatile RDM platforms. As the research terminology and processes can differ greatly between research disciplines, it is expected that one RDM platform will not be enough.

At Monash, MyTARDIS has been used effectively by many scientific disciplines. Besides its officially supported disciplines of protein crystallography, electron microscopy and proteomics, it has also been used for medical imaging, quantum physics and material science. Monash also provides researchers with access to Arcitecta Desktop, a web operating system for metadata and data that enables users, from individuals to distributed groups, to ingest, discover and share any type of data. This tool is a commercial product for which Monash has a site licence.

5.6 Sustainability of technical research data management infrastructure

Monash's approach to promoting the sustainability of its RDM infrastructure involves:

- thinking about sustainability from the start, when deploying or developing new RDM infrastructure

- making a strategic assessment before deciding to support any new discipline-specific infrastructure at Monash
- considering cloud-based solutions, in order to reduce operational costs and outsource specialist support
- adopting or adapting a community solution before developing a new one from scratch
- promoting a sense of ownership by the relevant researchers and their community in discipline-specific infrastructure. This encourages adoption and provides better funding opportunities, because a community can access a larger amount of funding than an individual institution
- providing a nursery to nurture and develop new RDM services
- devolving responsibility for RDM to the Monash community.

5.7 What's next? – the Virtual Lab

Generally, RDM infrastructure has been independent of other research components. A new Australian research infrastructure project, the Characterisation Virtualisation Laboratory (CVL), integrates high-performance computing, direct data capture from key instrumentation, RDM, data storage and visualization infrastructure with analysis and imaging tools to support next-generation instruments. The CVL (see Figure 8.6) is a cloud-based environment for the analysis and visualization of multi-modal and multi-scale imaging data. It is being developed by four universities (Monash, the University of Sydney, the University of Queensland and the Australian National University) together with four national imaging facilities (Australian Microscopy and Microanalysis Research Facility, National Imaging Facility, Australian Nuclear Science and Technology Organisation and the Australian Synchrotron). This remote desktop environment allows researchers access to a wide range of existing tools and services provided through a centrally managed environment.

So, as RDM infrastructure becomes more tightly integrated with other research infrastructure and as RDM practices become a common part of researchers' everyday practice, it is foreseeable that RDM will become indistinguishable from other aspects of the research process. The CVL takes the next step along this path.

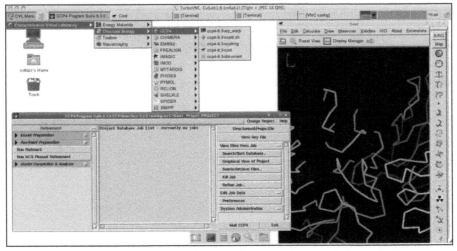

Figure 8.6 The Characterisation Virtual Laboratory desktop environment being applied to structural biology

6. Conclusion

Between 2006 and 2013 Monash University took a strategic approach to RDM that aligned with the goals of the institution and its research agenda, while also providing infrastructure based on discipline and researcher needs. To build RDM capabilities, key areas of the university with specialist skills have worked together with senior management in a collaborative environment. This has created a pool of expertise in RDM with a shared focus on common outcomes, which will drive Monash forward as researcher needs and university goals evolve.

At an institutional level Monash has created and endorsed RDM policies and strategies; established organizational structures to plan, implement and promote RDM; developed an RDM website, guidelines and other resources; developed programmes to build capability; established technical infrastructure and deployed a number of RDM platforms; created a large and widely accessible institutional digital data store; and established the Monash University Research Repository. Jointly this provides Monash with flexible research infrastructure for the future.

From the researcher's perspective Monash offers a range of discipline-specific RDM platforms, provides advice and has started conversations on the process of curating and exposing research data collections. In strategically significant areas Monash is providing discipline-specific RDM platforms and for more general areas it is providing one or more versatile

RDM solutions to meet these needs. Monash will continue to develop infrastructure to meet the ever expanding and diverse needs of its researchers.

Monash embraced RDM to improve research practice, attract researchers and research income, and to encourage the reuse of data to increase research impact, validate research outcomes and reduce legal risk. For this to be sustainable Monash strives to integrate RDM within all research processes, practices and training. The goal is for RDM to be standard research practice, including being part of research funding. The complex infrastructure now in place represents the first steps towards maximizing the value of the institution's research.

7. Websites

1   http://rdsi.uq.edu.au.
2   www.nectar.org.au.
3   www.ands.org.au/about/approach.html#ardc.
4   http://researchdata.ands.org.au.
5   http://tardis.edu.au.
6   www.aaf.edu.au.
7   http://ands.org.au/guides/cpguide/cpgrifcs.html.
8   www.datacite.org.
9   www.policy.monash.edu/policy-bank/academic/research/research-data-management-policy.html.
10 www.collaborativedrug.com.
11 http://hfb.its.monash.edu.au.
12 http://interferome.its.monash.edu.au/interferome/home.jspx.
13 http://mytardis.its.monash.edu.au.
14 www.openmicroscopy.org.
15 http://ozflux.its.monash.edu.au.

8. Citation

National Health and Medical Research Council (NHMRC), The Australian Research Council (ARC) and Universities Australia (2007) *Australian Code for the Responsible Conduct of Research*, Australian Government, www.nhmrc.gov.au/_files_nhmrc/publications/attachments/r39.pdf.

CHAPTER 9

Case study 4: a national solution – the UK Data Service

Matthew Woollard and Louise Corti

1. Introduction

Data management has been succinctly defined by the editor of this volume in an earlier work as 'an active process by which digital resources remain discoverable, accessible and intelligible over the longer term' (Pryor, 2012, vii). Research Data Management (RDM) to the present authors is a subtly different process, which can be seen as the activities that are undertaken by a researcher or team of researchers as part of the research lifecycle, which precede but complement the activities of a data service or data service infrastructure. Theoretically, the breakpoint between the responsibilities of the two streams of activities is the transfer of data from the data producer to the host repository but in practice this is not so black and white. In this case study we outline the key activities and services carried out by the UK Data Service that support research data management as they relate to the production of research data in the social sciences. We explain how our services, together with those delivered by other providers, can contribute to the much-needed wider portfolio of training and professionalization in RDM in the higher education sector.

The UK Data Service began its new life in 2012 as an integrated service funded by the Economic and Social Research Council (ESRC). Aiming to create a more unified service and identity for the ESRC's data services in the UK, it consolidates the former Economic and Social Data Service (ESDS), the

Secure Data Service (SDS) and much of the data service component of the ESRC's Census Programme. The primary aim of the service is to provide users with access to easily discoverable and relevant data to enable and expand social and economic research. However, there are subsidiary aims which stem from this primary aim, and one of those is to inculcate better research data management practices amongst researchers and data creators. The service is run from the UK Data Archive at the University of Essex in strong collaboration with a number of significant partners, including Mimas and the Cathie Marsh Centre for Census and Social Research at the University of Manchester, along with the Geography Department at the University of Southampton.

2. The structure and functions of the UK Data Service

The overall structure of the service is based to a large extent on the functional model provided by the Open Archival Information System (OAIS) reference model (ISO, 2012). The model has been adapted to provide a robust foundation for the existing and future needs of the service. Figure 9.1 shows the major areas of activity across the whole service: it simplifies an even more complex visualization showing the major activities in scope, and demonstrates the considerable number of interactions and dependencies within the service. The figure also highlights a semantic issue between the worlds of digital preservation and research management, where both communities use the term 'data management' to mean different things.

The OAIS reference model is a helpful model for the delivery of digital preservation services, but for services which are not expected to provide permanent access to digital files it may be rather too complex. The key consideration in whether or not a service should follow this model is whether or not access is to be provided to digital assets on a 'permanent' basis, or only for the anticipated lifespan of software in which the digital files were passed into the custody of the repository. Regardless of the complexity or holistic fit of the OAIS model, it provides a very useful approach to managing the workflows of digital assets in repositories, from ingesting a submission information package (SIP) of data through to the ultimate creation of a dissemination information package (DIP).

As a distributed organization, the UK Data Service is structured around key functional areas which have interlocking activities. These are explored in more detail in the subsections that follow. The service provides outreach and capacity building across all of these functions, in particular at pre-ingest

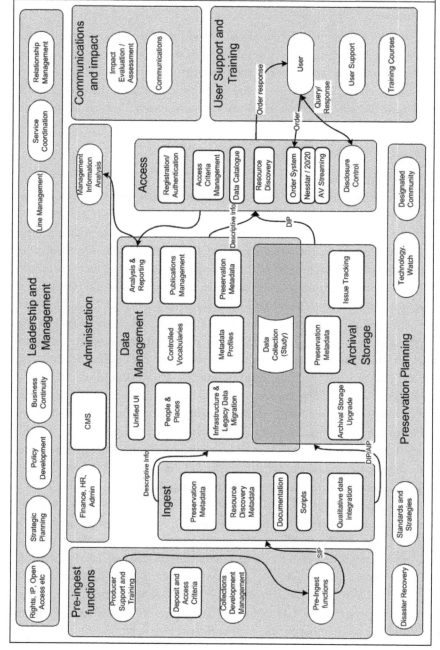

Figure 9.1 Generalized scheme of the main activities of the UK Data Service (*reproduced courtesy of the University of Essex*)

and ingest stages, which aim to instil best practices in RDM so that research data is offered for deposit in the best possible shape.

2.1 Pre-ingest

Pre-ingest activities consist of all those activities which take place before data is formally introduced into the service. For the service there are two key pre-ingest functions: producer support and training, and collections development. These functions are likely to be the most critical for other organizations which offer or plan to offer research data management services.

Producer support and training

The service works with a wide range of data producers, mostly government departments, international agencies, research centres and groups and individual researchers to ensure that the benefits of best data management practices are accrued to the producers and the service itself. The producer support function offers data producers guidance and advice on those elements of the research data lifecycle which precede the formal 'deposit' or transfer of data to the service or another repository. This includes consideration of all data-related aspects of planning research, from costing data activities and establishing roles and responsibilities of key players through to the use of shared protocols in data collection; formatting, organizing and storing the data; quality control; validation; documentation and contextualization. Particular attention is paid to the areas that are most likely to result in precluding data sharing, namely, ethical and legal considerations, including consent and rights management. The overall approach is to explain the responsibilities of researchers to create high-quality shareable data resources and the benefits that good data management and sharing can accrue to the researcher.

The service has worked very closely with the ESRC since 1995 to develop and implement its *Research Data Policy* (ESRC, 2013), providing guidance for grant applicants, award holders and grant peer reviewers. We have also guided the Medical Research Council in creating its data policy. Finally, the service has been a key player in the Jisc Managing Research Data Programme[1] in the form of advice, peer review and running dedicated projects. This programme has provided a timely co-ordination of effort, injected funding and engendered great collaborative spirit across UK higher education institutions (HEIs) to manage local research data assets. In turn this has demonstrated the pivotal role of data centres, such as the UK Data Service, in utilizing their domain expertise to help develop a more unified landscape for RDM services.

Collections development

This function ensures that the most relevant, highest-impact data is selected for ingest, and actively identifies and negotiates for new data. The service's track record in negotiating with data owners and producers to secure access to critical data sources and agree rights and licensing issues – which can be complex and prolonged – means that we are able to maximize the alignment between the needs of users and data owners. A *Collections Development Policy* (UK Data Service, 2013a) for the service has been designed to maximize the value of the data brought into the service's collection, since it is not possible to acquire or ingest all the data which may have value to the ESRC's target research communities or which needs to be kept for some period of time. Any policy must be robust and implementable, yet flexible enough to accommodate changes in scope or direction resulting from external drivers, high-level policy changes, or indeed user demand. Our policy is supplemented by an internal cross-functional Collections Appraisal Group, which ensures that the policy is implemented appropriately.

As outlined in Chapter 5, any organization with an obligation to hold research data should design and implement a selection policy that sets out the key parameters of what will be kept, under what mandate, for how long and with what level of descriptive metadata. Such a statement provides clear boundaries for these activities, and should be backed with higher-level buy-in, support and relevant resources. At the UK Data Service, once a data collection has been though its appraisal process, a 'processing plan' is created that sets out licensing matters, how much value to add, and appropriate access (i.e. what delivery mechanisms and under what terms and conditions). The service has a valuable role to play in training new data archives and institutional repositories in this bespoke appraisal process as it relates to the handling of social science-type data.

2.2 Ingest

Ingest is the activity by which data is prepared for long-term access. The activities carried out in this process range from error and integrity checking, ensuring appropriate levels of anonymization and checking confidentiality, compiling user documentation, cataloguing and indexing, and preparing data for preservation and access. Much of the metadata created during the ingest process is used as preservation-level metadata. The skills involved in the ingest process are probably the most diverse in a single function, which is why we place a particular emphasis on their importance, especially surrounding the ingest processes for large-scale complex surveys. The key activity within this function is to ensure that there are versions of deposited data which are not software-dependent, and will be able to be migrated by the service to more up-to-date formats when required. Institutional repositories will need to design or adapt processes to ensure that the data ingested into their systems is usable in the longer term, while maintaining its authenticity. This includes handling versioning of data and metadata in a robust way.

For many institutional repositories the ingest process is likely to be less discriminating, but the lengthy experience of the host organizations of the UK Data Service has shown that maximizing ingest processing efforts as early as possible in the process of digital curation ensures that long-term access is available at a lower total cost.

2.3 Data management

The OAIS reference model uses the concept of data management to cover a number of activities relating to the internal management of data. For the functional model of the UK Data Service we have elected to use the terms 'archival storage' and 'technical services' to cover most of these activities. Technical services, however, reach beyond the data management activities defined by the OAIS.

Archival storage

The archival storage function of a data service ensures that data is *available* in the long term. (In contrast, the *usability* of the data depends to a large extent on activities undertaken by the ingest and preservation functions.) The service provides persistent data access, maintaining and allowing for the reuse and citation of every major version of data. Changes in data files in our custody may be necessary, either for the purposes of augmenting documentation, adding new waves to longitudinal surveys or simply correcting previously undetected errors in the data. Ensuring the logical integrity of files over time is also important, ensuring that users of data are able to validate previous research with the same data files as used in that research. The archival storage function also ensures that the various versions of files which we hold in our preservation system are the same as each other, providing for data integrity. The UK Data Archive (as one of the host organizations of the UK Data Service) has assessed itself against the Data Seal of Approval[2] and is continuing to play an instrumental role in helping other national data archives in Europe to attain this benchmark. It is vital that institutional repositories consider what level of archival status they are seeking to attain; the term 'Trusted Digital Repository' should be used with care and caution, as it denotes the implementation of standards at the higher end of archival practice.

Technical services

These are closely linked with internal infrastructural activities and the overall web services. Technical services have a profound effect on all aspects of the data service infrastructure. Almost all activities within the service have some technical aspect, though many need human operation from the specific function. Technical services provide the protocols for a single technical infrastructure for the service, including internal access control mechanisms (essential to ensure integrity and provenance of data and retaining compliance with ISO 27001, a specification for an information security management system), preservation metadata, user identity and user access management. The last two points are particularly valid for institutional repositories, which may have an obligation to make certain research council-funded data available for reuse, but also prevent access to other materials to which the public may not have the right to access (most likely for rights or commercially sensitive reasons).

Technical activities are increasingly managed in a single integrated workflow, for example covering a collection negotiations database, data transfer mechanisms and tools for data producers. Such seamless workflows can help to reduce both the information required from data producers and the manual activities of the data ingest team. Changes to data collections need to be fully documented in a generic and automated way, and the creation of explicit preservation-level metadata is essential. These activities can help to streamline the underlying work of any data service, so that interlocking functions are able to work closely with each other and prevent redundancy of effort.

The UK Data Service and its predecessors have been around for some 45 years, making it challenging to rebuild internal 'legacy' systems without affecting the services provided themselves. For any repository dealing with data it is important to plan as far into the future as is possible, since changes in the culture of data sharing, in access conditions and delivery mechanisms, and in the requirements of others are likely to change over time. Anticipating these changes is a *sine qua non* of any service or institutional repository wishing to remain efficient, up to date and meaningful in a research world which is being increasingly driven by metrics and proof of impact.

To this end the service has been proactive in developing access control mechanisms that better meet the requirements of the Open Data agenda, while protecting data which has the potential to be disclosive, especially when linked with other data. Our development program has included a unified user interface for internal management information, part of which can provide valuable externally facing self-service reporting.

2.4 Access

Increasing access to, and usage of, data are high priorities for a funded data service or repository. While making research data and related research outputs available is important, ensuring they are easily findable and accessible regardless of where they may be physically located is perhaps even more critical. Seamless resource discovery is the ultimate goal for any web-based resource provider. In addition, it is vital that the existence of materials is known and documented, even if they are not accessible for certain reasons, such as confidentiality, rights or other restrictions. In these cases the provision of relevant descriptive metadata is essential. Part of the rationale for the UK Data Service is to integrate the data delivery systems for data which are generally accessible and 'secure data', provided by the (former) Secure Data Service. Owing to the sensitive nature of the data supplied via secure access, and the formidable restrictions to access, it is not possible to harmonize these data delivery systems. However, it has been possible to ensure that the metadata catalogues for both access systems are cross-searchable. Metadata have been harvested from the ESRC Data Store – our self-deposit system for ESRC-funded researchers – to populate Discover,[3] the service's unified catalogue. Fields have been mapped where metadata differed slightly. This allows effective cross-searching across resources previously held in different catalogues and provides a step towards enabling unified resource discovery for social science data in the UK. The service has been contributing to national efforts to specify and agree core metadata for data collections. Our own desire is to see a scenario whereby users can easily locate ESRC-supported research data regardless of where it is held.

Much of the technical infrastructure of the UK Data Service is based on a service-oriented architecture, including the website. All of our data are delivered via the web in one way or another. It is important to keep in mind the importance of web mechanisms that will be used by repositories to provide access to data, since users demand functional, intuitive, reliable and effective web services. Therefore, data must be easy to find, and the mechanisms for finding it easy to use. Institutional repositories have exactly the same challenge. It is most likely that external users will be directed to an institutional repository from a reference to a research output which is embedded through an electronic citation. Users must feel confident of the status (or version) of the digital materials they find. The situation is no different for digital data; services must be able to provide proper persistent identifiers for the citation of the data and related objects they make available.

Efficient access to data resources not only depends on effective and user-friendly systems for resource discovery; for the UK Data Service, systems for user authorization and user access management are also essential. Authorization deals with a number of variant licence regimes; for example at the time of writing, census microdata available from the service is limited to researchers in the UK, and some of this microdata is further limited to those with Approved Research status.[4] Access management is important because it not only helps us understand how data collections are being used, but because it also allows us to provide this information back to the data producers and data owners. This helps to demonstrate the value of secondary analysis to both these groups as well as the funders of the UK Data Service. While most HEIs do not require complex authentication systems for their research output repositories, finding an appropriate method to collect management information is essential. For those data repositories that need to justify their user-oriented activities or secure more funding, such management information can become a vital lifeline.

For the UK Data Service, secure access, as opposed to managed distribution, will almost certainly remain the exception for data access, but the service's portfolio of 'sensitive' data will grow, as will the demand for access. The service increasingly requires secure access methods to allow researchers to use personal sensitive data. While data owners recognize that this data can provide considerably more research value, they cannot legally allow researchers to use it without stringent usage conditions being in place. These secure forms of access are unlikely to be requirements for HEIs, but those running data management services in HEIs should be aware of the provisions of the Data Protection Act if they are required to provide access to data which might be considered to be personal. Many social surveys are indeed considered to include personal data. The 2012 guide on anonymization published by the Information Commissioner's Office provides further valuable advice (ICO, 2012). HEIs need to be aware of the variety of specialist services which are available to provide advice and other services.

At the UK Data Service, access to disclosive data is provided through a secure 'portal'. However, it should be borne in mind that the costs of running such a secure access service are much more strongly related to the volume of demand than those of the 'non-secure' services and it is therefore essential to monitor usage and impact carefully. A vital part of delivering secure access services is in providing mandatory user training, appropriate analysis software, auditing and disclosure control functions for users. This stream of activity is highly labour- and cost-intensive and also relies on the service conforming to the ISO 27001 information security standard (ISO, 2005), as well as further accreditation processes.

2.5 User support and training

The UK Data Service provides both generic and expert user support; the former is carried out across the entire service and the latter is provided for data collections that fall into the core service at its outset. The vision for user training is to raise wider awareness of key data and to build capacity among four key groups of users: academic undergraduate and postgraduate students; academic research and teaching staff; non-academic users; and the non-traditional user.

Any effective service needs to provide some kind of assistance to users in finding what they require. In turn, this requires staff to have an understanding of the range of complexities of the data resources they provide access to. The service has a team of expert staff, with strong research skills, focused on providing dedicated user support, advice and training. It is perhaps unlikely that many HEIs will have the resources to provide this level of support, so it becomes essential to provide as much relevant information within the dissemination information package to allow end-users to be able to understand and use the data with confidence.

The UK Data Service makes use of a single web-based help enquiry system, providing federated support for the whole service. We have a strong vision to have a rich and growing bank of expert online resources for academic and non-academic users to access information and advice quickly and easily. These resources can take the form of pre-prepared help guides; multimedia training on a wide range of topics; a suite of thematic web pages; and a public-facing, searchable, web Q&A forum where communities of researchers can assist each other. These resources enable users to more rapidly find support that is tailored to their needs. We focus our specialist support on those collections relating to complex, large-scale surveys including longitudinal data, international macrodata and qualitative and mixed methods data.

A data service can never seek to replace more traditional academic methods of training, but can complement and supplement these avenues of education. Where appropriate, we point users to alternative sources of relevant information and training. In specialist areas of training such as that surrounding the use of sensitive data through our secure access systems, we focus on the practicalities of assessing confidentiality and ensuring disclosure control in microdata. These analysis-oriented training sessions complement the data management training we deliver for data creators; users benefit from having an appreciation of the factors involved in collecting data to make it sharable.

2.6 Communications and impact

Although these activities are not part of the official OAIS functional model, they are a requirement for any data service infrastructure. Institutional repositories may have a lesser requirement for these dedicated activities but there should be a clear rationale to improve the use of services provided at an institutional level. Visibility of resources, in addition to the quality of those resources, lead to increased use; increased use is a demonstrable impact measure and quality impact secures additional resources. This money-go-round is essential so that services are sustainable in the longer term.

In the service's communications plan, *Communicating for Impact* (UK Data Service, 2013b), we emphasize and explain our key focus on data use, data reuse and data sharing. We proactively target non-users, by undertaking discipline-specific focus groups, and by promoting ourselves more prominently with existing and potential data owners, in non-academic user networks and international audiences. We also seek to exploit the benefits of closer working with the key owner and producer stakeholders such as the Government Statistical Services (GSS), national survey organizations and international statistical organizations like the World Bank. An internal communications team focuses on promoting our funder's impact agenda through the exploitation of the management information we collect. This function also co-ordinates, monitors and promotes educational and research impacts, working closely with ESRC and other data suppliers.

2.7 Preservation planning

The service ensures that its preservation-based activities are fully grounded in international best practice, and liaises with key organizations and networks over these activities. We maintain our own standards and technology watch to ensure that the best value for money is maintained for our funders. In addition, we provide informal training and mentoring for other international social science data archives that are setting up data preservation services.

We do not touch on management and administration of the service in this chapter, but suffice it to say that management commitment is vital for the smooth running of the UK Data Service; likewise, HEIs will need to provide dedicated resources for the management of their repositories if they are to be successful.

3. Conclusion

This overview of the UK Data Service shows how our activities, many of which are standards-based, can influence and complement research data management infrastructure in HEIs. Five interlocking factors are causing HEIs to rethink their research data management services:

1 Researchers' responsibilities towards their research data are starting to change.
2 Research funders are increasingly mandating open access to research data which they have funded, requiring relevant data management planning and practices in order to maximize transparency and accountability of all research areas.
3 Governments are demanding transparency in research.

4 Journal publishers increasingly require submission of the data upon which publications are based for peer review.
5 The economic climate is requiring much greater reuse of data.

Together these drivers mean that researchers will need to improve, enhance and professionalize their research data management skills to meet the challenge of producing the highest-quality research outputs in a responsible and efficient way, with the ability to share and reuse such outputs. These initiatives also mean that HEIs will have to step up to the mark in their activities to support long-term access to this data and to manage the ethical and security risks of their data assets. Their responsibilities will change, and investment to develop capacity will be required.

Data centres can play an invaluable contribution to building capacity in a number of areas, particularly where there are discipline-specific issues surrounding the data resources and known user needs. One of the UK Data Service's host institutions, the UK Data Archive, has worked on a number of projects which provide research data management advice to universities, institutional repositories and researchers. Both the UK Data Service and the UK Data Archive expect to carry out these activities into the future, and we can provide bespoke advice and capacity building to the emerging institutional data repository landscape.

4. References

4.1 Websites and notes

1 Jisc Managing Research Data programme 2011–13: www.jisc.ac.uk/whatwedo/programmes/di_researchmanagement/managingresearchdata.aspx.
2 Data Seal of Approval: http://datasealofapproval.org.
3 UK Data Service Discovery interface: http://discover.ukdataservice.ac.uk.
4 Access to ONS Data: www.ons.gov.uk/ons/about-ons/who-we-are/services/unpublished-data/access-to-ons-data-service/index.html.

4.2 Bibliography

ESRC (2013) *Research Data Policy*, www.esrc.ac.uk/_images/Research_Data_Policy_2010_tcm8-4595.pdf.
Information Commissioner's Office (2012) *Anonymisation: managing data protection risk. Code of practice*, http://ico.org.uk/for_organisations/data_protection/

topic_guides/~/media/documents/library/Data_Protection/Practical_application/
anonymisation_code.ashx.

ISO (2005) ISO 27001: 2005. *Information technology. Security techniques. Information
security management systems. Requirements.*

ISO (2012) ISO 14721: 2012. *Space data and information transfer systems. Open archival
information system (OAIS). Reference model.*

Pryor, G. (2012) Preface. In Pryor, G. (ed.), *Managing Research Data,* Facet
Publishing.

UK Data Service (2013a) *UK Data Service Collections Development Policy,*
http://ukdataservice.ac.uk/deposit-data.aspx.

UK Data Service (2013b) *Communicating for Impact,*
http://ukdataservice.ac.uk/about-us/impact.aspx.

CHAPTER 10

Case study 5: development of institutional RDM services by projects in the Jisc Managing Research Data programmes

Simon Hodson and Laura Molloy

1. Introduction

This chapter offers a preliminary overview of the development of research data management (RDM) services by projects in the second Jisc Managing Research Data (MRD) programme, which ran between 2011 and 2013. Reference is also made to the first MRD programme and projects within this, where appropriate. The second MRD programme encouraged projects to adopt a coherent approach, to share ideas and resources at an early stage and to look to the Digital Curation Centre (DCC) for guidance. Therefore, it is hoped that details of how the programme was designed and managed, and the approaches emerging from the projects, will be of interest. It should be stressed, however, that only a few of the projects have been completed at the time of writing, and so the detail of RDM services developed and conclusions about effective approaches can only be partial.

1.1 The data management impetus

The good management of research data is not, of course, an end in itself but is commonly perceived as an essential component of good research practice. An increasingly vocal community of researchers considers making research data easily available for verification and reuse to be an essential component of good scientific practice. Indeed, Geoffrey Boulton argued in his keynote at the MRD workshop in March 2013 that publishing research findings without simultaneously making the underlying data (in other words, evidence) available amounts to malpractice. Where data are the product or record of unrepeatable observations, sound data management, curation and long-term preservation strategies become imperative.

Meanwhile, certain research disciplines are becoming increasingly 'data-centric' and the creation, sharing and reuse of data are a core focus of activity. Some disciplines have been revolutionized by the community adoption of open data principles. The innovative and transforming potential of data reuse, re-combinations or 'mashups' – for example those combining data with geospatial location components – is a growing source of interest and is generating palpable excitement both within and beyond the academy. The integration of data in metastudies is regarded as essential for more robust results in various areas of health studies and clinical trials, for example as practised by the Cochrane Collaboration.[1] Government and funders are increasingly cognisant that the research grand challenges, such as climate change and responses to aging societies, require interdisciplinary research programmes underpinned by the infrastructure to support good practice in data sharing.

Conventionally, the task of long-term curation of valuable datasets is seen as belonging to national and international data centres with specific missions and appropriate expertise. Additionally, certain data collections or specialized databases have been developed in response to research needs. Registries of data repositories such as Re3data[2] and Databib[3] demonstrate the proliferation of such resources. Yet, it is readily apparent that there is not – and in the short-to-medium term there *will not be* – an appropriate home for all types of data produced by research projects conducted in universities. Where coherent data services exist, catering to the needs of particular research disciplines, or to the curation of particular data types, these are preferred. But universities, as research institutions, also have important responsibilities in the management of research data.

1.2 The role of universities in supporting research data management

The second Jisc Managing Research Data programme addressed a strategic need to develop RDM services in UK universities. It responded directly to the increasing realization that universities have an essential role to play in supporting RDM through the research lifecycle, as explored in Chapters 1 and 2. Universities have tended to do this by providing training and tools for researchers and, where subject-specific data centres are not available or where the university considers it appropriate, by developing data collections in an area of research specialization, looking after the data assets in the long term via institutional data repositories.

Universities have two specific roles in the support of good RDM and the development of research data infrastructure, covering the early and later stages of the research lifecycle. The first is to provide an excellent environment for the conduct of research. In relation to data, this means supporting researchers in meeting funders' requirements in developing data management plans (DMPs), providing appropriate training, resources and tools to facilitate good practice. The second is to contribute to the information infrastructure that allows the management, discovery and reuse of research outputs. Universities, like research funders, have an interest in developing better oversight of their research outputs, including data. Where there is not an alternative home, universities will have a responsibility to retain and curate at least the data that underpins published research findings, but also those datasets that may be considered a significant and reusable output of a given research project.

Recognition of the need for universities to develop RDM services has been emerging for a few years. Prior to 2009 a number of reports, many of them Jisc-funded, sought to cast light on the growing data management challenge for UK universities (for example, Beagrie, Chruszcz and Lavoie, 2008; Green, Macdonald and Rice, 2009; Lyon, 2007; Swan and Brown, 2008). In February 2009, the UK Research Data Service (UKRDS) Scoping Study published preliminary proposals for a co-ordinating body and a set of pathfinder projects. It is fair to say that these proposals met with some resistance from stakeholders. The UKRDS co-ordinating body was viewed – perhaps unfairly – as potentially duplicating activities of existing data centres and the DCC. With more validity, the proposed set of four pathfinder institutions was considered too narrow and self-selecting. It was in this climate that the first Jisc MRD programme was established.

2. Developing a vision and structure for Jisc research data management support

2.1 The first Jisc Managing Research Data (MRD) programme

The first Jisc Managing Research Data programme[4] which ran between 2009 and 2011, took the recommendations from the aforementioned data-related reports and, with an investment of c. £4.3 million, implemented a broad range of activity. Given the context and the uncertainties around the proposed UKRDS, the programme approach was deliberately exploratory, seeking to prototype solutions and build understanding of how RDM capacity might be developed. The programme was divided into four strands, as follows:

1 eight large projects to develop **research data management infrastructure** (both human and technical) in institutions or specific disciplines, together with a DCC-led support project that provided a number of functions and developed the CARDIO tool to assess RDM readiness
2 six projects to improve and make a case for **research data management planning** in direct response to funder requirements
3 six projects to develop **research data management training** materials (termed 'RDMTrain') to improve capacity and skills in the sector, including the Data Management Skills Support Initiative (DaMSSI), which provided a supporting role
4 eight projects to promote open **data publication** and explore mechanisms for citing, identifying and linking research data.

An emerging focus on institutional RDM

Because of its exploratory nature, the RDM infrastructure strand of the first MRD programme – and indeed the programme as a whole – sought to achieve a balance between projects looking at the needs of particular research disciplines and those taking an institutional approach. It became apparent, however, that a more explicit focus on the development of RDM services in institutions was required.

The first set of institutionally focused infrastructure projects was necessarily exploratory and the programme encouraged a variety of approaches.[5] For the ADMIRAL[6] (Oxford) and MaDAM[7] (Manchester) projects, the focus was on understanding requirements and providing technical solutions for specific research departments, though both projects found that a broader institutional approach was needed. The Incremental[8] (Cambridge and Glasgow) project focused on the human side of the challenge, producing a set of very useful training and guidance materials. Finally, the Sudamih[9] (Oxford) project focused both on training materials and a prototype research database hosting service.

All projects produced benefits statements and developed business cases for embedding their outputs. Despite this activity, it seemed there was not yet sufficient momentum or high-level support for the provision of RDM services without further external investment, probably from Jisc. Further work was necessary to develop the scope, content and delivery of RDM services and to make the case within these and other institutions. The IDMB project (Southampton) had perhaps taken things a little further in developing an institutional 'blueprint' and a broad ten-year roadmap for the development of an RDM service, and this seemed to point the way towards more holistic work in a further programme.

What had become apparent during the first programme was the considerable appetite in certain support divisions within institutions to provide RDM services. The need to join up activities across IT services, the library and the research office had been made clear by the work of several projects. Their lessons, gathered at MRD programme and DCC events, notably the Research Data Management Forum (RDMF) series, indicated an appetite and potential for senior support in a number of universities. Furthermore, the outputs from the MRD programme, particularly guidance and training materials, had created a fertile ground on which further work could seed and grow.

2.2 The second Jisc Managing Research Data programme

It seemed appropriate and timely for the second MRD programme to be more coherently directed towards the development of institutional RDM services and somewhat more prescriptive in its approach. Planning was undertaken during the initial MRD programme, with the first internal Jisc proposal for a second MRD programme submitted in January 2011. This prioritized the development of institutional RDM services and required that large infrastructure projects would secure senior management support, develop an institutional research data policy and put forward a business case for embedding a pilot service.

Three significant developments, which all took place in spring 2011, confirmed this direction and contributed to the final shape of the second programme. The first was the publication of the EPSRC *Policy Framework on Research Data* (EPSRC, 2011), which crystallized the need for universities to provide RDM services. The second significant development was the publication of the University of Edinburgh's *Research Data Management Policy* (2011). Although firmly aspirational in tone, this indicated intent, caught the attention of other universities and has served as a reference in the subsequent development of institutional RDM policies. The third development was the use of monies from the HEFCE Universities Modernisation Fund (UMF) to expand the role of the DCC, from March 2011. As a result the DCC initiated a programme of Institutional Engagements, offering tailored support to increase research data management capability.[10]

Requirements in the Call for Projects

As indicated above, the Call for Projects[11] was more prescriptive and ambitious than in the first programme. Released in June 2011, the call allowed for two channels of large infrastructure projects: A1 was to pilot RDM service in institutions that had done little or no work in this area; and A2 was to enhance or extend RDM services in institutions where a pilot already existed (for the most part these institutions had been a project in the first programme). This approach was explicitly to encourage institutions new to the programme to propose projects. Nevertheless, both channels were demanding in what the projects should do and how they would be supported and constructed.

To ensure that the large infrastructure projects had genuinely strong institutional support and were aligned with local strategy, it was a requirement of funding that each project should have a Steering Group including a member of the university senior management team, for example a Pro-Vice-Chancellor for Research or equivalent. To the same end, it was required of A2 proposals, and encouraged in A1 proposals, that the university should provide matched funding.

Building on the activities and findings of the first programme, the call also specified a number of activities that each project should undertake. These were defined at a relatively high level, leaving each institution to develop services that would fit with existing provision, approach or ethos. Nevertheless, the intention was to encourage a set of projects which would undertake a set of similar activities together, as a programme, and produce broadly comparable outputs. The programme set out to encourage projects to reuse, refine and build on existing work, and an annotated bibliography of outputs from the first programme and from the DCC was provided to facilitate this.[12]

All projects were required to undertake a requirements analysis and were encouraged to use the DCC Data Asset Framework[13] or CARDIO quiz[14] as a basis for this. Similarly, projects were asked to produce guidance materials, training and support activities, being directed to the work of the Incremental, Sudamih and RDMTrain[15] projects as good examples. For the development of a technical infrastructure, the use of existing systems and those in development by UMF pilots[16] was encouraged. Projects were expected to support good practice in storing and handling 'active data' during research activity, as well as repositories to curate and share data after that activity's completion. The programme also asked projects to explore the potential of the SWORD protocol for data deposit and strongly encouraged the use of DataCite DOIs (digital object identifiers).

Projects were asked to examine business processes and define roles and responsibilities for RDM throughout the lifecycle. The call also stressed the importance of 'human infrastructure' and called for projects to develop and implement a programme of liaison activities, training and guidance to ensure effective join-up between researchers and support roles in the institution. Finally, projects were required to contribute to the development of overarching institutional policies on RDM and to present a business case to transition the pilot RDM activity into an ongoing service.

Programme structure and projects

The structure of the first MRD programme had been validated, so this was broadly retained in the second, with strands addressing the challenges of data management planning, producing training materials and piloting innovative ways of encouraging data publication. However, at the centre of the programme was a set of large projects to develop institutional RDM infrastructure and services. This can be seen in Figure 10.1.

The call provided an opportunity for particularly innovative or timely proposals, or for projects to develop RDM approaches, systems or solutions for specific subjects that might have a wider application. The call also encouraged the participation of established data centres. So it was that two projects were funded to look at approaches to metadata and deposit challenges in specific research areas. A further project focused on the development of metadata elements for research data in CERIF, the Common European Research Information Format and continued by implementing this profile and developing services at the University of Glasgow. The remaining 14 funded projects took the institutional approach that had been prioritized in the call. Table 10.1 lists the large infrastructure projects included in the second Jisc programme.

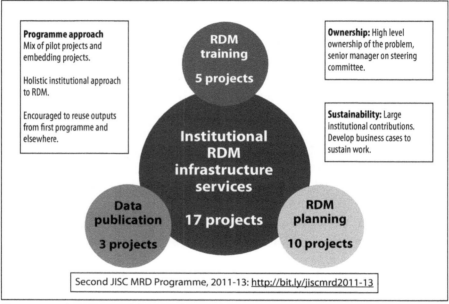

Figure 10.1 The structure of the second Jisc MRD programme

Table 10.1 Large infrastructure projects (strand A) of the second Jisc MRD programme			
University of Reading, University of Bristol, British Atmospheric Data Centre	PIMMS	http://proj.badc.rl.ac.uk/pimms/blog	Subject Specific Metadata
University of York, Archaeological Data Service	SWORD-ARM	http://archaeologydataservice.ac.uk/blog/sword-arm	Subject Specific Deposit/Costing
University of Glasgow, University of St Andrews, University of Sunderland	Cerif 4 Datasets	http://cerif4datasets.wordpress.com	Consortium (CERIF)
University of Bath	Research 360	http://blogs.bath.ac.uk/research360	Single Institution (A1)
University of Bristol	data.bris	http://data.blogs.ilrt.org/project-blog	Single Institution (A1)
University of the Creative Arts, Goldsmiths, University of the Arts London, Glasgow School of Art	KAPTUR	http://kaptur.wordpress.com	Consortium of Institutions (Creative Arts) (A1)
University of Essex	RD@Essex	http://researchdataessex.wordpress.com	Single Institution (A1)
University of Hertfordshire	Research Data Toolkit Herts	http://research-data-toolkit.herts.ac.uk	Single Institution (A1)
University of Leeds	Leeds RoaDMaP	http://blog.library.leeds.ac.uk/blog/roadmap	Single Institution (A1)
University of Lincoln	Orbital	http://orbital.blogs.lincoln.ac.uk	Single Institution (A1)

Continued on next page

Table 10.1 (continued)			
University of Newcastle	iridium	http://research.ncl.ac.uk/iridium/	Single Institution (A1)
University of Newcastle	ADMIRe	http://admire.jiscinvolve.org/wp	Single Institution (A1)
University of the West of England	UWE RDM Pilot	http://blogs.uwe.ac.uk/teams/mrd/default.aspx	Single Institution (A1)
University of Exeter	Open Exeter	http://blogs.exeter.ac.uk/openexeterrdm	Single Institution (A2)
University of Manchester	MiSS	www.miss.manchester.ac.uk	Single Institution (A2)
University of Oxford	DaMaRO	http://blogs.it.ox.ac.uk/damaro	Single Institution (A2)
University of Southampton	DataPool	http://blogs.ecs.soton.ac.uk/datapool	Single Institution (A2)

Programme co-ordination

The Jisc MRD programme was run with a particular ethos and approach, presenting a strategy and vision for how such innovation and change programmes can be designed and managed. The objective was to be a coherent programme rather than a set of disparate projects. This approach was undertaken in the belief that the effectiveness and influence of such interventions and investments is far greater when a set of projects work closely together to exchange ideas, to share developments and learn from each other. By such means, developments may be accelerated during the lifetime of the programme, providing savings of effort through the reuse of material and shared learning. Furthermore, the approach provides institutions outside the programme with a set of coherent activities and outputs with which they can engage.

Adapting an approach used by recent Jisc 'Rapid Innovation' work, projects were required openly to blog regular updates on their work (as opposed to submitting progress reports to the programme manager). The JISCMRD and RESEARCH-DATAMAN mailing lists[17] were widely used as was the Twitter hashtag #jiscmrd, which became a sort of pinboard of updates and announcements from projects. Three part-time 'evidence gatherers' (EGs) were seconded to the programme with the specific task of producing a report substantiating the benefits achieved by the projects and the programme as a whole. Another aspect of the EGs' role was to provide more general assistance with communication and engagement within the programme. Significant programme developments, events and other reflections were reported on the programme manager's and the EGs' blogs.[18] It is fair to say that with the support of the EGs and DCC staff, the MRD projects membership embraced the approach and became a particularly vibrant and engaged community.

An additional feature of the programme's approach was to have regular workshops to share ideas and updates. As far as possible these were developmental in that they responded to emerging needs. So the programme launch meeting presented the ethos and strategy, provided an introduction to the use of blogs and Twitter, and encouraged projects to consider outputs from the previous programme and the DCC. In March 2012, in response to project requests, a workshop was held to support the development of institutional RDM policies. Other workshops followed for projects to engage with training materials, the evidence gathering approach, to consider the use of the CKAN data portal for RDM and to explore issues around storage of research data.[19] An additional support function was provided by the British Library, which as the DataCite member for the UK ran a series of six workshops with support from the Jisc MRD programme to explore and overcome challenges and encourage the use of DataCite DOIs by universities that provide data repository services.[20]

3. An emerging model for the development of RDM support services

The MRD programme progress workshop held in October 2012, in conjunction with the DCC,[21] presented an opportunity for the projects to consider their work across a range of areas and to form a high-level view of what is required for an institutional research data management support service. The workshop was organized into thematic sessions, relating to projects' activity. These areas are represented in Figure 10.2, which seeks to provide a useful, high-level visualization of the areas addressed by projects in developing an RDM Service. It does not pretend to be a detailed representation of the service components, but a guide to the areas of activity and consideration; and at a programme level it played a useful role in facilitating group discussions and interchange between projects.

Each project in the Jisc MRD programme addressed all or most of these areas. At the time of writing, not all the projects have been completed and it is not possible to provide a full summary of all the areas described above, nor to draw examples from all of the projects. It is fair to say, however, that progress has been more rapid in some areas, while others remain – necessarily – at an early stage of development.

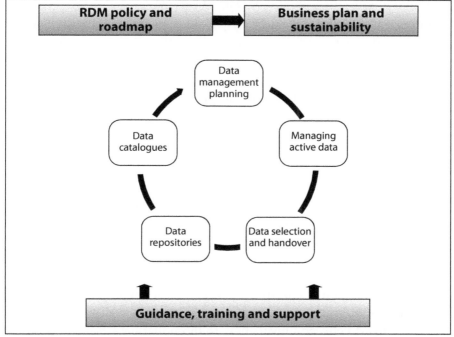

Figure 10.2 Components of research data management support services (reproduced from *How to Develop Research Data Management Services – a guide for HEIs*, by permission of the Digital Curation Centre)

In what follows, we shall provide an overview and examples from a number of projects covering the following activity areas:

- requirements analyses and data asset surveys
- institutional RDM policies and strategies
- guidance and training materials
- . provision of robust storage and services for 'active' data
- data repository services
- business cases for continuation of RDM pilot services.

This structure closely parallels that of Chapter 5 on developing RDM infrastructure and services, so the two chapters should be read in conjunction. While this case study focuses on the achievements of institutional projects within the second Jisc MRD programme, Chapter 5 takes a broader perspective, incorporating examples from other UK universities, DCC work and international initiatives.

3.1 Requirements analyses and data asset surveys

An important step that cannot be by-passed is to conduct a requirements analysis, so this was made obligatory in the MRD Call for Projects. Most projects used DAF or CARDIO, often in adapted forms. More detail on these tools is available in Chapter 4. Projects typically conducted broad surveys followed by more detailed analyses to understand the nature of research data being created and how these were stored, managed and shared. Projects often worked closely with a set of departments or research groups to identify requirements and then co-design training, DMP support or the provision of technical infrastructure. A number of projects, including those at Bristol and Bath, had intended to pilot activities in a single school or faculty. However, they soon found levels of demand for support across the institution obliged them to broaden the scope of activity.

Survey results

Although it is difficult to effectively summarize the findings of the surveys, there does not appear to be a great number of marked differences in the practice of RDM between universities. To those that have been working in this space the findings may sound very familiar. Most projects[22] found that:

- there was a lack of central policy and co-ordination of RDM
- RDM practice, understanding and awareness varied widely within institutions
- few researchers have experience of completing a DMP
- researchers use a wide variety of storage solutions, with varying degrees of robustness and security
- most researchers' storage requirements exceed their current institutional provision
- data was held in a wide variety of formats and volumes, and often required specialist knowledge to describe and manage it
- awareness of legal, IPR and policy issues relating to RDM – particularly those of research funders – are relatively low
- there is strong evidence of demand for advocacy, training and support, particularly in developing DMPs as part of grant applications
- systems to support RDM during research projects and institutional data repositories would be valued by researchers.

The surveys showed that storing and sharing research data in a controlled manner during projects were researchers' most pressing concerns. Bar a few exceptions, research data management practice was found to be short-termist, with solutions being *ad hoc* and local. Most projects reported very mixed attitudes to the idea of data sharing; some researchers expressing considerable resistance, while others expressed enthusiasm at the provision of repository systems to describe and share data.

Data volumes and data loss

Surveys have allowed projects to estimate the data volumes produced and held.[23] Estimates of current data storage requirements range from as little as 150–170 Tb in a new university, through to up to 2 Pb in a 'research-aspirational' university, to 2–4 Pb in a number of Russell Group universities. All such figures are estimates and many may be wide (and low) of the mark! Many projects reported along these lines: 'the more groups we go to talk to, the more we're hearing of significant data holdings on external hard drives and small RAID systems'.[24]

Projects uncovered some evidence of significant data loss. In one institution's survey, nearly a quarter of researchers reported having suffered significant data loss, with roughly 8% reporting having lost one day's work and a similar number one week's work. The project made a rough and deliberately conservative estimate that the cost of such data loss amounted to £25,000. This was the absolute cost of data loss uncovered by the survey, rather than an extrapolation across the university. It serves as an indication that the price of investment in RDM services may be mitigated by reductions in the cost of data loss. Most projects have understandably been unwilling to publish such results for fear of reputational damage, yet such figures and examples are by no means unusual and seem to be mirrored in most institutions. Further-more, many projects have encountered instances where data representing a significant investment were being managed in circumstances with a high risk of failure, and a few have uncovered examples of catastrophic data loss.

Although individual requirements analyses uncovered few surprises when compared to previous studies, it is invaluable to present university managers with empirical evidence of current practice and likely demand. Without such evidence based on current practice, they are unlikely to be persuaded of the need to invest in RDM services. Perhaps even more valuable is that the very act of conducting the surveys and interview is a necessary step in raising the issues, engaging researchers and preparing expectations for necessary but incremental interventions.

3.2 Institutional RDM policies and strategies

The creation of an institutional RDM policy is a keystone activity in the development of RDM services. An RDM policy can signal intent, attribute responsibilities and – as the DCC *How to Develop RDM Services* guide stresses – 'policy development is an important outreach and engagement activity in its own right' (Jones, Pryor and Whyte, 2013, 6). For this reason, it was an activity stipulated of all large infrastructure projects in the second MRD programme. Inevitably, however, there were different ways of going about the activity, reflecting institutional culture, the relationship between policy and strategy and the interaction between key service units (such as the library, IT services and research office).

Policy development was an area where projects benefited substantially from discussion within the programme. In response to demand, a workshop was held in March 2012, hosted by the Leeds RoaDMaP project. Most sessions of the workshop were held under the Chatham House Rule[25] in order to allow projects to speak frankly about their approaches and the challenges faced. Although the focus was ostensibly on the development of institutional RDM policies, in practice, it became more than that. In particular, projects discussed the relation between policy and implementation, the appropriate distribution of responsibilities within the institution and the task of making the case for investment. As such, the event was welcomed as a timely opportunity to speak frankly about a number of related challenges at a formative early stage in the projects' work.[26]

Approaches to RDM policy development

Many institutions have adopted the approach of formulating and agreeing a set of high-level and general principles, often similar to and modelled on Edinburgh's avowedly aspirational policy. It would then be the task of the RDM strategy, often expressed in an EPSRC roadmap, to put these principles into practice. Differing levels of detail may be observed in the published policies – most notably adding precision to the responsibilities of researchers and linking directly to related policies, supporting documentation or guidance, as is done, for example, in the Southampton policy.[27] The University of Leeds policy[28] is in most respects similar to the general approach of the Edinburgh policy. However, it adds some precision in terms of compliance with other legislative frameworks and PI responsibilities at the completion of a project. Neatly, the policy links at specific points directly to FAQs and guidance documentation and is followed by statements of the benefits of the policy and improved RDM.

The Open Exeter project gave two distinct slants to their policy work, in order to align it more closely with institutional priorities and project activities. First, Open Exeter worked closely with postgraduate students on a number of project activities: testing new technologies, documenting experiences and methodologies, and supporting some of the embedding activities. Fittingly, therefore, the project prepared two policies, one for postgraduate research students (PGRs) and another for researchers.[29] Second, the policy is combined with Exeter's Open Access policy. The documents lay out, therefore, the responsibilities of researchers and of PGRs to deposit their published work and appropriate data with Open Research Exeter, the university's research archive.

3.3 Guidance and training materials
Online RDM guidance materials

The first Jisc MRD programme served as a catalyst to a more sophisticated awareness of research data management. Institutions have increasingly produced online guidance resources since, containing high-level definitions and concepts of RDM tasks. A list of some of these RDM guidance web pages is provided by the DCC.[30] As one of the preliminary activities conducted by institutions, these resources attempt to cater for researchers with no knowledge or experience of RDM, as well as those who might just be looking for a particular, institution-specific detail. The websites typically define skills likely to be required by researchers in the course of their work, and provide named individuals from IT services, the research office or the library who could provide support. The production of online guidance resources often signals the institution's commitment to improved RDM practice, as they demand ongoing maintenance after the project lifetime.

The Incremental project's web resource[31] has proved helpful to various subsequent MRD projects as an indicator of the sorts of content required by institution-wide guidance resources, as well as a way to present the information for easy navigation. More recent online guidance web pages cover similar ground; but there are indicators that topics to help researchers exploit their data, such as licensing of data and the use of persistent identifiers for datasets, are becoming popular as these areas mature. Important areas of RDM that are less often covered in institutional training and guidance include data citation, use of persistent identifiers for researchers and datasets, the costing of RDM and the selection and appraisal of data for curation.

RDM training projects (RDMTrain)

Five projects were funded in the first MRD programme to design and deliver training materials for postgraduate and early career researchers in named research disciplines. These projects were commonly identified as the 'RDMTrain' strand of the programme. The projects worked closely with named academic departments, incorporating discipline-specific terminology and examples within the generic guidance. Four projects were subsequently funded to design, pilot and test training materials in the second MRD programme. This strand saw a widening of the intended audience to include research librarians and other information professionals requiring research data management awareness and skills. Further subjects were also supplied with discipline-specific resources. The outputs of both RDMTrain strands are openly available and have been deposited in JORUM. The projects are noted in Table 10.2.

Table 10.2 RDMTrain projects from the two Jisc MRD programmes	
Project (University)	**Discipline coverage**
CAiRO (Bristol)	Creative arts and performance
DataTrain (Cambridge)	Archaeology and social anthropology
DATUM for Health (Northumbria)	Health studies (using qualitative, unstructured data)
DMTpsych (York)	Psychological sciences
Research Data MANTRA (Edinburgh)	Geoscience, social and political sciences, and clinical psychology
RDMRose (Sheffield)	Library and information science
RDMTPA (Hertfordshire)	Physics and astronomy
SoDaMaT (QMUL)	Digital music
TraD (UEL)	Psychology, computer science and library science

The large infrastructure projects were, of course, also occupied with guidance and training, as the programme design acknowledged the fundamental importance of awareness and skills development alongside technical development. Without investment in human infrastructure, projects risked losing researcher interest in and management support for improved practice. Some projects provided bespoke support for researchers seeking RDM advice and, in particular, help with the preparation of DMPs as a part of grant proposals. The data.bris (University of Bristol) team found particularly high levels of demand and provided support for approximately

60 researchers from all faculties of the university. To scale to these needs, the team contributed to the university's ongoing series of grant writing workshops. A number of other institutions, including the Universities of Bath, Southampton and Essex, have run similar events.

Training support projects and the reuse of materials

The first RDMTrain strand was supported by the Data Management Skills Support Initiative (DaMSSI), led by the DCC.[32] It was recognized that research data management skills were not yet embedded within UK postgraduate skills curricula, and in order to do so there was a need for agreement on what constitutes a basic set of postgraduate-level data management skills. The initiative demonstrated the relevance of RDM activity to wider researcher skills frameworks such as the Vitae Researcher Development Framework and the SCONUL Seven Pillars of Information Literacy by mapping RDMTrain outputs to these established models. Recommendations from the DaMSSI project, such as improving the findability of RDMTrain outputs, were pursued via the subsequent DaMSSI-ABC project.

Projects in the second MRD programme were encouraged to reuse and extend outputs of earlier work and they typically reused a variety of resources. Examples include the ADMIRe project, which used material from MANTRA and the concurrent TRaD project.[33] TRaD and iridium are amongst other projects that have also used MANTRA resources in their guidance. MANTRA's success in developing highly praised interactive training resources using the Xerte learning object software provided inspiration for the later KAPTUR and TRaD outputs on the same platform. In turn, MRD programme outputs have been useful for the DCC and others. For example, a DCC training event for research librarians at the University of Northampton[34] made use of the work of outputs from ADMIRe, MANTRA, Research360, RDMRose, RoaDMaP and TraD as well as the UKDA *Managing and Sharing Research Data* (Van den Eynden et al., 2011) guide.

3.4 Provision of robust storage and services for 'active' data
Data storage

A number of projects explored how the central provision of data storage could be improved to mitigate the risk of data loss and meet researchers' requests for robust and secure storage. The Research Data Toolkit Project at the University of Hertfordshire (RDTK Herts) was one of the projects to explore this in detail. The project found that the existing networked storage, Hertfordshire's local cloud, could supply the necessary functionality to the majority of researchers, with the exception of those requiring multiple terabytes of storage. The project surmised that 'the problem was that because of poor documentation, induction procedures and onward training most researchers couldn't use it effectively, thought it too limited in capacity, or were simply unaware of the offer'.[35] This indicates that the situation of low uptake of centrally provided storage – shared by most projects in the programme – can at least in part be addressed through awareness raising, support and training activities.

The costs of hardware failure and data loss have also been examined by the RDTK Herts project in an analysis that uncovers the significant hidden costs of *ad hoc* 'Data centre Under the Desk' (DUD) arrangements.[36] The study acknowledges the lure of cheap storage (when only the hardware costs are considered) and recognizes that risk analyses based on cost-reliability may play out differently for different types (and value) of data. Nevertheless, the evidence presented suggests that the hidden costs of *ad hoc* systems, including the higher risk of data loss and the staff time involved, makes DUDs extremely uncompetitive, between two and four times more expensive than centrally provided services. For a university such as Hertfordshire, consolidating 1 Pb of research data from *ad hoc* arrangements to a centralized data service could save nearly £1 million per annum.

The University of Bristol had already invested in a Research Data Storage Facility (RDSF), by means of which up to 5 Tb of storage could be assigned to research projects via a 'data steward'. During the life of the data.bris project, and in large part demonstrably the result of data.bris awareness-raising activities, the RDSF has seen a large increase in the number of 'data stewards'. Notably, many applicants explicitly mentioned their need to 'publish' research data – to make it available, with a persistent identifier – as the central reason for their application. This points the way to a potentially attractive feature of centrally provided data storage, above the avoidance of data loss.

Systems for managing and sharing data

In addition to adequate storage, researchers also need a facility to support in-project data sharing with collaborators external to their institution. The RDTK Herts project delved into the reasons behind the pervasive use of

Dropbox, finding that it is simply 'an order of magnitude easier to use than anything else currently on offer'.[37] However, the cost of Dropbox does not currently scale competitively for large data, and universities are concerned by security issues associated with the location of data in such third-party, cloud solutions. The project looked into some alternative 'Dropbox-like' solutions to support cloud-hosting, back-up and synchronization and sharing functions. DataStage, iFolder, SparkleShare and OwnCloud were each found to be too immature, of uncertain sustainability, or requiring too much support to consider seriously in the short term. There is undoubted appeal in the functionality of cloud-based back-up/sharing products, and calls for such services at institutional or national level. But there are a number of substantial issues – such as appropriate hosting, security, access, cost, usability – which need to be addressed before this can be a reality. At a minimum, institutions should raise awareness of the issues to consider. The Open Exeter project produced brief guidance on the use of cloud tools for storage and file transfer[38] which may be instructive in this vein.

Several benefits ensue when research data are held within university systems: the institution can be assured that security, data access and back-up can be robustly managed and opportunities exist for integration with other research systems. The data.bris system enhances the RDSF by providing a 'publish' mechanism, by which data already in the system can be made available and exposed, without the need for an arduous deposit and upload process. It is hoped – and usage seems to confirm – that the security and robustness of the RDSF provide good motivation for projects to use it. Once in the system, the barrier to publishing data is lowered. Where the data is not already in a university support system, then lowering the barriers to data deposit and supporting the transfer of large datasets are important to the development of effective RDM services. A number of projects experimented with using the SWORD2 protocol for deposit of research data. The data.bris project trialled BitTorrent for robust transfer of large datasets, while the University of Hertfordshire has used Zendto. The Open Exeter project, meanwhile, developed a tool for depositing large datasets into DSpace, taking advantage of the SWORD2 protocol and using Globus for asynchronous data transfer.[39]

An even more effective way of improving RDM than simplifying deposit is to persuade researchers to use institutional RDM systems early in the process of data creation. To this end, a number of projects sought to explore how research data services can support the full research lifecycle and join up existing or desired institutional systems to support research project management. This is particularly relevant, as RDM is just one aspect of the research process (for researchers) and just one aspect of administering the research process and projects (for universities).

Integrated RDM systems: the case of using CKAN in the Orbital project

Realizing that data management cannot easily be isolated from other aspects of the research lifecycle, the Orbital project at Lincoln took the view that RDM 'was not simply a planning and curatorial exercise'[40] and so support and systems should address not only the planning and deposit stages. The project adopted CKAN,[41] taking advantage of its APIs, data store and data visualization features to join up research systems and provide a place where researchers can create a 'research data environment' to manage data during the active phase of research projects. It is hoped that providing visualization tools and linking to other university systems will make this a useful and robust platform in which researchers will be willing to keep their data during the research project.

The tool joining everything up is the Researcher Dashboard.[42] This links to the Awards Management System and Nucleus (Lincoln's staff registry), and allows the creation of a research data environment. When a dataset is complete and can be made available, or a metadata record published, this, too, is managed through the Researcher Dashboard, which will link to the DataCite API to assign a DOI and deposit a record of the dataset in Lincoln's EPrints repository. These processes can be seen in Figure 10.3.

The Orbital project reports that this approach helped them significantly in two ways: (1) in engagement with researchers who could see the benefits of managing data in the CKAN platform; and (2) in preparing their business case in a university which was more receptive to the benefits of a joined-up approach to research information management than the specific needs of research data management.

The Orbital project's adoption of CKAN was influential for other Jisc MRD projects, particularly as they facilitated a workshop to look at the possibility of using CKAN for RDM in universities. This workshop was used by Joss Winn of Orbital to prepare an evaluation of CKAN for RDM in an academic context.[43] The software was explored by the KAPTUR, iridium and data.bris projects, with the latter now using CKAN to provide data portal functionality.

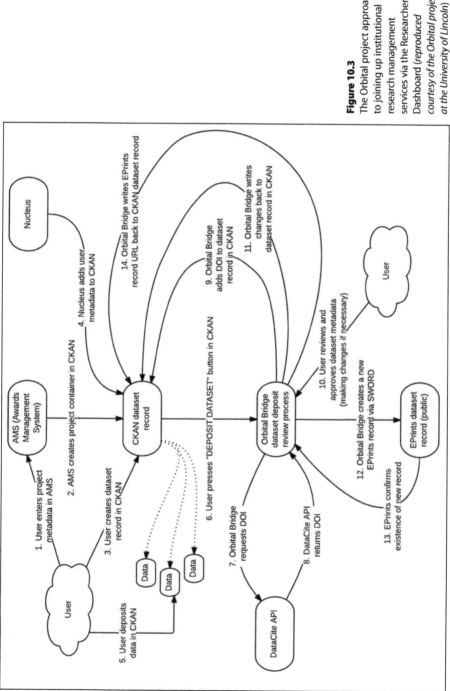

Figure 10.3
The Orbital project approach to joining up institutional research management services via the Researcher Dashboard (*reproduced courtesy of the Orbital project at the University of Lincoln*)

3.5 Data repository services
Extending institutional repositories for data

All universities involved in the MRD programme had an institutional (document) repository of some form (typically DSpace, Fedora or EPrints instances) and most adapted these for data. Although primarily used as document repositories, such software may in principle be used for any type of digital content. Fedora, after all, is used by the UK Data Archive, and DSpace underpins the Dryad data repository. Many projects felt that it was important to use a platform that was already supported in the university, to take advantage of existing expertise and awareness.

The RD@Essex project worked with the existing EPrints institutional repository and undertook extensive customization to make the software more suitable for curating and presenting research data. This work focused on adapting and extending the EPrints metadata profile to allow the capture of detail necessary for describing a diverse range of research data collections. As with many institutions, Essex has a broad research base, producing varied data types. The shared challenge for institutional data repositories is to develop a metadata profile that meets requirements which seem to pull in opposing directions. The metadata must be generic and flexible enough to describe and present data from any of the disciplines in the institution, yet descriptions should be detailed and specific enough to allow reuse. In addition, the information requested should not make the deposit process so arduous and complex that it deters users and presents a barrier to uptake. As the project reports, such considerations impose 'a necessary compromise between ease of deposit and the need for sufficient information to fully enable re-use'.[44]

Developing metadata profiles for research data

Deploying the UK Data Archive's expertise and approach to social science data curation, the RD@Essex project built on previous work, adapting a three-layer metadata model proposed by the Southampton IDMB project in the first MRD programme, as seen in Figure 10.4. Similar three-layer models have been discussed by Alex Ball of the DCC,[45] and a comparable division, featuring 'a structured, semantically-rich model for contextual metadata' has been proposed by the Engage project and Eurocris (Houssos, Jörg and Matthews, 2012). For the University of Essex schema, the core and detail metadata were put together using elements from DataCite 2.2, INSPIRE 1.2 (for geospatial information) and DDI Codebook 2.1 (for social science

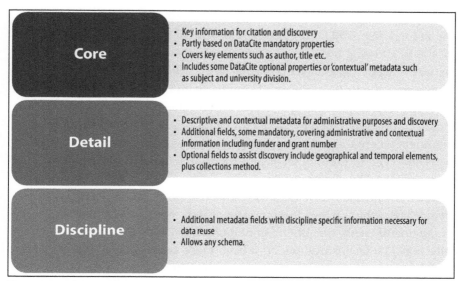

Figure 10.4 The RD@Essex three-layer approach to metadata, adapted from the IDMB project
(*reproduced courtesy of the RD@Essex project*)

studies and data collection). The metadata profile has been published[46] and mapped against these standards and the profile used by DataShare, the digital repository of the University of Edinburgh. The DaMaRO project at Oxford has taken a broadly similar three-tier approach.

The RD@Essex project worked with specific research groups, ingesting sample datasets into the repository and testing usability. The datasets covered a range of research areas and data types, including large-scale proteomics and bio-imaging data; data relating to artificial intelligence research; management research data, typically spreadsheets; and socio-linguistic data. Adaptations were made to the user interface to enable clearer presentation of the extended metadata and of data elements within collections. Through collaborative work with the DataPool project, these adaptations and the metadata profile are now available as an app or plug-in for EPrints called ReCollect, available from EPrints Bazaar.[47] The plug-in allows other institutions to set up their own EPrints data repository with the expanded metadata profile for describing research data and the redesigned interface for presenting complex data collections. The RD@Essex project also produced a user guide[48] for preparing and depositing research data in the institutional data repository and a set of policies[49] covering the 'depositor agreement', the 'rights and responsibilities' of the repository service and the 'terms and conditions' for end users of the data.

British Library DataCite workshops and the use of DOIs

The second Jisc MRD Programme has sought to raise awareness of the possibility of using DataCite DOIs in university-based data collections, and has encouraged projects to take this step. With support from the MRD Programme, the British Library's Datasets Team ran a series of six very well received workshops looking at issues around the identification and citation of data.[50] Topics included metadata for citation and discovery, the best use of identifiers where there are issues of granularity or versioning, and practical issues involved in minting DOIs and the contractual arrangements with the BL as the UK's DataCite provider.

Some institutions have regarded the use of DataCite DOIs as a 'no-brainer': Bristol, Oxford and Southampton have made the necessary arrangements with the BL to mint DataCite DOIs for datasets in their collections. Other institutions have been more cautious and there has been useful debate within the programme, on the listservs and at the workshops, about the merits of DataCite DOIs as opposed to other forms of persistent identification.[51] On the one hand, there has been a view that DOIs might be too heavyweight a solution for institutional data repositories, which are emerging systems and commitments, for which the collection development and management trajectory is not yet certain. Some institutions, like the University of Essex, felt that a consensus had not been reached as to the real benefits of adopting DataCite DOIs for institutional data repositories, viewing Handles or internal persistent identifiers as sufficient. The contrary view, expressed in these discussions, is that assigning a DataCite DOI to a dataset implies that a set of important decisions have been made in terms of the dataset being fixed, permanent and of a certain quality level.

If using DataCite DOIs, it is perhaps not *essential* for university-based data repositories to take on these responsibilities, but some argue that it helps to communicate that such a responsibility has been taken to depositors and users. One of DataCite's core missions is to encourage the citation of data in the scholarly literature. Again, a DOI is not *essential* for a well crafted and workable citation – but there is a widespread perception that researchers trust DOIs and will buy into data citation more readily if they are used. It is a widely held view that has motivated the adoption of DataCite DOIs by a range of data centres, including UKDA and BADC (Callaghan et al., 2012) and by initiatives such as Figshare, Zenodo and Dryad, which view assigning DOIs as an important step in encouraging researchers to share data outputs.

3.6 Business cases for the continuation of RDM pilot services

The business cases put forward by the projects demonstrated how best practice in RDM would benefit an institution and help strengthen partnerships with external collaborators (which may require robust and secure RDM infrastructure). The Research 360 project at Bath also produced a document to show how improved RDM could contribute to research excellence and specifically to the university's performance in research assessment activities.[52]

One of the key examples of success in this area comes from the data.bris project. Through a more ambitious business case than originally envisaged, the team secured internal funding for five members of staff for a 2½-year pilot to further develop the data.bris RDM service. The pilot will cover:

- continued development of the University of Bristol RDM website
- delivery of advice and training for researchers, including DMP support and consultation
- a pilot research data repository service, with CKAN providing the data portal access
- exploration of the possible integration of the data.bris portal with the University's Pure Research Information System.

Arguments that carried weight were the need to meet the requirements of funders and, increasingly, academic publishers, but also – and importantly – that the availability of datasets would benefit research in the university, forming the grounds for innovative new projects, particularly those examining the potential of knowledge extraction from 'big data'. Perhaps the most telling case, particularly for the projects at Bath and Bristol, was the ability to point to the rising level of researcher demand for support.

Projecting return on investment in the data.bris business case

In challenging economic times for universities, it is also important for business cases to address 'the bottom line'. There are three main areas in which it might be proposed that RDM services could obtain financial benefits for the institution:

- by reducing the risk or the actual cost of data loss, which may be incurred directly through the cost of recreating data or indirectly through secondary effects (damage to reputation, loss of research income)
- through increased research efficiency, by supporting researchers in

RDM, thereby freeing them for core tasks
* through an increase in research income from more successful grant proposals, where DMPs or strong RDM infrastructure may be a factor.

The data.bris business case addressed each of these issues and did so in part by setting targets for the pilot project, which will continue the work of the MRD project. First, the risk of data loss can be assumed to be reduced by increased use of the university's centrally provided storage and the project provided examples of high-value data (the result of considerable investment) that was now securely housed in the RDSF.

Second, it is recognized that researchers already spent a proportion of their time on handling their data, but often this is not in the most efficient or effective way. On the basis of the project's work with researchers, it was estimated that the RDM service (training, support and infrastructure) could free up at least 2.5% of an average PI's time from data management activities, 'an efficiency of significant monetary value'. In the business case, the new data.bris pilot service undertook to demonstrate such efficiencies through four individual case studies per year.

Finally, the data.bris project had provided direct support for the preparation of DMPs. In one case, this came when peer reviewers had rejected the technical appendix for an £800,000 research proposal to the AHRC. The data.bris team helped rework the technical appendix and the resubmitted proposal was successful, with the data management and sharing plans now described as 'exemplary'. On the basis of this and other work to support DMPs and grant writing, the data.bris business case undertook to demonstrate a 1% increase in grant income attributable to high-quality DMPs, again through four individual case studies per year.[53]

Progress on business planning and prioritizing resources

Several other projects in the MRD programme have also been successful in securing ongoing support from the institution for the RDM service development initiated by the Jisc project. At Southampton, a dedicated group of six staff in the library, equivalent to three full-time staff, will take a lead on research data management support, focusing on the further development and extension of RDM services piloted by the IDMB and DataPool projects. Similarly, the Research 360 project's business case led to the creation of two permanent and full-time data management roles at the University of Bath in order to continue the work of the project. As noted previously, the Lincoln business case proposed the development of joined-up 'research information services' and this was felt to be more attractive to the university than focusing uniquely on RDM. The success of this proposal has led to the creation of a new post of research services developer to continue development of the Orbital RDM system and the regrading of a librarian's post to support this work. The university has created a new steering group for research services and an annual DAF-based survey will be performed to track progress.

The business case for local investment in data infrastructure was not compelling at all universities. At Essex, a 'route map' was approved, outlining how the high-level policy would be implemented, not least in order to meet EPSRC expectations, though this was not the single and unique objective. The 'route map' works at a high level and covers such issues as the provision of training and support, the allocation of storage and the creation of a suitable register for data created in the university but stored elsewhere. Importantly, responsibility for each of these areas is assigned either to the Research and Enterprise Office, the university's Research Strategy Committee or ICT Steering Group.

The emphasis in the RD@Essex sustainability plan, however, is on raising awareness, training and building capacity. The further development and maintenance of a repository infrastructure for the long-term preservation of data was felt to be beyond the current capacity of the university to sustain.[54] In a time of considerable pressure on university budgets, in which establishing systems to support REF (Research Excellence Framework) reporting have taken priority, investment in RDM infrastructure – beyond the human services – can struggle to gain traction. The University of Essex 'Sustainability Plan' states:

> the University is uncertain as to whether a single-track investment in local data infrastructure is the best way forward and that a federated approach with, for example, their 94 Group colleagues might be more efficient and less cost-intensive. It needs to be recognised that there is already both formal mandatory data sharing policies in place that are working and national expertise in data centres who already deal with sharing research data. Smaller universities, such as Essex, would be better using national shared infrastructure services, like [Jisc/JANET brokered] services for cloud storage and possibly specialist off-site data appraisal and advice on preparation, such as that provided by the UK Data Archive for all ESRC research data. Any longer-term preservation comes at a huge price and should utilise a shared service.

> (www.data-archive.ac.uk/media/402398/rde_sustainabilityplan.pdf)

Exploring the possibility of data infrastructure services that are shared between institutions will be important if some smaller institutions are to be able to provide RDM infrastructure for their research-intensive departments. This points to the ongoing need for national co-ordination and strategy in the development and provision of RDM services.

4. Where next? Institutions and the data infrastructure

The projects in the Jisc MRD programme demonstrated that it was important and feasible for universities to develop RDM support services and provided evidence that benefits could thereby be achieved. Nevertheless, it should be stressed that, even in the most advanced and successful cases, these remain pilots. There remains a long transformation before any institution has a fully implemented, 'nose-to-tail', RDM service.

It remains to be seen what scale of service will be most appropriate for each institution and therefore what level of investment may be required. Few institutions are assessing the situation and thinking that there is no need for *any* adaptation and investment. A significant number of research-intensive universities in the UK regard the development of RDM services as a necessary step to achieving a core part of their mission and as a means to stay competitive for research grants and, potentially, steal the march in a world of more data-intensive research. The impetus is no less strong, however, among some universities that are 'research-aspirational', perhaps largely teaching institutions with certain departments or groups with excellent research credentials. For such universities, the gain or loss of a research grant can be significant and there is marked ambition not to lose ground to the research-intensive institutions.

There have been calls to explore regional or national solutions. Implementing and running expensive infrastructure, like RDM storage solutions, represent a cost – and a benefit – that could potentially be shared between institutions on a regional or national collaborative basis. Although many institutions felt that there were clear benefits of developing data infrastructure as part of their local RDM capacity, others felt that the university could provide awareness raising, guidance and training, but that long-term preservation was something that should be tackled by a shared, national infrastructure, perhaps working with existing data centres.

A number of areas of activity will clearly repay further attention. For example, there is a need to address the usability of key components of the RDM infrastructure, from spaces for managing and sharing 'active' data, through VRE-type tools, to the deposit and repository functions. A number of projects have pointed to the need for further work to join up RDM services with existing systems which support the management and reporting of research projects.

One-to-one services are not scalable and full lifecycle support for RDM can only be achieved through strong researcher engagement, as well as through researchers being better equipped to help themselves. Projects have indicated that researcher demand for support in the preparation of DMPs, for storage and sharing facilities, and even for mechanisms to 'publish' research data, have provided the most eloquent passages in their business cases. Continued advocacy, training and preparing the capacity to respond to demand as it develops will be essential in the ongoing development of RDM services.

The landmark Royal Society report, *Science as an Open Enterprise*, makes a forceful case for 'intelligent openness' to allow access and reuse of research data. Among its recommendations is that 'JISC's Managing Research Data programme, or a similar initiative, should be expanded beyond the pilot 17 institutions within the next five years' (Royal Society, 2012, 73). This call is echoed by the projects in the MRD programme. Most projects felt that they benefited from being part of a co-ordinated programme and there are numerous recommendations for the approach to continue, with more direct involvement of the DCC. As the data.bris team writes:

> Without the existence of large-scale Jisc Innovation programmes of this type, valuable sector-wide cross-fertilization and accelerated progress is unlikely to occur through the independent normal operation of disparate institutions. The new Jisc and its client institutions should look to the old JISC's MRD programme as an exemplar model for future innovation programmes.[55]

5. References

5.1 Websites, project reports and notes

1   The Cochrance Collaboration is an international network of more than 31,000 dedicated people from over 100 countries that works together to help healthcare practitioners, policy-makers, patients, their advocates and carers, make well-informed decisions about healthcare, by preparing, updating, and promoting the accessibility of Cochrane Reviews. Further details are available at www.cochrane.org.

2   Re3data list of repositories: www.re3data.org.

3 Databib list of repositories: http://databib.org.
4 Jisc MRD programme 2009–11:
   www.jisc.ac.uk/whatwedo/programmes/mrd.aspx.
5 It should be mentioned, for the sake of balance, that two of the more
   discipline-focused RDM infrastructure projects in the first programme also
   produced excellent work. I2S2 provided a valuable and detailed analysis of the
   research lifecycle and data exchange in research using facilities of various
   sizes, and contributed to the STFC's ICAT data management system. FishNet
   developed a data archive for the Freshwater Biological Association, an
   infrastructure which has gone on to be used to underpin the DEFRA-funded
   Demonstration Test Catchment Archive. Notwithstanding these successes, it
   was clear that the Jisc programme needed to prioritise effort to help
   universities address the need to provide RDM services.
6 www.jisc.ac.uk/whatwedo/programmes/mrd/rdmi/admiral.aspx.
7 www.jisc.ac.uk/whatwedo/programmes/mrd/rdmi/madam.aspx.
8 www.jisc.ac.uk/whatwedo/programmes/mrd/rdmi/incremental.aspx.
9 www.jisc.ac.uk/whatwedo/programmes/mrd/rdmi/sudamih.aspx.
10 DCC Institutional Engagements: www.dcc.ac.uk/community/institutional-
   engagements.
11 Jisc MRD02 programme call:
   www.jisc.ac.uk/fundingopportunities/funding_calls/2011/06/
   managingresearchdata.aspx.
12 Annotated list of MRD01 project outputs:
   www.jisc.ac.uk/whatwedo/programmes/mrd/outputs.aspx.
13 Data Asset Framework: www.data-audit.eu.
14 CARDIO tool and quiz: www.dcc.ac.uk/projects/cardio.
15 RDMTrain projects:
   www.jisc.ac.uk/whatwedo/programmes/mrd/rdmtrain.aspx.
16 UMF pilot projects (strand A3):
   www.jisc.ac.uk/whatwedo/programmes/umf.aspx.
17 JISCMRD listserv: www.jiscmail.ac.uk/cgi-bin/webadmin?A0=JISCMRD and
   the RESEARCH-DATAMAN listserv:
   www.jiscmail.ac.uk/cgi-bin/webadmin?A0=RESEARCH-DATAMAN.
18 Programme manager's blog: http://researchdata.jiscinvolve.org/wp and the
   evidence gatherers' blog: http://mrdevidence.jiscinvolve.org/wp.
19 A full list of the workshops and events run by the programme is available at:
   www.jisc.ac.uk/whatwedo/programmes/di_researchmanagement/
   managingresearchdata/events.aspx.
20 British Library DataCite workshops:

www.bl.uk/aboutus/stratpolprog/digi/datasets/dataciteworkshops/index.html.

21 MRD progress workshop: www.jisc.ac.uk/whatwedo/programmes/
di_researchmanagement/managingresearchdata/events/
ComponentsofInstitutionalResearchDataServices.aspx.

22 A flavour of the published requirements reports can be obtained from the
following three studies: 1) Summary Findings of the Open Exeter Data Asset
Framework (DAF) Survey, https://ore.exeter.ac.uk/repository/handle/10036/3689;
2) ADMIRe project Research Data Management Survey,
http://admire.jiscinvolve.org/wp/2013/02/07/university-of-nottingham-research-
data-management-survey-results; and 3) University of Essex Staff Research Data
Survey www.data-archive.ac.uk/media/391114/rdessex_staffsurveyreport.pdf.

23 Given the immaturity of practice, it is less easy to estimate the volume of data
which will need to be retained and archived in the long term. A common rule
of thumb is 10% – more robust estimates may emerge from the programme,
but were not readily available at the time of writing.

24 These figures and the quotation are unattributed by agreement.

25 Chatham House Rule: www.chathamhouse.org/about-us/chathamhouserule.

26 Summary of the Jisc MRD policy workshop: http://mrdevidence.jiscinvolve.
org/wp/2012/03/16/chatham-house-at-weetwood-hall-emerging-themes-from-
the-jiscmrd02-institutional-rdm-policy-workshop.

27 Southampton RDM policy: www.calendar.soton.ac.uk/sectionIV/research-data-
management.html.

28 Leeds RDM policy: http://library.leeds.ac.uk/research-data-management-policy.

29 Exeter PGR policy: https://ore.exeter.ac.uk/repository/handle/10036/4279; and
the general OA and RDM policy:
https://ore.exeter.ac.uk/repository/handle/10036/4280.

30 DCC list of RDM guidance web pages: www.dcc.ac.uk/resources/policy-and-
legal/policy-tools-and-guidance/policy-tools-and-guidance.

31 Incremental web pages at Glasgow: www.glasgow.ac.uk/datamanagement and
Cambridge: www.lib.cam.ac.uk/dataman.

32 DaMSSI: www.dcc.ac.uk/training/damssi.

33 See details at: http://admire.jiscinvolve.org/wp/2013/04/22/adapting-using-and-
re-using-rdm-training-materials.

34 More details at www.dcc.ac.uk/news/rdm-training-librarians.

35 RDTK Herts Final Report.

36 Bill Worthington on RDTK Herts project blog: http://research-data-toolkit.herts.
ac.uk/2013/05/the-cost-of-a-bit-of-a-ddud/ and http://research-data-toolkit.
herts.ac.uk/2013/06/data-loss-in-the-ddud.

37 RDTK Herts Final Report.

38 Cloud storage guidance for the University of Exeter:
http://as.exeter.ac.uk/media/level1/academicserviceswebsite/library/documents/
openexeter/Basic_Cloud_Storage_Guidance.pdf .

39 See http://blogs.exeter.ac.uk/openexeterrdm/blog/2013/01/25/dspace-
submission-using-globus-and-sword2-update/ (final output not yet available at
the time of writing).

40 Orbital Final Report.

41 CKAN is an open-source software, developed by the Open Knowledge
Foundation, that has become the worldwide default for government data
portals. See http://ckan.org.

42 The Research Dashboard is described in detail at:
http://orbital.blogs.lincoln.ac.uk/2013/05/07/throw-down-the-sword.

43 See http://orbital.blogs.lincoln.ac.uk/2013/06/07/open-data-and-the-academy-
an-evaluation-of-ckan-for-research-data-management.

44 RD@Essex Final Report.

45 See for example www.bl.uk/aboutus/stratpolprog/digi/datasets/
workshoparchive/ball-metadata-citation.pdf.

46 RDE Metadata Profile for EPrints:
www.data-archive.ac.uk/media/375386/rde_eprints_metadataprofile.pdf.

47 ReCollect is available from the EPrints Bazaar: http://bazaar.eprints.org/280.

48 ReCollect user guide:
www.data-archive.ac.uk/media/391123/rdessex_recollectuserguide.pdf.

49 ReCollect policies:
www.data-archive.ac.uk/media/391126/rdessex_recollectpolicies.pdf.

50 Outlines of these workshops and presentations are available from
www.bl.uk/aboutus/stratpolprog/digi/datasets/workshoparchive/archive.html.

51 For details see the archive of the Jisc MRD JiscMail list: www.jiscmail.ac.uk/
cgi-bin/webadmin?A1=ind1210&L=JISCMRD&X=54EF84403399358C8A&Y#2.

52 See http://blogs.bath.ac.uk/research360/2013/06/research-data-management-
and-ref2014.

53 Stephen Gray 2013, data.bris Benefits Report.

54 RD@Essex Project Final Report to be published. The allocation of effort in the
sustainability plan was not public at the time of writing.

55 data.bris Final Report.

5.2 Citations

Beagrie, N., Chruszcz, J. and Lavoie, B. (2008) *Keeping Research Data Safe: a cost model
and guidance for UK universities,*

www.jisc.ac.uk/media/documents/publications/keepingresearchdatasafe0408.pdf.

Callaghan, S., Donegan, S., Pepler, S., Thorley, M., Cunningham, N., Kirsch, P., Ault, L., Bell, P., Bowie, R., Leadbetter, A., Lowry, R., Moncoiffé, G., Harrison, K., Smith-Haddon, B., Weatherby, A. and Wright, D. (2012) Making Data a First Class Scientific Output: data citation and publication by NERC's Environmental Data Centres, *International Journal of Digital Curation*, **7** (1), 107–13, doi:10.2218/ijdc.v7i1.218.

EPSRC (2011) *Policy Framework on Research Data*, www.epsrc.ac.uk/about/standards/researchdata/Pages/policyframework.aspx.

Green, A., Macdonald, S. and Rice, R. (2009) *Policy-making for Research Data in Repositories: a guide*, DISC-UK DataShare report, www.disc-uk.org/docs/guide.pdf.

Houssos, N., Jörg, B. and Matthews, B. (2012) A Multi-Level Metadata Approach for a Public Sector Information Data Infrastructure. In Jeffery, K. G. and Dvořák, J. (eds) E-Infrastructures for Research and Innovation: linking information systems to improve scientific knowledge production, *Proceedings of the 11th International Conference on Current Research Information Systems* (6–9 June 2012, Prague, Czech Republic), 19–31, www.eurocris.org/Uploads/Web%20pages/ CRIS%202012%20-%20Prague/CRIS2012_2_full_paper.pdf.

Jones, S., Pryor, G. and Whyte, A. (2013) *How to Develop Research Data Management Services – a guide for HEIs*, DCC How-to Guides, Digital Curation Centre, www.dcc.ac.uk/resources/how-guides.

Lyon, L. (2007) *Dealing with Data: roles, rights, responsibilities and relationships*, www.ukoln.ac.uk/ukoln/staff/e.j.lyon/reports/dealing_with_data_report-final.pdf.

Royal Society (2012) *Science as an Open Enterprise*, http://royalsociety.org/policy/projects/science-public-enterprise/report.

Swan, A. and Brown, S. (2008) *Skills, Role, Career Structure of Data Scientists and Curators*, Key Perspectives, www.jisc.ac.uk/media/documents/programmes/ digitalrepositories/dataskillscareersfinalreport.pdf.

University of Edinburgh (2011) *Research Data Management Policy*, www.ed.ac.uk/is/research-data-policy.

Van den Eynden, V., Corti, L., Woollard, M., Bishop, L. and Horton, L. (2011) *Managing and Sharing Data: best practice for researchers*, third edition, UK Data Archive, http://www.data-archive.ac.uk/media/2894/managingsharing.pdf.

Index